When Are You Going Back?

A memoir of the sea

Harry Nicholson

Dharmashed

Copyright © 2023 by Harry Nicholson

All rights reserved.

No portion of this book may be reproduced in any form without written permission from the publisher or author, except as permitted by U.S. copyright law.

For those who did not return.

Cover picture from a watercolour by Bill Wedgwood which shows Liverpool docks. The tug 'Throstle Garth' has the liberty ship ss 'Sandsend '(Headlam of Whitby) in tow. The vessel in the background is possibly the 'Warkworth', owned by Dalgliesh of Newcastle.
Image: courtesy of Joan Price

Contents

1. The Bus To Port Clarence 1
2. Tees 9
3. Native Shore 17
4. Blind 25
5. Weser 34
6. Scheldt And Thames 41
7. Biscay 49
8. The Gully Gully Man 58
9. Sovereigns 66
10. The Burning Coast 76
11. Sheba 83
12. South Of Socotra 90
13. Gan Island 96
14. The Grand Oriental Hotel 103
15. The Miller Of Dee 114

16.	Hooghly	122
17.	Chowringhee	132
18.	The Black Hole	139
19.	Homeward Bound	146
20.	Visakhapatnam	154
21.	Mrs Ferguson's Tea Set	163
22.	Monsoon Seas	171
23.	Kitchener Country	178
24.	July Wedding	185
25.	Drydock	195
26.	Cliff Land	201
27.	Mahronda	206
28.	Pickled Egg	213
29.	Malta	219
30.	Equator	227
31.	Tuticorin	236
32.	Madras	242
33.	Chittagong	249
34.	Homeward Bounders	258
	Appendix	262

About the Author	264
Also by	265

1

The Bus To Port Clarence

Monday, 23 February 1959.
Mist rises from the salt marsh — mist too shallow to hide a standing goose. It will soon burn off. Concrete posts poke through every ten yards or so. Twice as tall as a Coldstream Guard, the sentinels stand ready to mangle and smash off the wings of any of Hitler's gliders should he try an airborne invasion. Other crude structures, blunt and slitted, rise from the white vapour. In case they came by landing-craft, the War Office studded these flat-lands with pill boxes and tank obstacles. The slab-sided, concrete machine-gun posts and anti-aircraft gun positions are abandoned these past fourteen years. They squat here and there — mute, blind, lonely places now, except when whooped through by urchins who play at commandos, or when sneaked into by courting couples, or investigated by bare-kneed entomologists on the lookout for hibernating moths. My insect collection holds a specimen with scalloped lilac-grey wings splashed with orange blotches, the Herald moth, *Scoliopteryx libatrix,* gathered from just such a place.

The sun has been up for an hour and brightens the steel of the North Sea. Twenty miles to the south-east, the tremendous sea-cliffs of North Yorkshire stand in blue relief: Hunt Cliff, Boulby, and Hummersea, the tallest cliffs in England. Directly south, the anvil shape of Roseberry Topping, North Riding's little Matterhorn, juts out of the hazed plateau of the Cleveland Hills. There's a lawn of sheep-cropped grass on the summit of Roseberry where Beryl and I sunbathed. Roseberry ... It's curious how names become unglued over time, the Danes who settled at its foot called it Odinsbjarg, the hill of their god Odin. The Danes also gave the name to this district, their new conquest: Cleveland, the Land of Cliffs. The village of Great Ayton nestles in the dale beneath Odin's Hill. Captain James Cook, the great navigator, went to school there as a boy. The Cook family cottage is now in Australia, rebuilt in Melbourne and clad with authentic Yorkshire ivy.

My leave is over, and there'll be no more greetings in the street: 'Oh, hello, Harry. Home from sea again? When are you going back?'

I'm on my way to sign articles for another deep-sea voyage with Thos. and Jno. Brocklebank Steam Navigation Co. This time I need not journey from Old Hartlepool on the Durham coast, to cross England by train to Birkenhead; the ship is in Middlesbrough for three days loading, so this trip is a mere ten miles by bus. After helping with the handover from the relief coasting crew, my boss from Lancashire will say, 'See you tomorrow, Harry. Get yourself off home to the bosoms of loved ones while you can.' At least, I hope so.

The clippie works her way along the aisle. 'Any more fares?' It's Maggie, six-foot tall and smart in her United Bus Company conductor's navy-blue uniform edged in red piping. She's grown into a handsome woman. I'm impressed how she carries her height proudly now; during our few weeks of awkward courting she would stoop a little so as not to be two inches taller than me. I've since seen her walking out with a fellow who matches her height. She's good at baking: once I was invited to her little terraced home when her parents were out. She'd been making cakes. We sat before a blazing coal fire and ate a few. They had currants in them. She kept her pinafore on all evening.

'Hello, Harry. Still at sea? I hear you're getting married. And you're only twenty. When's the big day?'

'Morning, Maggie. It'll be in July, if I'm home in time. The arrangements are all down to Beryl.' I hold out my fare. 'I'll be twenty-one by then. Single to Port Clarence, please.'

She smiles and gives a little shake of the head. I pocket the shilling. Today I'll be travelling free — she must know the ticket inspector is on a different route. She clips a notch into the weekly ticket of the chap beside me. 'You make sure you're back in good time and don't disappoint the lass.' She moves on. 'Any more fares?'

Morning throats are cleared on the top deck and windows shoved open amid billows of pipe smoke — strong stuff, that Battleaxe Bar and Walnut Plug. I'm seated half-way down the shuddering rows of seats, surrounded by shipyard workers. Mates are comparing notes about their weekend:

'Do any good at the dog track, Henry?'

The speakers are in the pair of seats in front. They've got muscular necks. 'Nah! Had five bob on a black bugger from Horden, a hot certainty, name o' Flash Harry, but he left the trap like the most constipated greyhound you ever set eyes on. Fly the birds, did you?'

'Just a short one. Pedalled a basket of pigeons up to Hart. Watched them take one turn about the windmill, then head straight home. At least they knew the way and all I had to do was freewheel downhill.'

'You keep them on Yankee corn; I've telt thee afore, birds never fly for the joy of it if they're out of condition. Dad allus reckoned to feed the best carlin peas he could afford. On top o' that he would tip a drop o' cider vinegar into their watter. He was never without a trophy on the mantlepiece.'

I give up listening to the pigeon men, there's rabbit talk in the seat behind me. I've an interest; along with my dad, I used to keep and show Blue Beverens and Flemish Giants.

The rabbit man has a gargly voice. 'At the Liberal Hall up Park Road, a tortoiseshell English went best Fancy. You don't see many torts. Breeder by the name of Wilks from Blackhall Rocks. A big man with Dutch'.

His mate has a similar rattle. 'Oh, aye? And what did thee think on it? That Cuddy Wilks is a right dab hand with the tweezers. Yon's a well-known plucker. Should be cautioned by the British Rabbit Council.'

'She was a bonny enough doe. I was stewarding and had hold of her. A balanced pattern and never a white hair in any of the spots, nor down the spine. Judge looked at the definition and shoved her straight to top o' table, and she stayed there. Mind you, I did notice a tiny white hair on her nose — on her butterfly, that is.'

'There you are then, the tweezers missed that one. Cuddy's eyes must be knackered. I get fed up with all the plucking in the Fancy. I've a mind to give up the Tans and get into Fur. Been offered a mated Blue Beveren by a chap whose overstocked on Wynyard Road. She weighs fourteen pounds, lovely colour, dense coat that rolls back nice and slow. Good type — a bold Roman face and grand mandolin haunches. He asks fifteen bob.'

'Well, if the strain turns out not to be a winner, at least you'll be able to put summat on the dinner table and at the same time make a pair o' mits for your lass. Tans make hardly enough for a sandwich, and they've nowt of a coat... That reminds me, after the show a little lass brought her Lilac Rex to judge Coulson, to ask why she didn't win a card. What she could do to make it a better exhibit and suchlike.'

'Oh, aye? And what did Clogger Coulson have to say?'

'Not much. He picked the Rex up, looked at its hocks — a bit bald they were — stretched out the forelegs — they were bowed like bananas — and said, "Now then, honey, you'd best get this'n under a pie crust". Poor bairn went off in tears.'

The double-decker bus leans at a disconcerting angle while she negotiates a bend in the road. She throbs to a stop at the tiny settlement of Graythorp, where a third of our cargo of shipyard workers dismount to hurry across the road to William Gray's drydock enterprise.

Two sea-fatigued ships: an anonymous little collier, and an eight-thousand ton vessel of the Hogarth line, stand high and dry. Cradled by huge timbers, their life support is delivered by cable and hose. The Hogarth funnel is black, adorned with a red band sandwiched between two bands of white, reminiscent of a rasher of cheap bacon, hence the fond term for the company: *two of fat and one of lean*. Among seafarers that company has a reputation for poor feeding. There's a ditty that goes:

*You've heard of Hungry Hogarths?
The worst feeders on the sea
Their salt beef sailed with Nelson
Aboard the Victory.*

A tall crane hovers nearby, waiting for the day to start.

At the bridge over Greatham Creek we sway and lurch as if aboard some vessel in mid-Atlantic. The morning has a nip to it, so passengers are snug inside heavy coats — tired army surplus for the main part, but some will have returned with their owners in 1945. Their flat caps, once bought for Sunday best, are black with engine grease or red with shipyard rust. The young fellow crammed next to me wears a cap impregnated with white powder.

He points. 'Plenty of fat geese on the flats.' A host of heads lift through skeins of evaporating mist. 'Any one of 'em would go down a treat with sage and onion stuffing. Be right canny for Sunday dinner.'

I nod. 'And with roast spuds in crispy skins, peas out of the garden, and a dollop of buttered swede.'

'My missus won't touch swede. Gives her bellyache. Me, I'm partial to frosted snagger.'

In one motion, black fronts and pale bellies take to the air. Wintering Brents from Spitzbergen. Honking, they form into groups that head for the estuary margins to feast on eel grass. They sense the tide is on the ebb.

He glances at my navy-blue bridge coat. 'Merchant Navy?'

'Yes. Been on leave for a month after the best part of seven months away. She's alongside in the Tees. I'm to sign on today.'

'I've not had a proper morning tab yet. Late up.' He opens a worn tobacco tin. Most of the blue paint has gone but it remains embossed with the head of an Indian chief in full war bonnet. He fishes among the Rizla papers to lift out half a hand-rolled cigarette, then lights the nipped end with a Swan Vesta match. The tab looks to have enough length to give him a few draws. 'What's your job?'

'I'm second radio officer on the *Mawana* — she carries two. Last trip was her maiden voyage, so she's in good nick. A steam turbine.'

'That sounds grand. Meself, I'm a pipe lagger at Smith's yard. Just about finished the engine room of the *Galway*. She's diesel powered. A Doxford engine by Hawthorns up at Hebburn. She's out on sea trials any day now. We've done her nice and tidy. It sometimes gets on the chest, does lagging with asbestos.'

I nod. 'My dad worked at Smith's. Rivetter by trade but ended up helping the ship platers when welding took over.'

'Not there now, then?'

'He'd have been on this bus, but we lost him a twelve-month gone. Should have reached his pension come November.'

'That's a shame. It's hard graft in the yards. A lot don't see their pension.'

'The war didn't help. The Great one, that is. Wounded on the Somme, baked to a frazzle in Salonika, then malaria. That generation don't make old bones — so Mam reckons.'

The bus slows for Port Clarence junction. My smart *Felca* wristwatch with luminous dial, bought in Aden, says we are running late. There's the clatter of nailed boots hitting the pavement as men jump off before she comes to a halt.

'My stop. You have a good trip. Enjoyed the bit blather.' My neighbour gets up, hitches his army haversack (tea can poking from the top) over his shoulder and joins the file of workmen that press towards the stairs. He blends with eighty others who hurry across the road towards the slipways and yards of Haverton Hill, anxious to clock on. The shipyard hooter is sounding for the start of the day.

The lightened bus manoeuvers less heavily as she turns left, then dips beneath the railway bridge, takes a sharp right and a left into the final stop. The last score of passengers leap off and run for the Transporter. The suspended gondola fills with cyclists, mostly workmen with cans of tea hung from handlebars. There's a matron or two in headscarves and a sprinkle of office girls. The man who attends the gondola and collects fares shouts in my direction, 'Come on, lad! Let's be havin' yer'. But my seagoing kit is cumbersome and I'm the last to squeeze aboard as the gates clang shut.

The deck is a sea of cyclists, with one Cameron's brewery lorry a silent hot island in the centre. The Bedford is loaded with wooden barrels of strong beer brewed in Stranton, West Hartlepool, for the parched throats of steelworkers. The covered areas to either side are full, so I lug my two bags up the stairs to the top deck from where the view is worth the trouble.

The gondola clanks into motion and we begin our 300 yard journey across the river Tees, suspended by cables from a bogey that travels along a lattice of steel girders fifty yards above us. The ingenious contraption is hauled back and forth by an engine in the motor house on the Middlesbrough bank. A fellow can climb to the top by a winding metal staircase and walk across the draughty upper bridge if he wants a thrill. I've done so in the past, mostly for a lark. The Tees Transporter is the most majestic of three such crossings in Britain.

My ship, SS *Mawana*, is moored to the wharf just a couple of hundred yards downriver. Despite her recent six-month maiden voyage east, she looks smart in the morning sun. Cranes already lower slingloads of steel into her holds. It's a dry day. I'll walk.

Mawana astern of Malabar (Liverpool)

2

Tees

I drop my bags in the cabin and go in search of the chief. He leans on the rail outside the wireless room and watches our loading proceed. Suspended from cranes, sling after sling of steel girders are persuaded to lay snug beside their comrades somewhere in the chasm below. Such a hollow din rises from the innards of the *Mawana*. Echoes of thuds, clatters, and expletives escape through the hatches. Middlesbrough dockers are at work; their accent slices the air with an edge of flint that would startle an industrial worker from any other part of Britain.

An incomprehensible yell erupts from below, directed at the signaller fellow who peers into the hold from his position by the hatch coaming. He's a broad man, in muffler, donkey jacket, and flat cap, who directs the crane driver with rigid arm movements and subtle flutters of his fingers. I imagine how the brim of his cap will have embossed a permanent groove across his forehead, as did my father's own buttoned-down working cap. I catch the second yell: 'Ca canny up top! We're bluddy strugglin' down 'ere, man. Not so wick wi' the buggers. It were Baltic when we kicked off and now we're boiling, like.'

My boss, Don Butterworth, raises a ginger eyebrow. 'Harry, being a local, I suppose you'll understand these people.'

'Near enough, like. *Ca canny* means to proceed with caution. The chaps below want the job to be less rushed, they can hardly keep pace with the crane, like. For something to be *Baltic* means it is perishing cold — they reckon it was nithering when they began, but now they're in a lather of sweat, like. Folk in these parts like to end a sentence with *like,* like.'

'You sound somewhat similar when you forget yourself, old son.'

'Not too much, I hope. My lot hail from Old Hartlepool, an ancient place with archaic families. Our lingo can be a touch sweeter on the ear. West Hartlepool is a new and mongrelised town, same as this place, so folk from all over the shop moved in; Scots, Welsh, Irish, Scouse, Germans.'

'Ah yes — Middlesbrough! Gladstone declared it to be an *Infant Hercules.*'

'There was nowt here before the ironworks, Don. Just marsh, estuary, and a cluster of farms. It used to be a feeding spot for migrating ducks and geese, but when the railway came, the wildfowlers netted thousands and sent them by train to the London markets. No good for geese now — look at the river.'

We peer over the side. The ebb is gathering, and with it an opalescent sheen of colour drifts to the sea. A sprinkle of shore birds pick about on the exposed mud of the far bank — turnstone and redshank, they look to be. Thin gleaning for them in this polluted place.

'See the muck floating down from Stockton and Thornaby. And to think my mother's uncles, Bass and Smokey, made a living of sorts hereabouts as late as 1914, netting the last of those salmon that remembered where they were born and tried to make it through the soup.'

'You spin a good yarn, Harry boy. How do you know it was 1914?'

'Easy. Family tales and Arthur Mee's Childrens' Encyclopedia. In 1914, Kaiser Bill's battleships, flying British ensigns, stood off Tees Bay and opened up on Hartlepool. A hundred and thirty died. Folk ran for the hills, but my grandmother, Dolly Mush Horsley, stood on the cliffs wrapped in her shawl, feet in clogs, and watched the whole thing — mind you, she was a touch eccentric. The first shells dropped short and plopped into the sea around

Bass and Smokey's little fishing coble. They had to row like Billy-o, raise the sail, and put ashore at Redcar.'

'Like I said, you spin a good yarn.' He clears his throat. 'Can't wait to sail. This air reeks of ammonia. Never seen so many belching chimneys. ICI chemicals is chucking it out.' He rubs a finger along the gritty surface of the hand rail to reveal the shine of varnished mahogany. 'And the ironworks dump red muck all across our paintwork. Still, there's profit here, no doubt.'

'I've cousins in Haverton Hill on the north bank. It's handy for the ICI. Their dad's a chemical worker. They reckon Monday's washing rots on the line before it's gathered in, and it's not safe for bairns to be left outside in their prams unless there's a breeze off the sea.'

He grunts. 'On another matter; now that you're determined on wedlock, and being a native, I suppose you'll be hoping to slope off whenever you can?'

'Well, once I've done any outstanding jobs, extra time at home would be brilliant.'

He stokes his chin. 'Yes, fair enough, it's rare for us to be on the North-East coast. This trip could be seven months, so treat these few days as a bonus. We'll check out the gear before lunch. First job for you is to read the specific gravity of the batteries and note them in the log. Be sure to top up the electrolyte and grease the terminals. Then we'll go through the spares inventory. Signing ship's articles is at three o'clock in the saloon, after which you can clear off to the bosom of your family for the night. Be back aboard by ten in the morning and we'll take it from there.

Of the eight cinemas in West Hartlepool, the Regal is our favourite. The back rows have cosy double seats in red plush, especially designed for courting couples. It might scare a decent girl if a fellow suggested the double seats on a first date, but Beryl and I are well acquainted and rush to one side of the projectionist's box to claim the last vacant double.

The beam of light blazes through a thin veil of cigarette smoke to throw the image of a white cockerel onto the screen. The handsome fowl perches on a weathervane. He thrusts out his neck, lifts his wings, and throws back his head to utter a strident clarion call that makes the loudspeakers rattle. *Pathe News* must be short of current stories, for what follows is a visit to Her Majesty's Stationary Office where *Hansard* is printed. The publication reports verbatim on the proceedings of the British Parliament. It is *Hansard's* golden jubilee. We catch little of it. After folding up our damp raincoats and stowing them under the seats, we've turned our attention to those around us.

On my left is a beefy lass with a mass of blond curls. Can't be long since she took her curlers out. When she shuffles about, our seat moves in sympathy. Her boyfriend is a lean fellow with owlish spectacles. He reminds me of Buddy Holly, he who tragically died in a plane crash only three weeks ago. Such a massive loss to modern music. Who can tell what his legacy will be? Buddy's hits pull crowds onto the floor, jiving and bopping at the Queen's Rink. *If you knew Peggy Sue, then you'd know why I feel blue ...*

Beryl is on my right, and beyond her a runtish Teddy Boy lounges with his arm around a flashy bit of stuff. Dressed in velvet-collared jacket of a crumpled tourquise that apes the fashion of the Edwardian era, he has his built-up crepe-soled shoes on the back of the seat in front. That is, until the usherette shines her torch along the row to show the way for a burly bloke and his woman. The big man arrives surrounded by the aroma of strong beer. I recognise his demeanour, hefty shoulders and thick neck — he's probably a boiler maker, and hence a man who commands respect in these parts. The fellow sits directly in front of the Teddy Boy, who now has to lean to his right to see the screen. The couple in front of us are short beings, so we are ok,

I whisper to Beryl, 'Swap seats with me — I don't like the look of that Ted.' The Ted sniffs as I sit beside him. He lights a fag to show he's tough, but he can't be that tough — it has a cork tip.

The bit about *Hansard* has run out. Only lonely folk in a bored daze took any notice of it. Next comes a piece on the history of Berlin. Wobbly footage shows Kaiser Wilhelm II reviewing his troops on the occasion of his 25th accession to the throne. The narrator goes on at length about the Hohenzollern dynasty. Someone down the slope calls out, 'And a right load of bastards, the lot on 'em!' There's a response, 'Too true, mate. Should all be strung up!' The usherette flicks her torch beam along the rows. 'Quiet, please, or I'll send for the manager.'

By now Beryl has opened the box of Maltesers I bought at the kiosk. She leans into me to whisper the advertising slogan: 'Time for a less fattening centre.'

'Why not?' I reach out to examine her centre. She's got a delightful waist, enhanced by the spinal corset she wore for months after her fall from the crags of Great Gable when climbing in Cumberland with her previous fiance. Soon after I returned from a trip to India eighteen months ago, she ended her engagement to the rock climber. That caused a great fuss in the family, but they seem to have got over it. When I walk Beryl home now, her mother serves me with scrumptious corned beef and potato fritters.

I roll the ball of chocolate over my tongue and crunch on it as King Hussein of Jordan inspects the debris site of a crashed airliner. Many dead in the desert. The audience has grown sombre. Next, a twin-engined plane filled with tourists has gone down into the sea off Buenos Aires — there's one survivor. End of *Pathe News*.

To cheer us up, they treat us to a Bugs Bunny cartoon, *Hare Way to the Stars*. Bugs has foolishly mixed radish with his carrot juice, which causes him, by some garbled reasoning, to be launched into space. He collides with Russia's Sputnik and gets into a fight with Martians intent on destroying Earth. He defeats them all.

Beryl nudges me: 'That was a dog's breakfast. A right *bake*, as your mother would say.'

'It was. Shall we ask for our money back?'

'What does she mean by a *bake*?'

'Don't know. Never enquired. She has odd expressions. Maybe a *bake* is a lot of leftovers, useless for anything apart from being thrown together in a dish and shoved into the oven under a pie crust.'

Through the interval, we discuss my mother's use of quaint words. The lights have gone up and four ice-cream sellers have taken their stations. Queues trail down the sloping floor for tubs and lollies packed onto trays hung around the girls' necks, but we can't be bothered to move from our cosy back row.

I dip into the Malteser box; the chocolates are growing tacky with our warmth 'For instance, Mam says *sneck* where others say *latch*, and she says *spelk* instead of *splinter*. She calls a flea, a *lop*, and a pig a *gissy*. Maybe they're bits of dialect from when the town was just a fishing spot. By all accounts, her people have been on the Headland for hundreds of years, just fishing. Dad's came down from the Tyne — his lot were ironworkers and proper Geordies. The Danes settled around here. Could be that Mam's words are Old Norse.'

The lights lower and the big film begins. We enjoy the fight scenes on the longships, the costumes and the scenery of the fjords. It is a hefty saga. As we leave, after standing for the National Anthem, Beryl links my arm and says, 'So that was *The Vikings*. I thought Kirk Douglas looked the part. Did you enjoy it?'

'Most of it. Right up to the last fight, in fact. Up to where Tony Curtis kills Kirk Douglas and then says in a nasal Bronx accent: "Why did he hesitate?" If that was supposed to be Old Norse, well I'll go to Shields. Apart from that phoney scene, I was impressed when they sent Kirk's body out to sea on a burning longship. I wouldn't mind a send-off like that.'

'Kirk's got a dimple on his chin, a bit like yours.'

'Is that so?' Despite the rain, I throw back my shoulders as we hurry for the bus.

For two more days I take the double-decker bus to Middlesbrough, make myself useful around the wireless gear, then slip off home as soon as I might. On Tuesday I'm home early enough to venture into the sand dunes a mile distant to give my dog a run. Not that Peter needs exercise, he is usually out all day in search of bitches. He shared my days when I was a boy and now goes wild with joy when I return from a five-month voyage. But I hear he can be a nuisance when I'm away. He wanders the town and can be gone for a couple of nights. I comb the cotters out of his wavy black-and-tan coat and meet his brown spaniel-collie gaze. What to do about my bold, and getting old, mongrel dog? I don't know.

Beryl and I spent much of my month's leave decorating Mam's main bedroom. It will be our living room after we marry in July. Bits of furniture have appeared, bargains that Beryl has accumulated. A secondhand three-piece suite, grey-blue and barrel shaped. An end-of-roll length of carpet from a sale. On the carpet stands a Kashmiri table; the top is a chess board fashioned from black walnut and buffalo-bone squares. It stands on three legs, each leg the head and trunk of an elephant. It is the best thing I've brought back from India.

Beneath the window stands a hand-wound gramophone on Queen Anne legs; it has rested there for as long as I remember. Cousin Eric hoped to buy it but never saved up the five pounds. The lid lifts to reveal a turntable set into sumptuous red velvet that invites fingers to stroke and linger. It has an acoustic pickup that transduces into an internal horn. The volume is controlled by opening and closing the doors. We try to remember to change the steel needle after twenty plays. A side compartment holds a collection of shellac records my parents bought in better times. Beryl and I played them as we pasted and hung lengths of wallpaper.

Begin the Beguine is Mam's favourite, she still dotes on the singer. Chick Henderson was a crooner from our town, a local lad from humble beginnings, who had a great future but died of shrapnel wounds during the war. The Beguine has been played so much, the surface is almost smooth and the sound now so thin and faint it is as though Chick is far away.

A record by Billy Williams must be old because he died in 1915. It has a hollow sound, as if copied from an early waxed cylinder, and goes:

When Father papered the parlour, you couldn't see Pa for paste
Dabbing it here, dabbing it there, paste and paper everywhere
Mother was stuck to the ceiling; the kids were stuck to the floor
I never knew a blooming family so stuck up before.

We've almost worn out the grooves of a 1926 Colombia record by *Gid Tanner and His Skillet Lickers*. They pick fast banjos while Gid sings:

Hand me down my walking cane
Oh, hand me down my walking cane
Hand me down my walking cane
I got to leave on the midnight train
For all my sins are taken away ...

Gid Tanner has us jigging around the floor and we set Peter off barking. There are heavier crackly shellacs from long ago: *Rock of Ages, Abide With Me, Rescue the Perishing.* The needle rarely rides those sombre valleys nowadays.

3

Native Shore

River Tees. Friday 27th February 1959.

Loading at Middlesbrough has been a blissful interlude, a mere bus ride from home. Yesterday, Beryl rushed here after work to arrive in time for dinner in the saloon. Three officers remembered her visit to Liverpool before *Mawana's* maiden voyage five months ago, and welcomed her vivacious presence at the table. But today we make ready for high tide and the sea.

Departure day starts with echoing hoots of fussing tugs: cargo vessel *Galway* is leaving her birthplace at the Haverton Hill shipyards. Astern of her, a few hundred yards upstream, behind the soaring steel lattice of the Transporter Bridge, two oil tankers break the skyline: *San Ernesto* is fitting out, and *Majola* sits in the stocks where she has grown in stature in the last four days.

From the shipyards come clatters, bangs, hammerings and grindings — and booms that seem to reverberate from a satanic cavern. The din muffles the thud of *Galway's* Doxford engine as her 6,500 tons glide past on her way to sea trials. She makes just enough speed to keep station in midstream. Her new paintwork bright in the morning sun, she is led by an elderly tug, the *Acklam Cross,* with a second securing her stern. They will return to nurse our own ship around the final two bends of the Tees.

Our gangway, that rose and fell with the flood, is already cleared away — last night, Beryl made a dainty descent of it in her high heels. Now she has gone, I'm in subdued spirits.

My chief will open the station once we clear the estuary. Meanwhile, I idle on the boat deck with a mug of tea, coming to terms with the pungent fish kedgeree served at breakfast. I need to stand on deck and watch the landmarks go by, for this is my native shore.

An hour later, the tugs have us moving downstream against the last push of the incoming tide. To starboard, stretch hundreds of acres of ancient marsh, now sealed beneath hillocks of a strange gunmetal rock shot through with gas holes — a hundred years of dumped blast-furnace slag make for a desolate tomb. The South Gare, a breakwater built of the same waste, reaches out for a mile and more. The Gare hides the river entrance from the violence of the North Sea. It holds a fishermen's harbour known as Paddy's Hole, for it was mostly Irishmen who toiled on the breakwater. Propelled by oars, a gaggle of cobles: blue, green, and white, slip from the Hole to round the Gare and check their crab and lobster creels sunk onto the Redcar reef. Our wash makes them dip and bob. Redcar lies just around the corner to the south, a seaside resort of cafes, fun palaces and boarding houses — there'll be few footfalls this February Friday.

Wrecks litter the reefs and shoals of this coast. In the last days of 1906, a fierce blizzard drove a 6,000 ton Japanese cargo liner, the *Awa Maru*, into Redcar's West Scar Rocks. With typical courage, rowers in fishing cobles and the lifeboat rescued all 102 souls on board. To lighten ship and help her refloat, the owners chartered a local vessel, SS *Clavering*, to retrieve the shipment of machinery, girders, and pitch. One month later, the *Clavering* sailed from Middlesbrough for Japan loaded with the salvage, but she lost control in a gale and struck North Gare. Known to locals as the Slag Wall, that second protective breakwater now slips by on our port side. The sea bed hereabouts is littered with *Clavering's* parts. Our Indian lascar sailors are busy on deck, making shipshape for deep water. They will be unaware that eighteen of their countrymen, so far from home, drowned at the head of North Gare not a half-mile from where they coil ropes this fine morning. The orange-billed oyster catchers that stand in rows on the

Slag Wall, huddled like sextons in black coats and white shirts, are indifferent.

Three vessels, down to their Plimsoll marks, ride at anchor in Tees Bay; iron-ore carriers waiting a berth. Samuel Plimsoll, the 19th century Member of Parliament, took holidays at Redcar. On his walks to the South Gare, he was appalled at the number of wrecks — where ships had capsized, overloaded by greedy owners. He called them 'coffin ships' and pressured Parliament to legislate that vessels must display safe-loading marks. Scrooge owners hated Plimsoll for threatening their profits. The new law left it to shipowners to paint the marks wherever they saw fit. A few had Plimsoll's lines painted on the funnel! It was an outrage that ended in 1890.

A mile out, a tanker approaches at a leisurely pace. She has timed her arrival to perfection. It is a waste of fuel to be early, before the tide is full enough for the river to take a deep ship.

Beyond North Gare, on the Durham shore, crouches the Zinc Works. It squats in isolation, a scruffy factory that makes sulphuric acid in safety amid salt flats and tidal creeks. Two miles on, the sun brightens the promenade, the cottage rows, the pubs and shops, of the ancient village of Seaton Carew. It is where Beryl spent her early years.

All being well, we shall marry in July at Seaton's Holy Trinity church. The Victorian bell tower that will fling out peals for us, peeps above the roof of the Seaton Hotel. A lump grows in my throat — we have said goodbye for perhaps six months. Last night I snipped a lock of hair from her tresses. Tied with a scrap of lace, it nestles between the pages of my *Wireless World* diary.

On Seaton shore, at extreme low tides, half-fossilised tree stumps appear; a forest from the end of the Ice Age when tribes of hide-clad hunters, armed with sticks and flints, walked here from Europe. In an old house by that beach, Beryl's grandmother has a hairdresser's business. In her cellar, just above high water mark, a stone slab stares up from the flagged floor. I've asked, but no one admits to what it hides. Sometime, after a few beers, a couple of us men must heave on its rusted iron ring and lift the slab. We might find steps to a smuggler's tunnel.

Five miles further north is the Norman church of St Hilda that presides over Hartlepool Headland. For centuries, my mother's fisher-folk ancestors buried their kin just yards from its flying buttresses. It stands on the site of a monastery once governed by Abbess Hilda, a lady of the royal house of King Edwin of Northumbria. That was in the 7th century. I stare at the old town and its battlemented walls and wonder how life was, thirteen-hundred years ago, when a chain stretched across the harbour mouth to keep out Scots.

My ruminations end when a little collier emerges from Hartlepool. She's one of Everards, deep-laden with coal for the Thames. As soon as she clears the piers, her pilot descends a rope ladder, jumps into a launch and motors across to a sea-stained vessel waiting to enter. The timber ship lists as if her stack of deck cargo has shifted in wild weather: a deadly load of Baltic fir, cut to pit-prop length, ready to shore up the workings of Durham mines. Though loaded with timber and slow to sink, ships of that trade have drowned many.

'A bit busy in these parts, Sparky.' Alf, our Liverpool carpenter, stops beside me and fishes a crumpled Woodbine from his boiler suit. He's just come off watch on the bows. In narrow waters, it's his task to drive the windlass and drop anchor should there be a mishap. 'It can be dodgy coming out around here, what with that dredger, and her tug with its string of hoppers.' While I shield the flame of his lighter, I note how his fingers are twice the size of mine. The Woodbine ignites at the third attempt. He straightens the broad frame of his Scouse torso and blows out a perfect smoke ring. 'A collision at sea can ruin one's entire day.'

I chuckle. 'Droll! Did you make that up?' Alf is a well-read man, a poet and balladeer, so I expect surprises.

'Nah!' he replies. 'Some reckon it's by an ancient Greek gaffer, name of Thucydides, but I've my doubts.'

'Never heard of him, Chips. Sounds like one of Alfie Holt's Blue Funnels — Antilochus, Eurybates, Ulysses, and such.'

'You mean to tell me you've not read Thucydides' *History of the Peloponnesian War*? It's a bugger when a man must crew with the uncultured.'

'I'll get around to it when I've finished Lady Chatterley.'

'Progress! You've moved on from Zane Grey, then! What are you up to now? Watching your auld town slip away? I recall you confess to being a monkey-hanger. Tell me again why you hanged the hairy little man.'

'I admit nothing of the sort. It was well before my day. That monkey, dressed in soldier's clothes, paddled ashore from a wreck during Napoleon's war. One local, who'd been abroad a time or two, reckoned it to be a Frenchman, and when they got nowt but gibberish out of it, they were convinced. So they took it to the magistrate. He declared it a French spy and ordered it strung up in the gibbet on the beach.'

'No RSPCA in those days, then. Is the story true? What do you reckon?'

'Some believe it's a skit put about by snooty Victorian incomers to the new town of West Hartlepool. They enjoyed poking fun at the fisherfolk of the Headland — thinking them quaint. Historians say the tale is not found in print until well after the old queen took to wearing black. But I've heard there used to be a pub half-way down Northgate that displayed a stuffed monkey in a glass case. It had rope burns around its neck.'

Alf's great nose gives a sniff. 'There was a time when, if you called a chap a monkey hanger, it could start a fight.'

'Not these days. Headland folk are proud of the story, and won't have it denied. There's a verse that celebrates the gallows crew. It starts:

On the sands the fishermen stood,
Horsley, Pounder, Coulson, Hood.

Those surnames are in my mother's ancestry, all of them decent fisherfolk without benefit of education.' I struggle with a sense of family pride mixed with shame at what was done to the hairy man.

'Then you are a proper monkey-hanger! He slaps me on the back. 'You look a touch hang-dog yourself. Join me for a Guinness when you can. Keep smiling through!' He strides away. I button up my bridge-coat against the nippy breeze and return to my reverie.

Out there, half a mile offshore from Seaton, the ocean covers the twisted frame of a German Zeppelin. In 1916, searchlight fingers caught her whilst she bombed the district. Captain Pyott, a twenty-one-year-old South African, flying a Bristol Fighter biplane, brought her down in flames. Beryl's father, Frank Scott, was in short trousers at the time. It's a favourite family story. He watched the whole thing, right from seeing Captain Pyott roar past in a canvas-covered tender on his way to the aerodrome as the town's gun battery opened fire. The gunners claimed the victory, but Beryl's dad tells how, 'The biplane seemed to flutter like a butterfly above the Zeppelin, then fired into the gas bag so that a tongue of flame shot up'.

There were no survivors. The commander of *Zeppelin L-34* was one Kapitanleutnant Max Dietrich, the uncle of Marlene Dietrich, a girl of fifteen destined to become a famous singer and Hollywood star. Captain Pyott survived the war to take over his father's biscuit factory in South Africa, where he oversaw the creation of the famous Romany Creams. Beryl's father sings a ditty that spread around the town after the Zeppelin fell. It's a parody of a 1915 song: *Back Home in Tennessee*:

Way down in Monkey Town,
They brought a Zeppelin down,
There were searchlights gleaming
People screaming,
All the sky was bright.

The soldiers cried: 'What Ho!'
'We'll give that zep a show.'
They fired shells one by one,
It won't be a Zeppelin long.

Back home in Germany,
That zep will never be.
All they got to greet them,
Was the deep blue sea beneath them.

They never got back,
Oh, they never got back,
To their home in Fatherland.

Ten miles inland, where the pastures and ploughlands of County Durham roll, I see a derelict windmill above Elwick village, its sails a skeleton. It was there I laboured for a few shillings during school holidays, mucking out cow byres, gathering potatoes behind the plough, hunting for hen's eggs laid in obscure places. The plodding, kindly old farmer invited me to work for him full-time when I left school at fifteen. His eyes twinkled. 'Yes, I'll give thee a job, sonny. You look to be a useful sort of lad.'

Thanks to the encouragement of my seagoing brother-in-law, an engineer with Elder Dempster, to apply for South Shields Marine College, rather than stacking cow clap in that clarty yard, I'm on this fine ship with a modern trade at my fingertips and a three-course lunch promised that features Madras chicken curry instead of an apple, a lump of cheese, and a hunk of bread.

A grey seal raises her head from the low swell to inspect us with soft hazel eyes. She must be a vagrant from the Farne Islands to the north, for there are no colonies here. Many years will pass before her kind breed again on these polluted shores.

But that time comes. After sixty years, the blast furnaces and foundries are cleared away, the poisoned Tees is healed and salmon once again shiver and flash their way upriver. The acres of dumped furnace slag at South Gare, colonised by rare lime-loving plants, become a Site of Special Scientific Interest. The Zinc Works is no more. A nuclear power station crouches on the skyline, silent and ominous, while a boisterous colony of seals gets on with life around its skirts. Nearby, a thriving nature reserve rings with the yelps and hoots of Arctic geese and swans. Visitors sip coffee, eat chocolate cake, and gaze through visitor-centre cafe windows, astonished that avocets and egrets have come to breed. Cargoes of pit props are no longer hauled from the Baltic. Profits gone, the coal pits die; the dark workings where ponies hauled coal trucks, and men squatted with picks (my grandmother's forebears among them), collapse and flood. Shipbuilding exists only in the memory of old men playing dominoes and sipping pints of beer in bars where they may no longer light a pipe. Yet, the little Graythorp drydock is busy dismembering redundant oil rigs, and worn-out ships as mighty as the French aircraft carrier *Clemenceau*. My old radio college in Ocean Road at South Shields is a crowded modern theme pub. The rooms upstairs, where I studied for my Radar Maintenance ticket, can be hired for wedding receptions. Times change, but the brunette curl of a twenty-year-old lass still beckons from between the pages of my 1959 diary, when we two are gone grey.

Our tugs and pilot have departed, the Headland slips astern, and *Mawana* leans — we've altered course for the German port of Bremerhaven.

4

Blind

Friday, 27th February 1959. North Sea.
The Morse from GCC, Cullercoats Radio close to the entrance to the river Tyne, comes in with the precise hand of a British coast station:
  Low FASTNET 985 expected LUNDY 995 by 0600 tomorrow, losing its identity. Outlook for the next 24 hours. TYNE HUMBER FORTIES SE3 or 4 veering SW later. Moderate. Showers. Visibility good, occasionally moderate. FISHER SE 3 or 4. Moderate. Clear. Drizzle later. Good to moderate. DOGGER GERMAN BIGHT SE2 or 3. Sea slight. Fog. Poor.
  I pass the weather forecast for the North Sea into the chartroom. The First Mate scans it. 'Humph! Losing its identity. I know how it feels. As for blankets of fog, it's to be expected, what with a perishing brass-monkey sea topped by warm southern air. We'll be blind soon enough.'
The pink tinge to his blue eyes is a sign of weary hours, or maybe he's just come off a bad spot of leave.
  'The radar's in good nick. We serviced it yesterday. Changed a load of valves. Forty-mile range is top-notch.'
  He replies in tones that lack his usual refined modulation and are a touch vexatious, 'That might be so, Mister Marconi, but the five-mile range will be more vital. There are those without radar. Packs of drifters, Seine netters, and what-not, floating about on Dogger Bank. Decrepit Sam-boats. Flags of convenience manned by officers who bought their tickets for ten quid in Athens. Radars rid-

dled with faults. Bottlenecks at the Weser approaches. The North Sea, the Viking's Whale Road, their bloody Vomiting Gannet's Bath, can be a swine. I want to know what the Dutch and German stations have to say — if you can spare the time, that is.' He slams shut the chartroom hatch.

Oh dear! The mate has got the hump. A phrase comes to mind, one often heard at sea: 'Shipmates, Board of Trade acquaintances, and other bastards I have sailed with.' But I put that out of my mind. He is an accomplished officer and we need to get along, for we all rely on each other. There are thousands of miles to go.

George, the First Mate (he prefers the more correct title of Chief Officer) is a cultured fellow from the Home Counties who has yet to forgive me for defeating him at darts on our previous voyage. We held the ship's sports day in the officers' smoke-room as Mawana glided across shimmering sunset glass in the Red Sea. It was expected that the mate's notorious skill would, as usual, defeat all comers. He was drawn against me in the first round but, to the astonishment of all, I knocked him out of the competition with the most terrible accuracy. An engineer from Birkenhead, one eye puckered against his fag smoke, demolished me in the next leg.

It's odd how a mediocre player like myself can sometimes strike a vein of genius. Twenty years later, it would happen again — in a tavern on the Isle of Skye. Our party of four climbing friends had abandoned the Cuillin Ridge to deliver our fallen leader to hospital to have his injuries stitched; the volcanic gabbro rock of the Cuillins makes a harsh surface to take a tumble on, composed of large crystals that can lacerate a leather boot. Whilst fairy-like and freckled Hebridean nurses attended to Mike, we three uninjured repaired to the inn. In no time, we were challenged to a darts match by a gang of boisterous Irishmen enjoying a day off from laying tarmac on Skye's narrow roads.

It was to be 301 Down, start and finish on a double, the best of three. Loser buys the beer. At first we did well – the tarmac gang had already imbibed a skinful before we arrived. We won the first round, they won the next. The third leg would decide the winner. Both teams briskly chased down their scores from 301 to a point where the contest could be decided by a single dart. I felt in best form: fit, tanned, supple, poised, and relaxed after our adventures in the mountains. Before each throw, the elbow warm and loose, I would pause for two seconds to allow the beery fug in my mind to clear. A team-mate presented three darts with apologies for leaving me with the cul-de-sac score of 3 to break. All was predetermined. My first dart must find the single 1. The second dart must find the double 1. To hit the 20 or the 18 on either side of 1 would make us bust.

I checked how I stood. Rocked a little in my climbing boots, lined up the 'arrow', and launched. Thud. I groaned. Instead of hitting the broad and easy wedge of the single, my first dart had found double 1. The Irish cheered. We were stuck with 1. A double to finish was impossible. We were done for.

An interested drinker at the bar called out, 'Dinna fret, mon. Split the elevens! It's allowed here.'

'What do you mean?'

'Sink yer dart twixt the wee wires that make the number 11, and the game is yern. She's a wee bitty bit bigger than the bull's ee.'

I squinted at the board. Blinked. The public bar had fallen still. All eyes turned my way. I waited for the mental haze to clear. The dartboard fell into pin-sharp focus. The pair of rusty wires that composed the number eleven seemed to smile. I wiggled my elbow, then launched. The dart thudded deep into its target. It brought the house down.

An hour later, Sheveningen Radio PCH, on the coast of Holland, signals: DOGGER SE3, wave height 1.0 m. Fog. GERMAN BIGHT SE2 later veering S3. Fog, visibility poor to nil.

Then Norddeich Radio DAN, in Lower Saxony, gives: EAST FRISIAN COAST and HELGOLAND, southeast about 2, shifting south to southwest, Wave height 0.5m. Fog. I pass the reports through the hatch to the mate.

'Thanks, Sparks.' He grunts. 'I hope I was not too uncivil earlier. Fog is the worst villain a seaman can meet. Concentration by only a sixth sense in such muck can wrap the stomach in knots enough to sprout an ulcer.'

'Goodness!' I think. 'That might be an apology. Maybe I'm forgiven for the Red Sea darts match.'

On our approach to the southern edge of Dogger Bank, the radar shows a gaggle of slow echoes to the north — a fishing fleet. An echo returns from two miles astern — a ship on the same course, but making our speed. The twenty-mile range yields a scatter of distant traffic that will need to be watched in case some cross our track.

We steam on reduced revolutions. Fog climbs the bows, enfolds the winches, streams across hatch tarpaulins, tugs at masts. The funnel divides it, the whip aerials slice it. Fog rolls so thick along the flanks of the hull that none can note the condition of the sea. To stare into the sodden quilt is to fancy it hangs with the shadows and shapes of phantoms. Imagination figures a parade of shrouded ghouls that step out a slow dance towards the stern. Every vertical streams with wet. Every horizontal drips its share. Our lights burn: green to starboard, red to port, white at the mast head and the poop — they fade and grow bright as the veils come and go. Atop the foremast rides a bold and murderous gull, a greater black-back, Larus marinus. He's been perched for an hour, taking his ease. Now and again his white head glints with a golden shine, as though the sun breaks through somewhere up there.

Just when the gloom seems endless, a rent in the fog might open for a bare minute. At obtuse angles to our hull, a watery sun uncovers rafts of clown-faced puffins, and razorbills in dapper black and white. The fishing is good here, plenty of herring and sprat. Once upon a time, the North Sea was inhabited dry land and marsh, with

Dogger Bank a range of wooded hills three quarters the size of Holland. But after the Ice Age, the sea returned to prompt our ancestors to gather their spears and shift camp to the western hills. The water rose as the ice caps melted. It took a few thousand years to creep back until the day when the great wave came. Dogger was the last place to drown. Now, bottom-scouring trawlers might haul up half-fossilised lumps of oak and pine, the tusk of a woolly mammoth, worked flints, and even bits of amber among the gasping mass of flapping plaice and skate.

Though ears strain for steam whistles and the thud of diesel engines, all is muted, even the whine of our turbines is hushed. The clink of a bridge officer's coffee cup set down in its saucer can make one start. Secunnies (Indian seamen), buried in yellow oilskins, stare out from the extremity of each wing of the bridge; they are puree-wallahs, lookout men. Without radar, we would steer blind. The Lascar crew refers to the radar machinery as e'Steam Puree-Wallah: the steam-driven lookout man. They understand electricity to be a species of steam, it being the ultimate motive force on a vessel like ours. Every two minutes, as is the regulation for safety at sea in poor visibility, steam erupts from the ship's whistle, bolted to the funnel, and Mawana announces her presence with one long blast. Two minutes pass until a secunny in the wheelhouse pulls a lever and the harrumphing blast swells out again. So it goes on, hour after hour. For those on watch, there is no ease while they strain for any muffled response. But when men are in their bunks, they sleep sound — unless the engine stops. Should vibration cease to throb through a seafarer's bunk, his eyes will open with a start.

Cold air spills into the wireless room as Jamil enters with coffee on a tray. He's from Bengal. In his late fifties, short cropped beard — the mark of a hajji Moslem who has made the pilgrimage to Mecca. He's been with this company for years, one year on and one year off as is the regulation in India so that other seamen have the chance of a wage.

'Coffee she come, sahib. With chhota (small) cake from galley.' He sets down the white coffee cup and saucer, both blazoned with the Brocklebank house flag, half blue, half white. Next comes a plate that bears a little sponge cake with half a glazed cherry on top. 'Tigh coffee, sahib? Todha cheenee she cook (only a little sugar added).'

I take a sip. Once again, my gums don't cringe in horror, I seem to have persuaded Jamil to go easy on the sugar and condensed milk. Today's brew has a bite akin to bitter mud, but I don't let on. It will do. 'Coffee thig (good), Jamil.' He's eyeing the little cake with a cocked eyebrow, so I take a nibble. Light. Almost as good as Mam's baking. I raise a thumb. 'Cake bahut achcha (very good). Tell cook, this like cake at home.'

He waggles his head from side to side, in the manner of Indians when they concur. On his way out, he glances at the cover of the book by my elbow. 'Jamil son have this book, sahib. Clever son! Mother clever bibi (woman). Teacher!' He smiles in recollection, then leaves.

The whistle begins another five-second blast just as my boss comes in. He waits for it to subside. 'Just checked the radar; it's running hot with all this work. Echoes looked thinner than normal. Changed an EF50 and it's a deal better.' He picks up my book. 'Teach Yourself Esperanto!' He looks at the blurb on the back. 'I don't know anyone who speaks it. Do you?'

'La Unua Libro', I offer.

'What's that mean?'

'The First Book.'

'So you speak Esperanto?'

'Not yet, but I live in hope. The name Esperanto translates as One Who Hopes. Zamenhof invented it seventy years back. A Polish chap. He reckoned a universal second language would foster world peace.'

Don turns a page. 'Since then we've had two world wars. He'll be a touch disappointed.'

'Well, Jamil tells me his son in Calcutta has a copy. So it's getting around.'

He flicks through the pages. 'Some of it reads like the Latin they force-fed us at Grammar school. Did you take languages?'

'Not we oafs at Galley's Field Secondary Modern. We were destined to be layers of bricks, hewers of coal, and rollers of iron. But we did ask for French. Teacher said the school would consider it once we'd learnt to speak proper English.'

'And how far did you get with that project?'

I choose to ignore Don's wit. 'Speaking of language, the mate called the North Sea the Gannet's Bath and the Whale Road. What's he on about?'

He snorts. 'You'll have to read the Sagas. Mr Mate can't help airing his knowledge. Expensive education. Studied Beowulf, don't you know. But he's a competent chap, and highly thought of in Cunard Buildings.'

'I've heard of Beowulf. It's a Norse Saga that could have taken place around Hartlepool. In those days, it had plenty of caves and swamps that could hide a monster.'

'Shh! Listen'. He cocks his head at the far off rumble of a ship's horn. 'Hear that?'

The wheelhouse telegraph rings, then sounds again as the engine room acknowledges. The speed drops and our steam whistle blasts out. A mournful reply drones through the murk, this time more muffled. The call and response continue for long minutes until our telegraph sounds a final ring and speed picks up.

A head pokes through the chartroom hatch. It's the chief officer. 'Captain's on the bridge. Wants D/F fixes. Can you do us three beacons: Spurn Point, Nordhinder, and the Weser lightship? If they're not transmitting, we'll have whatever else will make a decent cocked hat.'

I flick switches to warm up the direction finding gear and ask, 'How close was that ship we heard?'

'Two miles ahead. On track for the Humber. There's more to come.' He shuts the hatch.

Don throws it open. 'I want the crew's aerials lowered, and all else illegal that they've rigged. If that tangle stays up, the bearings can only be approximate.'

'Right! I'll send a secunny to drop the halyards and clear away whatever else he finds.'

'You can't trust the buggers,' Don grumbles. 'I took a stroll around before we sailed. Heath Robinson aerials sprouting everywhere — mostly from the engineers' ventilators. We never had this problem in the days before these new-fangled Jap transistor radios. Now everyone expects to have entertainment on tap. Move over. I'll take the watch while you take the bearings.'

He glances at the clock on the bulkhead. Two red zones mark the dial — two silent periods for the distress and calling frequency of 500kc/s. The red sectors permit no transmissions from 15 to 18 minutes and 45 to 48 minutes past the hour when all ships must listen for distress signals. In every ocean, ships fall silent. Woe betide anyone who flouts that rule. The offender will hear from the authorities.

The main receiver is now worked by my chief. He tunes for the Portishead traffic list, with all the warble and splutter that entails. On the end of the bench, the 500kc/s watch receiver spits out sundry callsigns on loudspeaker. The room fills with the fluting din of transmitters scattered across the triangle of the North Sea, from the treacherous tidal-race of the Pentland Firth, across to the yawning Skagerrak, and south to the Goodwin Sands. I make my headphones snug to mute the racket, and turn to the Direction Finder — pleased that the boss trusts me with such vital work.

The Spurn Lightvessel at the mouth of the River Humber, where Yorkshire meets Lincolnshire, comes in loud and clear. Her call sign MMH is followed by a long dash that I chase with the broad dial of the Bellini-Tosi direction finder to hunt for the null point in the tone. The zero is crisp — the secunny has wasted no time in lowering the crew aerials. I note the bearing of Spurn relative to our ship's head and jot it down. Nordhinder, off the Dutch coast, and the Weser lightvessel off the German shore, have broader nulls, so that I must swing the variometer to either side several times to determine the centre. The three bearings intersect to form a triangular space on the chart — shaped like the headgear Napoleon wore at Waterloo. We can assume Mawana is within that triangle. The watch officer has his 'cocked hat', and one small enough to keep him happy for a while. Though the bridge is content for the time being, I suspect we'll be on D/F duty until the radar picks up the entrance to the River Weser. Broken sleep is ours tonight, but we should be alongside in Bremerhaven by breakfast time.

5

Weser

Icy air nips the ears tonight as three of us clatter down the gangway. Carpenter Alf is buried in a capacious old duffle-coat. The bulk of Henry, our Birkenhead 4th engineer, is snug inside a woollen muffler and three-quarter black coat adorned by a blotched velvet collar — a Crombie overcoat once sported by some monied gent, but now looking just fine on a Merseysider with chipped fingernails. Behind the dense weave of a bridge coat, I'm protected well enough for a night out in the bomb-hammered town of Bremerhaven.

Mawana lies snug alongside in the river Weser, ready to load German exports: electrical machinery and Mercedes Benz engines. She's just astern of a tall Yankee freighter, a Victory ship. We inspect her lines as we stroll towards the dock gate. For all her rushed wartime construction, and the rust streaks and weld repairs, she is handsome in grey military livery.

Henry stares up at the tall funnel. 'Who's a sweet lass, then? Put together in short order, but too quick for the U-boats, you were. Lentz engine! Fifteen knots. Half as fast again as the poor auld Liberty ship. Yer in fine fettle, darlin'. Can't be over fifteen. A good ten years to go before the breakers get their mitts on yer.'

An American troopship is next — another grey being who looks to have done plenty of winter crossings of the Western Ocean. Her name needs a repaint, but could be *Geiger*. Squads of uniformed men in field caps, kitbags hefted on shoulders, have climbed her gangway all afternoon. They are going home. Armed guards are stationed, so we move on. Until 1949, ten years ago, Bremerhaven was a US controlled enclave within the British Zone of Occupation, a port of supply to the American sector after the surrender. The western sector of Germany is self-governing and prospers with Konrad Adenauer as chancellor, but the Allied army stays on to dissuade any adventures by the Soviet Union and its minions to the east.

Alf quickens his stride. 'Here she is!'

The US liner SS *America* dwarfs the end of the wharf. At 26,000 tons, she shrinks the 8700 tons of our steamer. She's abandoned the grey trooping colours and her wartime name, USS *West Point*, and is elegant again with black hull, white superstructure and two tremendous red funnels. Built in 1940 and conceived for luxury, she is now on her intended route, the passenger run between New York, Ireland, and Bremerhaven. Instead of 5,000 troops in bunks and hammocks, she carries 500 paying passengers in comfort. We loiter for five minutes, watching women in mink coats come and go.

Alf looks along the wharf. 'I wonder where it was The King landed. We should find out.'

Henry retorts, 'Which bleeding king?'

'I saw it on Pathe News at the Liverpool Odeon back in October. Only five months ago, on this very dockside, hordes of teenyboppers met the troopship *General George M. Randall* to rave over Elvis Aaron Presley. He'd been shipped to Germany to do his military service. US Army police had to shove back the squealing mob so Private Presley could disembark. I've got his records — *Heartbreak Hotel, Love Me Tender* — all good stuff.'

'So what will you do now? Kiss the dockside?'

Alf gives Henry a shove. 'Maybe on the way back. Once we've had a few bevvys. Let's be off.'

Rebuilt after fifty air raids, Bremerhaven is a lean and modern town. The RAF sent Halifax bombers by the hundred to cripple this critical base of Hitler's Kriegsmarine and his U-boat yards, and to seed the river with mines. One raid missed the docks but obliterated much of the town centre in twenty minutes. Other targets lay upriver: the Focke-Wulf aircraft factory and a massive, bomb-proof U-boat bunker. Six-thousand slave workers: POWs and German 'undesirables' perished during that bunker's construction — worked to death. An efficient system recorded the deaths of French prisoners of war, but not the Poles, Russians, and others deemed too sub-human to note down. The Nazis took away three hundred Bremerhaven Jews — only three returned. The town is under flurries of sleet tonight, but I imagine daylight helps these streets forget the horror that stalked them fifteen years ago.

After a much needed leg stretch past bomb sites and blocks of new flats with curtains drawn against the night, we discover smart shopping streets. All is deserted on this Saturday evening except for the occasional neon-lit bar. Music and American voices spill into darkness from the Rote Muhl.

Alf seizes our elbows. 'We'll give The Moulin Rouge a try. I'll get the ales in.'

We perch at the bar counter on high stools padded with leather. There are no signs of history. All is new, glossy and bright. Louis Armstrong's gravelly voice vibrates a speaker on the wall: *When the Saints Come Marching In*. Americans are ensconced on either side, drinking Becks bier from bottles. How can decent beer give of its best when it has not had chance to yield up its head and character in a shapely glass? They cannot experience the aroma. It's an insult to the brewer's craft. One might as well drink Guinness through a straw. I mutter as much to Alf.

Henry interrupts: 'That's no way to treat Pilsner. But they know not what they do, being raised on Budweiser.'

'Shush, you two. Don't upset the regulars.'

I glance along the bar to check for earwiggers. 'Asked for a beer glass in the States one time — a bar in Houston. The barmaid, a lass with dreamy green eyes, said: 'A glass! You want a glass? What are you? Some kind of wise guy?'

Alf gives a snort. 'Maybe you are. Try one of these.' He shoves a plate along the counter.

'What is it?' I take a bite from a cylinder of flabby, silvery layers impaled on a sharp stick. 'It's raw fish! Yuk. Did you pay for these?'

'On the house, to help work up a thirst. They're Bismark Herring, old son — pickled in vinegar and dill. Watch out for the capers. Did you never get rolled herrings at home?'

'We did. But Mam smothered them in oatmeal, then stuck them in a hot frying pan. Mostly on a Friday.'

'How do you find the Becks beer?'

I hold up the glass under a downlight; drain it and contemplate the froth that slides down the sides. 'A bit like that Tuborg Export we have on board. Crisp and hoppy, with a tang that makes you want more. I'll get them in.' The bartender is looking our way, so I hold up three fingers. 'I wonder if they sell Dortmunder.'

Henry inspects the pumps. 'Don't see any. Why Dortmunder?'

'It's just that when I joined the *Corburn*, a Cory collier in North Shields, the outgoing sparks had left a Dortmunder beer glass in my cabin. She was fresh back from Hamburg.'

'A collier out of the Tyne! How romantic. What was the feeding like?'

'When we tied up by Battersea power station, the cook, a huge fat bloke, chest hair poking through his string vest, sent the cabin boy ashore to buy a dozen sliced loaves, and fried fish and chips all round. Skipper was erratic — one day he would be leaving Bible tracts in my cabin, next day my little stash of pale ale had vanished and he'd left a note to say he'd borrowed it. The mate locked him in his cabin one time, to keep him off the bridge while we fought through a storm, miles off course. Next morning, rounding the tip of Cornwall, she broke down. Onshore gale and stuffed full with Welsh coal, drifting onto the Longships reef. Thought we'd had it. But the Geordie engineers got the engines going just in time. As to the feeding, it was filling, you might say. Were you ever on coasters?'

'No, always deep sea. Did two years on tankers. Persian Gulf, Venezuela, then the damned signal: *Land's End for Orders*. Quick turnarounds, pumping oil all day, hardly any time for a run ashore. No idea when you'd get leave. How about you, Chips?'

Alf sips the froth off his glass, then takes a deeper pull. 'First went to sea with the Bank Line. A decent company. Saw a lot of the Pacific. Tramping. For two years, we never knew where we'd end up. Interesting places right enough, Java, Fiji, Philippines, but two years away from home is a bit much when you've a lass waiting. I'll stick with Brocks for now. With Brocklebanks you've a fair idea when you'll see the UK again; never more than seven months, never less than five.'

We fall into thoughtful silence until I remember my first wireless rooms. 'I did two trips out east on a troopship. Whole regiments, plus military odds and sods to Singapore, Hong Kong, and Japan. The *Dunera* was British India owned, on permanent government charter. On docking after the second trip, I expected leave. But Southampton office dispatched me to Cardiff to sign Home Trade articles for six weeks on the *Hughli,* after which I could be sure of leave, they said. She was a Jimmy Nourse tropical tramp. Cabins opened straight onto the deck so as to keep cool. But the Marconi office tricked me into signing for deep sea, which meant two years away. After a lot of evasion by them, and threats from me that I'd rip up my discharge book and join the army, they found an Irishman to take over. I was rewarded with the little Tyne coal boat. Six weeks on her and I told Marconi to stuff their job and went back to college to study radar maintenance. Then came that slump in shipping. I tried Christian Salvesen whalers and then Bibby's, but no luck. I was getting anxious, but Brocklebanks took me on, them being keen on radar tickets.'

It is a fact that, despite a good dinner beforehand, when young chaps have a night out on the beer they usually want supper afterwards. So it is that our noses follow the vapours of fried onions to a caravan parked on a bomb site. We stand in line behind an army sergeant and a corporal. They show an interest.

'You guys Limeys?'

Henry is straight there. 'We are, right enough. Can't you tell from our scurvy-free complexions? Never a pimple on a British seafarer since the days of Captain Cook. We still keep a jug of the stuff on the saloon table, but I prefer to take a splash with my gin.'

'Gee, it's true then. You drink lime juice. On hard rations, we take vitamin C pills. There's no spots on us, neither.'

Alf is nervous of how this will proceed and gently squeezes the smaller Henry to one side. 'So as to combat scurvy, our German friends took pickled cabbage with them on long voyages. That's why we call them Krauts — when they're out of earshot.'

The sergeant is being served his pink and succulent Wiener sausage in a bun by an overweight man who makes the caravan rock as he moves. 'That's enough mustard, but you can add extra onions and sauerkraut. Say, Ulrich, these Brits here reckon you Germans lived on cabbages when you went to sea. Is that true?'

'Ja! Blutty kraut every day! That's why we won only *kleine* empire. Kraut give belly ache so bad we did not get past Finisterre. Without kraut it would have been Hamburgers who discovered Australia.'

'And you might have colonised America. And our revolutionary war would have been against you.'

'If it had been a German colony, we would not have lost.'

Alf can't contain himself. 'But it WAS you who lost. Much of the army of the Crown was Hessian and Brunswickian, brought over by Hanoverian George. So our side won! The American War of independence was yet another success for British arms.'

The corporal looks askance. 'Now look what you've started, Serge. Let's go sit on that pile of bricks and work through these frankfurters.'

6

Scheldt And Thames

3rd March, Antwerp.
 I offer a ten shilling note. The man in the sausage van rubs it between greasy fingers. 'You have American dollar?'
 'Sorry, that's all I've got left. Spent my francs.'
 'Ok, I give twenty francs for this.' He dips into his steaming sausage trough to fish out our wieners, lays the pink torpedoes into three white buns and anoints them with fried onion and yellow mustard. My change is counted out in alloy coins adorned with oak leaves, the head of a woman, and a miner with a lamp — yet another load of shrapnel to join the Indian annas and US cents in my tin of spare change.
 Which is best — the German slender sausage in a bun, or the short and fat Belgian? We three agree both are scrumptious and just the thing after a night out on excellent Pils. Henry prefers the Bremerhaven model, but I think the Antwerp version has the edge, if only for the way it bursts open when you take a bite. We sit in wiener and mustard contentment in the Grote Markt, on steps beneath a huge bronze statue that is green with verdigris, and contemplate the fragrant ladies passing by. I wonder if they are wearing 4711 *Eau de Cologne* — I'd bought a bottle of it for Mam when I was last here. The green man is Brabo, a Roman officer who cut off the hand of a brutal giant and hurled it into the river Scheldt near to where our ship is tied up.
 Restaurants and cafes line the square, nestled between ornate sixteenth century guildhalls. Alf gives one of his

considered sniffs. 'Surprising how these fine old buildings still stand. That depraved git and crap Austrian artist, Schicklgruber, cared little for architecture. Once the Allies took Antwerp, he had a blue fit and lobbed von Braun rockets onto the town. One went through the roof of the Rex cinema. Six hundred dead, half of them our soldiers. Anyway, I need to be getting back to the ship. A quick one in Danny's Bar on the way down Skipper Street. Any volunteers?'

Henry clambers to his feet. 'Only to keep you out of mischief.'

Schippersstraat is the prime spot in Antwerp's legendary red-light district. Rows of lit windows display alluring ladies. Each stands or reclines in her own window, each in her speciality costume, negligee or leather. She hires the room by the hour, including ornate armchair, chaise longue and bed. Drawn curtains hint at a client. So long as there is no public disorder, and except for street trade, none of this is against Belgian law. As we stroll past, there are smiles, beckoning fingers, and pouts. I find it difficult to give more than a glance, lest I catch their eye, but note the garter belts and suspenders and how red velvet plush is popular as interior decoration.

Henry loiters. 'Here's a bonny lass. And look here, fit as a butcher's dog, this'n.'

Alf calls back. 'Come away. Don't forget she's someone's daughter.'

Henry trots alongside. 'One or two could be someone's granny.'

Next comes a cluster of bars. I recognise the Buzz Bomb. 'This is a good spot. I was here in fifty-six, off a Jimmy Nourse tramp. The second engineer was a huge Pole. He did his party trick — a pickled egg washed down by a glass of lager. He did it twenty-one times, after which he offered to fight anyone in the bar who offended his friends.

Then he kissed his shipmates full on the lips and declared everlasting love.'

Henry makes a choked remark that sounds like, 'yuk'.

Alf slows his pace at the next bar, the Zanzibar. 'Keep out of there. The blokes inside are all women dressed up. Next one is ours.'

We find a corner in Danny's Bar. The mellow tones of Dean Martin and his *Buona Sera* fight against boisterous shouts and guffaws. The pumped beer is acceptable enough for a dubious joint on Schipper Street. There are some fine-looking women behind the bar and moving among the customers. One hovers a while to breathe into Henry's ear. Alf keeps grinning. She gives up on Henry and rubs her thigh against mine. Her long red locks are full of curls. 'Hello, sailor. Ver vill you sleep tonight?'

She smells like a Persian brothel — as they say. 'Sorry, luv, we're off early tomorrow. Anyhow, I'm spoken for.' I peep into a cleavage draped with rhinestones.

She flashes eyelashes of astonishing length and minces away. I glance at Alf. 'Something odd about that one.'

'No different to any of the others. The women in this establishment are all men dressed up.'

5th March, Thames Estuary.

With the river pilot collected out of the fog, *Mawana* creeps through the murk, bound for London's Royal Docks forty miles upstream. The pilot takes it steady. Somewhere to port is a broken-backed ship rotting on a sandbank off the Isle of Sheppey. In 1944, the American Liberty ship, SS *Richard Montgomery* had hauled 6,000 tons of high explosive and phosphorus bombs across the Atlantic, only to come to grief on a Thames shoal. Some cargo was unloaded before she broke in two, but 1,500 tons remain in her holds too lethal to disturb. As time ticks away, the bombs deteriorate. She's not a wreck that any pilot would wish to nudge. Her gaunt masts are visible to folk on the Isle of Sheppey. They will lose more than their windows should she ever detonate.

My chief enters to pace up and down the wireless room linoleum. He normally exercises on the boat deck, but this clammy fog puts him off. 'It's as thick as a Blackpool landlady's corset out there. I'll be glad to get alongside.'

'I had no notion the corsets of Blackpool were so dense.'

'It's my home town, so you can take it from me that they are. This fog gives me the creeps. One of our vessels was rammed in a Channel fog — right amidships. The poor bloody purser woke up with the bows of a Greek coming nicely to a stop just as they crunched into his bunk. He had a job to wriggle free. Imagine waking up to face a vertical mass of dripping rust and barnacles!'

'Blimey! That would put any bloke off the sea.'

Don raises his voice as the fog whistle begins its five-second blast. 'He never did get over it. Was inclined to take a tot of whisky with his bedtime Ovaltine after that.' He waits for the sonorous note to die. 'Once docked, we'll come off Home Trade articles and sign on Foreign. We'll be loading for a few days, and I'd like to nip off home. So you'll be caretaker. I'll leave a list of jobs. Ok?'

'That's fair enough. Take the chance while it's there. I had a decent stint of slipping off home at Middlesbrough.'

Eleven miles downstream from London Bridge are the Royal Docks. The entrance lock is said to be spacious enough to take the Cunard White Star *Mauretania*. Our *Mawana*, at a quarter of the great liner's 36,000 tons, can easily squeeze through, along with our tugs, *Titan* and *Sun*. Once the water level of the lock equals that of the dock basins, the gates creep open and the tugs draw us into the crowded Royal Albert Dock. The Albert is lined with ships of many nations — there must be twenty of them beneath the dipping cranes. On our left is the King George V, stuffed with vessels and lighters, but *Titan* tows us straight through the Albert and into Victoria basin.

The tugs nudge us alongside a vacant space on the quay, beneath four tall cranes mounted on railway lines.

Almost fifty ships are gathered in the three docks. Such glorious ranks of funnels to be admired: the buff column of *Chusan,* Peninsular and Oriental's great white passenger liner; a British India steamer's black smoke-stack with two white bands; the triple ostrich plumes of Prince Line; the blue and red chevrons of Stricks. Finest are the funnels of bright blue and black, the livery of 'Blue Funnel' cargo ships and their sublime architecture — this fleet of Alfred Holt carry Homeric names that stir the blood: *Cyclops, Hector, Jason, Ajax, Nestor, Memnon, Polyphemus.* Moored to a dirty dock, the two that lay here today seem like captive birds. But it's a glory to admire those Blue Funnels in their true home beneath tropical skies, gliding like swans on their sea tracks to the East, or bounding home with copra and tea, latex and teak.

These docks had 25,000 tons of bombs thrown at them, yet they survived to build much of the prefabricated Mulberry Harbour for the invasion of Normandy. A walk ashore reveals what survived the Blitz. The scents of Poplar, Canning Town and the Isle of Dogs join and merge. Odours from the soap factory, the abattoir, the Henry Edie brass and iron foundry, blend with smoke from the coal fires of crowded housing and the diesel fumes of London's red double-decker buses and a swarm of lorries. It is best not to breathe too deeply on a day of still air like this. The vapours merge in the fog to make the ripest of stinks, but helpful whiffs of banana and cinnamon leak from warehouses. And so we find it on our stroll through Silvertown, past the site of the terrible explosion of 1917 that killed seventy-three and flattened entire streets — all to purify TNT for the artillery shells that held back Kaiser Bill. The greasy pavements lead to the Round House, a handsome pub on the corner of Woolwich Manor Way and Albert Road. Sadly, it serves only Watney's Red Barrel, in thick and dimpled pint glass mugs with handles.

Henry's face is a picture when he takes a pull. 'I've heard about this stuff.' He shudders. 'It's even served on the

Queen Mary. How do they get away with it? And these ponsified southern glasses! Why can't we have a straight, thin glass — a decent sleeve? Drinking from this piss pot is like kissing a gorilla.'

Alf chuckles. 'You've got the makings of a poet, Henry. Though I agree. Proper ale in this country is dying a death with the craze for metal barrels and gas pressure. But the younger generation seems to like it this way. Consistency, you see. Never changes — bland and fizzy wherever it's served. What do you reckon, Sparks?'

'It's like bottled pop.' I hold the glass up to a lamp. 'But there's nowt floating in it. They haven't emptied the ash trays of pipe dottle and dog-ends into it to improve the body. Wooden barrels can be fine, if you can trust the landlord, but some ale I had in Cardiff looked like pond water — I half-expected to swallow a newt. It had no head, and was sour. At least this won't give you the trots. Is there a pub round here that sells Flowers bitter? That's half-decent, even by the standards of London.'

'Another budding wordsmith! So you're not too keen on Watney's?'

'It is consistent, but I suppose so is gnat's pee. It's safe — I'll give it that. Even so, I'd rather be at home with a pint of hand-pulled Nimmo's anytime.' I glance at my wristwatch — Swiss, a Felca bought cheap in Aden. 'I have to ring Beryl at eight o'clock.'

Henry pauses from filling his pipe. 'Your future in-laws got the phone in, then? You marrying into money?'

'Not quite. But she does have an umbrella.'

'There's posh!'

'I'll be ringing the phone box in Catcote Road, round the corner from her house. It's arranged. Let's hope there's not a queue for it.'

A tubby fellow on the next table leans over. 'You boys off a ship? I'm with P&O, off the *Chusan* with my mates.'

Henry responds: 'You'll be a steward.'

'Oh, my love, how did you guess?'

'Who else would come ashore in a fluffy pink Angora sweater?'

'Cheeky bugger! You want to make something of it?'

Alf intervenes. 'Don't mind our friend. Doesn't know any better, being from Birkenhead.' He mutters into Henry's ear. 'Leave off. The Round House is their watering hole. They're all here tonight, and some carry flick knives.' He drains his glass and stands. 'Right, then. I know a pub that sells Flower's bitter. Let's be off.'

As we wander through Silvertown, Alf recites:

From rocks and sands
And barren lands
Kind fortune keep me free,
And from great guns
and women's tongues
Good Lord deliver me.

'Where's that from?' I ask.
'Saw it carved into a piece of walrus ivory in the Liverpool museum. Sailor's scrimshaw art, about 1810.'
'What's it got to do with tonight?'
'Nowt. Just felt like giving it a run out. Poetry does not need permission to speak.'

The red telephone box smells of vinegar and fish and chips. I place a forefinger in the 'O', rotate the dial to full extent, then listen to the whirring tick as it returns. The operator responds, 'Hello, caller.' She sounds clipped and polished, with a hint of Cockney beneath the elocution.

'A long distance call to Hartlepools 5336, please.'
'For Hartlepools 5336, insert two shillings and sixpence for three minutes.'

I feed in a silver florin and a sixpence (almost two pints of beer) and pile up spare coins on a ledge.

Clicks and clacks sound for ten seconds before I hear the ringing tone, then: 'Hello?' It is Beryl's sweet voice.
'Caller, you are through. Press button A.'

I lean into button A — the mechanism needs oiling. The coins rattle into their secure metal box and we are in our own special world.

7

Biscay

12th March 1959.
Thursday today, mild and dry. With a scrubbing brush and plenty of soap, I've washed the London grime off our aerial insulators before the crew hoists the phosphor-bronze rigs up the masts. We had stowed the lowered aerials in a safe place to prevent them from getting chopped down by dockside cranes. With loading complete, hatches battened, high tide in the Thames, and sweeter air at sea, now is the hour to leave for India.

Once the ship is free of the Royal Victoria dock and established in the stream, the hoses are out. Our Lascar deck hands sluice the vessel clear of the detritus of a week of cargo work. Soggy newspapers, Player's Weights cig packets, spent matches, husks of pork pie, grit, spilt tea, scraps of freight-packing dunnage timber, and sundry unsavoury bits chucked aside by stevedores, vanish overboard into England's premier river. *Mawana* gleams again and is ready for the sea, but first the Trinity House pilot must thread her through flotillas of barges and their tugs, and past the occasional working dredger that disgorges massive buckets of noisome river silt into attendant hoppers. I'm loitering outside the wireless room, waiting for the Thames to broaden out and make it reasonable to open the station. A hundred and twenty watts of radio frequency energy into our aerial will swamp the joy of listeners to the BBC Light Programme along the terraces of London's East End. I'll wait until the dark flow widens.

The *Oceanspan* main transmitter warms into life with the hum of pleasure that comes when oscillators and antenna are in tuned harmony. The laminated plates of transformers whisper as I key on 500kc/s to attract the attention of GNF, Northforeland Radio, the local area station perched atop a chalk cliff on the Kentish coast. I offer a TR — a traffic routing report. He instructs that we both move to the 512 kilocycles working frequency. *GNF DE GWWZ MAWANA QTO LONDON QRD CALCUTTA VIA SUEZ.* He now knows we have departed the Thames, bound for Calcutta via the Suez Canal.

Northforeland acknowledges receipt and says he holds no traffic for us: *GWWZ DE GNF QSL QRU.* He will tell GKA, at Portishead in Somerset, of our movement. Once out of British waters, most of our traffic will be routed through Portishead, the busiest of the world's Morse stations.

Off Sheerness, the grizzled pilot, medal ribbons on his breast, descends by rope ladder to take a calculated leap into the heaving cutter, and we are free. He gave us flawless pilotage: 12th century England had a law that allowed a crew to behead any pilot who wrecked their ship.

To port, the Maunsell forts of Shivering Sands loom out of haze nine miles from the Kent coast. Even though the fortified towers are quadrupeds, they remind me of the three-legged invasion machines from Mars that blasted English villages with death-rays in H G Wells' novel, *The War of the Worlds*. It's my current bed-time reading, but images of striding Martian gunships prowl the dreams, so I'd best set that book aside for a while.

The forts are armour-plated structures arranged in circular groups. Each fort comprises seven giant platforms on long legs anchored to concrete blocks. They stand thirty feet above high water. Rusted and gaunt, they look menacing. Armed with searchlights and anti-aircraft artillery, they served their purpose. Air Marshal Goering's plan was for his Luftwaffe bombers to locate London by flying up the moonlit ribbon of the River Thames. Goering did not personally crouch in the cockpit of a bomber as, according to a wartime ditty written to raise British morale, he was testosterone disadvantaged:

*Hitler has only got one ball,
Goering has two — but very small.
Himmler has something sim'lar
But poor old Goebbels has no balls at all.*

Fortifications in the Thames approaches were built in response to the Blitz; they shot down twenty-two enemy aircraft and thirty doodlebugs (V1 flying bombs). Three sets of forts guarded the river: Shivering Sands, Red Sands, and The Nore. Ships need to take extra care hereabouts — in 1953, the Swedish *Baalbek* rammed and demolished two of Fort Nore's gun towers, killing four of the caretakers. (Five years from now, cracks in the fabric of staid and homely Britain will appear when Screaming Lord Sutch, the musician of Horror Rock, invades the fort on Shivering Sands to set up an illegal pirate radio station. Radio Sutch will entertain the region with pop music and advertising, plus readings of the notorious, and just unbanned, D H Lawrence's *Lady Chatterley's Lover* by the notorious Mandy Rice-Davies.)

Don arrives to relieve me for lunch as we clear the Strait of Dover to join the English Channel. 'Scotch egg, chips, and mushy peas today. College pudding for afters — what an excellent repast!' He nods at the starboard porthole. 'The world's busiest shipping lane, so he's taking us close in. You can make out breaking surf on the Goodwins. There's at least one mast sticking out of the sands. You know, there's two of our own buried yonder. *Mahratta* ran aground and broke up in 1939. The spooky thing is that her wreck lies on top of the first *Mahratta* wrecked thirty years before. What about that?'

I'd heard the story many times, but don't let on. 'So that's how the Goodwins come by the name, *Ship Swallower*. A thousand wrecks, they say.'

Don takes over my chair at the operating position. 'And that amounts to fifty thousand souls. The last casualty was the anchored South Goodwin lightship, of all things. Broke free and went down in a storm five years back. Crew of seven drowned. Only man saved was a bloomin' Ministry of Agriculture chap doing a tally of migrant birds!' Don fits on his headphones, calls out, 'Enjoy your lunch!' and I head for the saloon, musing on the Goodwins. Kentish folk, so I've heard, on fine days of dead low water, venture out once a year to play a quick game of cricket on the exposed shoals before flood tide.

(The Goodwin Sands stretch for ten miles along the coast of Kent with a safe channel, known as *The Downs*, between the shallows and the shore. Shakespeare knew of the dangers. In *The Merchant of Venice*, he has Salarino declare: '*Why, yet it lives there uncheck'd that Antonio hath a ship of rich lading wrecked on the narrow seas; the Goodwins, I think they call the place; a very dangerous flat and fatal, where the carcasses of many a tall ship lie buried ...*')

I open the hatch to the chartroom — the dim space is empty. Those on duty will be in the wheelhouse, peering through salt-spattered windows. A press on the bell push brings Bill Evans. The third mate ponders the weather report beneath the dim red bulb of the night-time light. 'Sorry, Bill. Just in from Niton Radio, Isle of Wight.'

He purses his lips as he reads: *GALE WARNING. BISCAY AND FINISTERRE SOUTHERLY SEVERE GALE FORCE 9 INCREASING STORM FORCE 10 SOON. SEA STATE ROUGH OR VERY ROUGH. VISIBILITY MODERATE OR GOOD OCCASIONALLY POOR*. He glances at the bulkhead clock. It's thirty minutes to midnight and the end of our watches. 'This has been brewing. It's a bugger. I'm getting my head down in half an hour. Let's hope it's passed over before we are both on again. Thanks, anyway.'

'Is the radar behaving itself?'

'Well enough. Seems tough gear, the new BTH. Mind you, I've been having to turn up the sea-clutter knob for the past hour. Sea is building, so I knew muck was on its way. But I'm wary of that sea-clutter control. It wipes out the wave-top echoes right enough, but I worry about what else has gone.'

'That's right. Too high and it can make a trawler vanish, too low and you'll miss echoes from small stuff amid the clutter. It would help if all ships carried a radar reflector to make them more visible.'

The second mate stamps into the chartroom. He's early for the watch handover. Walter Fisk hails from the Suffolk coast. 'We could be in for it tonight, Billy old son.' He squints at the weather report. 'Wind on the stem and swell to starboard. Typical Biscay! I'll acquaint the Old Man before he turns in.' He lifts the Master's phone and winds the handle.

I close the hatch so that the wireless room lights don't hamper the bridge officers' night vision, and turn my attention to the second silent period of the hour when, from 45 to 48 minutes past the hour, stations must cease operations to listen for signals of distress on 500kc/s. When the minute hand of our radio room bulkhead clock leaves the white-enamelled part of the face and touches the red zone, the waveband falls silent. All apart from a distant Yugoslav who calls GPK, Portpatrick Radio at the mouth of the River Clyde. GPK responds with *QRT* (stop sending) *SILENT PERIOD*. The rasping note of the Yugoslav gives two dots — which is an abbreviated apology. The rest of the three minutes is free of Morse code, except that through the surges of static comes a wavering weak note from a dozy operator, maybe two-hundred miles away, who has the telegraph key depressed so he can tune his transmitter. Then a hush — perhaps he's glanced at his clock. The hand leaves the red zone, and signals crash through. Bedlam returns. Everyone else in Biscay and The English Channel seems eager to contact a shore station:

GLD Landsend, GNI Niton (Isle of Wight), GNF Northforeland, OST Ostend, PCH Scheveningen, DAN Norddeich. I lower the gain control of the Redifon receiver and copy one of those calls into the radio log to fulfil the regulation that operators must make an entry in the log every ten minutes as proof they are on watch. We note silent periods in the log, plus records of distress traffic whenever it occurs. During distress, stations must hold silence except for those assisting.

Two years ago, I was junior on SS *Mahanada*, out of Liverpool for Calcutta. Our vessel kept a lookout for a missing British-flagged vessel, the 1943 Canadian-built Liberty ship, *Nordic Star*. She was en route from Philadelphia to Le Havre, loaded with 8,000 tons of anthracite coal. She spoke on 27th December when she gave her estimated arrival at Le Havre to be 3rd January. When our vessel intersected her intended course, she was six days overdue. The Cunard liner, Queen Elizabeth, on a similar track to Nordic Star, reported hurricane-force winds and waves up to eighty feet.

Each time I pass this way, I wonder if *Nordic Star* might sleep beneath our keel. The tragedy has held me since I had a letter from my friend, Brian Marsden, then a radio officer on a Greek vessel. He had been in Philadelphia in the same dock as the lost ship and was approached by the wireless operator from *Nordic Star* for advice on his equipment. Brian, a talented radio engineer, visited that ship and found the gear not to be in best condition, but did what he could. The transmitter and receiver must have functioned well enough for her Master to send a message to the agents, and one to his wife, at 0100 hours 27th December 1956. Then silence forever. She could be anywhere — 1800 miles to the west of us in mid-Atlantic, or beneath us right now. Of her crew of 34, we have no word. But five months after she disappeared, a sea-worn lifebelt, bearing the name *Nordic Star*, washed ashore at Machrie Bay on the Hebridean island of Islay. The North Atlantic Drift (an arm of the Gulf Stream) would have borne that lifebelt to Islay — its current arcs across the ocean to sweep the shores of western Scotland as it heads for the Arctic. It has a speed of about 0.5knots which, over the 120 days since Nordic Star vanished, could have moved the lifebelt 1500 miles. The lost ship might rest somewhere, in a canyon, or on a ridge, among the submerged basalt mountains of the Mid-Atlantic Ridge, one or two miles down. The loneliness and pitch blackness of her grave is the ghastly thought that sometimes comes to mind when I stare into the sea.

Hands on rails, I turn sideways to descend the stairway to my cabin, which is the sensible way in a sea that grows by the hour. The bunk invites, so I climb in to snuggle between the bulkhead and the Dutch wife. She lays the length of my bunk, six feet long, and mute despite what I say. Turned on her side and trapped against the raised fiddle board of the bunk, in wild weather she prevents a fellow rolling out of bed. It is a long drop — the bunk is built on top of three deep drawers. Propped against a pillow, knees raised, and with drooping eyelids, I read *King Solomon's Mines* for half-an-hour until Rider Haggard's yarn has our adventurers scaling a mountain called Sheba's Breast. *Mawana* has produced a rhythmic roll that causes the blue curtain across my porthole to hang inwards at forty-five degrees for long seconds, then return. I watch it for a few minutes whilst pondering what Beryl might be doing at this time. She is asleep — there's a half-smile on her lips. I switch off the lamp, and stretch out.

The Indian stewards have doused the tablecloth with water so that dishes, cups, and condiments don't slide into our laps. As ultimate defence, the fiddle rails sit locked around the table edges. There are vacant seats at breakfast, some stomachs are tender for the first few days. We have a gale of wind on the bow and twenty-foot ramparts of Atlantic swell charging at our starboard quarter with nothing to stop them clear from America. I've been fortunate to have never missed a meal because of *mal de mer*. In fact I've never been sea sick, but too many days of this can bring on a groggy fatigue.

It's Dundee kippers for breakfast. With his freezer space crammed and cramped, the Chief Steward likes to use up the smelly stuff before we reach the tropics. In the first week of a voyage, we may have one serving of poached salmon steaks. When the noble fish get high, they end their days in the most sumptuous dish of all time: Aberdeen salmon curry. I can't wait! It is the most memorable dish I've had so far. I place it just ahead of a fried egg sandwich prepared by a lady in a cottage that catered for cyclists. I'd ridden off the rain-drenched Cleveland Hills, into the village of Great Broughton in the North Riding of Yorkshire, after navigating the moorland from Lastingham via a disused mineral railway. I was fourteen and soaking wet, bruised and cut after plunging into a ditch. The fried egg sandwich cost a shilling. As I sat exhausted, and dripped like a half-drowned sparrow in her warm kitchen, it was the food of Paradise. That was a mere six years ago. How things change when you are growing!

Thank goodness the route to the wireless room is inside the bridge housing. I grasp the handrail tight. She yaws from the blow of another steep sea, rears up like a terrified mastodon, then plunges. I set off up the staircase, propelled by the sudden loss of gravity as her bows slide into a trough. My shoulder thuds against the bulkhead. She climbs again as I enter the wireless room, driving breakfast deeper into my stomach. The three paces to the chair are easy. It rides on a short chain bolted to the deck. I reach by my right knee and inch the rheostats clockwise. The inductor alternators and rotary transformers in the motor cupboard whir into life, then settle to a low and steady whine. I switch on both receivers, the latest Redifon R50M with its stiff and awkward waveband switch, and the wartime CR300, solid, easy, reliable. The valves glow and 500kc/s comes to life.

The sun is now bright in the east. From the porthole I glimpse a squadron of tiny birds, black with white rumps. Storm petrels, fluttering like bats over the swell. No bigger than a plump robin, they appear to walk on water as they tip-toe and patter across the heaving sea, picking at morsels. They rise as one, cross the ship, and flit into our lee, where the cook has jettisoned debris from his galley. Storm petrels do well by following ships. Those *Mother Carey's Chickens* have been sharing our breakfasts since the days of the cog and the caravel. They come ashore only at night, to visit their burrows on tiny islands.

We meet occasional small whales in the Bay of Biscay, but the huge Northern Right whale has vanished from here — the Basque whalers finished them off. I once applied for a job with Christian Salvesen whaling fleet out of the Tyne — I'd heard the money was good. Fortunately, for my future conscience, they had no vacancy.

At the close of my two-hour watch, we round the north-west corner of Spain and the fierce black cliffs of Finisterre. Southwards from this point, the weather should be kinder.

8

The Gully Gully Man

Wednesday, 18th March, 1959.
    Early morning, half-an-hour before my first watch. All is subdued, save for the muffled whine of turbines, the click and creak of wooden panelling, and the slap of the Mediterranean on the hull. *He who loves the sea loves also the ship's routine* — so wrote Joseph Conrad in his memoir, *The Mirror of the Sea*. I'd seized upon that book as soon as I'd scanned the list of library contents. It is good to be in the company of that thoughtful man; a chapter before sleep brings on contented dreams.
    I'm in charge of the library and so have first dip into the contents. About nine-hundred British ships plough the seas bearing a stout wooden box stencilled: *Property of The Mission to Seamen*. Two-hundred titles cram each crate, hence 180,000 books will be afloat around the world: an ocean of knowledge, edification, and comfort, intended by the charity for the improvement of the seafarer's mind. Our owners must concur, for they pay for the service. The crate holds an argosy of literature — everything a seafarer could wish, apart from sleazy stuff like the envy-inducing *My Life and Loves* by Frank Harris, or *The Kama Sutra*, written two-thousand years ago by an Indian chap — a citizen of Patna with an unpronounceable name. An interested reader must barter for such titles from Egyptian bum-boat wallahs in Port Said, or pavement vendors in Calcutta. If he is patient, there might be a dog-eared copy doing the rounds on board.

I've positioned the box, unlocked and unattended, in the officers' communal relaxation and games area known as the smoke room. There's a notebook for the recording of borrows and returns — we live in hope. A fellow can reserve a title that is already out. The system staggers when borrowers pass on books to a shipmate without routing them through the library. A book might disappear for weeks. Should a popular title be in a cabin too long, I rely on the frustrated reader to chase it up. If he fails, I'm appealed to and must negotiate. I check on the comings and goings each week, and ensure that the pencil I attached to the crate by a length of string has not wandered away. Having said all that, being in charge of this little world of literature brings on a warm feeling.

I'll become a nuisance soon enough: a scout, herder, hunter, and counter of books when I shepherd the library together in Calcutta. By the time we reach the Ganges, the officers will have read every Western and crime story in the box and must dip into Shakespeare's *Sonnets,* Homer's *Iliad,* or *Teach Yourself Esperanto.* They'll expect me to arrange an exchange of libraries with another vessel. I'll round up a volunteer to help lug the crate through the smelly puddles and monkey dung of Kidderpore dock and onto the other vessel, where we'll receive a hearty welcome before weaving our inebriated way back with the new library. When Indian Customs officers challenge us, we'll be detained while they examine the contents at the pace of constipated Amazon sloths. A bribe would help matters along, but I never play that game and know how they will ultimately yawn, preen moustaches, and dismiss us with an indolent wave of the hand.

I'm sharpening the library pencil when Don, my boss, strides into the smoke room — he strides everywhere, upright and ginger. He grunts a good morning. He's had a disturbed night. 'Got anything worth reading?'

I offer him the foolscap list of books, but he ignores it. 'You might like *Cruel Sea* by Nicholas Monsarrat. Born in Liverpool, it says on the flyleaf.'

'I'm not in the mood after last night. What else?'

'We've *Finnegan's Wake* by James Joyce.'

'Not blooming likely! The man's fixated on intestinal wind. You can never feel safe on a sofa these days.'

'Then, what about *The Land God Gave to Cain,* by Hammond Innes? Or there's, *Dr No,* the latest Ian Fleming — sex, snobbery and sadism, according to some posh London newspaper.'

'I'll take it.'

'The Auto Alarm bell got you up at two in the morning, Chief. Was it a genuine distress?'

'Eighteen hours astern. Yankee Liberty ship. *Valiant Effort,* Galveston for Calcutta, full of wheat. Perched herself on a reef off the Cani Islands. Ripped her arse out. They took to the boats. All thirty-seven got picked up.'

'I've not heard of the Cani Islands.'

'Italian for the Islands of Dogs. Off Bizerte, Tunisian coast. Well out into the Med, and a snare for the unwary should he take a track too far south when passing Sicily.'

'Radar wouldn't pick up the dogs, but they should have spotted the islands, surely.'

'Known in the trade as a radar-assisted collision, old son. Faulty gear will be the excuse. Radar can make the wheelhouse a touch nonchalant. Remember that ship at the foot of Finisterre? A three-hundred-foot cliff should give a decent echo, don't you think? Anyway, I'm off to my pit for an hour.' He strides out, clutching *Dr No.*

I saunter up to the wireless room. We have a choppy swell. She's rolling, but without menace. An occasional gout of green water and foam careers across the cargo hatches from starboard. Ah, the balm of the ship's routine, as Conrad might have put it.

There's a depression south of the Atlas mountains — swirls of packed isobars that will rearrange the Saharan dunes. As we trudged between Tripoli and Malta yesterday, the Sirocco wind lifted a vast plume of red dust out of the desert and draped it northwards across the central Mediterranean. It's at least three-hundred miles wide, for we've been half-blind for much of the day. The ship now wears an ochre overcoat as if she is down to the marks with iron-ore. Doors and portholes are shut, but Africa finds a way to penetrate. My boss grumbles that grit might have invaded the bearings of the radar scanner.

If the Sirocco gathers moisture on its track north across the Mediterranean, we could even have a 'blood rain', accompanied by thunder. Once we pass out of the dust storm, the crew will hose down the decks, derricks, masts, and our blue and white company livery on the funnel.

Eggs, bacon, and a slice of fried black pudding for breakfast. Dafid Jones, the 'first tripper' apprentice from Briton Ferry, in Glamorgan, declines the fry-up. I'm a quarter Welsh, with Evans and Morgan forebears from the same town as him, but have never needed the bucket. The poor lad's stomach has still not settled. He'll stick with toast and marmalade for now.

Paddy Rourke, the robust fourth engineer, shakes the HP bottle as if he were the barman of a cocktail lounge. 'That's a tragedy. You should get it all down yer, Taff. After all, tis part of yer bonny wages. But dinna fash yersel, the seas are easier east of Suez.' He lays a line of brown sauce by his black pudding, then fixes me with that Glasgow-Irish eye, a bold, mischievous gleam of challenge I suspect is reserved for Englishmen. 'Now for a more vital matter, Sparky pal. BBC Overseas will nae cover the Celtic v St. Mirren match tonight. Can you get the score for me? Celtic is my fitba team.'

Paddy's elbows are on the table — Mam forever told me off for that. I must never do such things amongst the officers at sea, she warned. She knew these things. Despite being descended from humble fisherfolk and coal hewers, she had hoped to become a lady's companion, and travel — see places like Florence and Venice. She answered an advert and had an offer from a London lady who spent time in Europe. The lady wrote to reassure Mam that she did not mind her scarred features from a childhood accident with fire. Mam's own mother, daughter of a Durham miner, would not give permission, so she became apprenticed to a tailoress. Thereafter, her adventures would be by bus, on chapel outings that advertised a trip around some cathedral, castle, or grand house of the nobility. That's not totally correct — there was the time she took me by train to London to stay with Dad's brother Jack and his brood of four. We children were crammed into one bedroom. What a night!

I snap out of my reflections. 'The end of the match will be close to midnight, ship's time. But I'll listen out for it. No Promises, though.'

'That's grand. And what else might keep the world agog this day?'

'There's fighting in Tibet. People have risen against the Chinese occupation. Mao's troops are hunting the Dalai Lama. Hawaii will become the fiftieth state of the USA. Eisenhower has just signed it into law.'

Paddy gives a snort. 'Bloody empires lording it o'er the wee fowk! The Irish ken it only too well.'

This is a good moment to butter some toast and think of Conrad ... *It is a great doctor for sore hearts and sore heads, too, your ship's routine, which I have seen soothe the most turbulent of spirits.*

Midnight news: The Dalai Lama has escaped across the Himalayas to reach India. St Mirren 1 — Celtic 0. Alas, poor Paddy. And sad for Tibet; will he ever go home?

Saturday, 21st March.

Into Port Said with the dawn. We know the exotic reek of the Egyptian town soon after we sight the low trace of the Nile Delta. The Canal builders positioned the new town of Port Said on dredged silt, and so it is a poorly drained place beloved of flies. On my third visit here, on the troopship *Dunera* in 1956, I went ashore with two shipmates. In a gloomy bar, glared at by locals as they sucked on a hookah, we tried the beer. Beer maintained Pharaoh's kingdom, say the Egyptologists — the sweating pyramid builders got through vast amounts.

We ordered the Al Ahram, an acceptable chilled beer of the Stella type, fermented in Alexandria at a brewery under the care of Heineken. Squadrons of alcoholic flies perambulated around the rims of our glasses, sipping at the foam. They took the shine off our pleasure. Not knowing where those hairy little feet had been before lining up for a sup, we brushed them away before we took a drink. As the beer shrank down the inside of the glass, the flies tottered in after the froth.

The HMT *Dunera* had been my first ship, but one whose days were in sunset. In 1956 she was bound for Singapore, Hong Kong, and Japan, one of many troopships that served British bases overseas. Moving regiments by ship would end six years later when aircraft took over. Aged seventeen, I had not travelled, except for streaking along the roads of Durham and Yorkshire on a road-racing bike. An exception was a trip to stay with relatives in Woolwich. From Uncle Jack's, Mam took me to London on VJ Day to witness the excitement when Japan surrendered. At last we had peace, they said. What was peace? I wondered.

That night, in Trafalgar Square, she kept tight hold of my seven-year-old hand among thousands of carousing, heaving revellers. London was in uproar. Soldiers, sailors, airmen, and girls sang and waved flags. Winding lines of tipsy uniforms and frocks danced the hokey cokey. Americans jumped into the fountains and sat on the backs of the great stone lions. Above that sea of swaying humanity, the huge bronze statue of Lord Nelson surveyed the city from his column high in the sky. In between kisses from American soldiers, Mam gave me a history lesson — she loved history. 'Now then, son, if Hitler had won the war, he planned to take down Nelson's Column and stick it up in Berlin as a trophy.'

I squint up at the brave admiral. 'But, Mam, Hitler didn't win. And so we can keep it.'

'And so we can, honey. So we can.'

Back to the *Mawana*: We've hardly moored at the buoys to wait for the Suez Canal pilot, before traders in bum-boats besiege us and cast their ropes over the rails. We rush to batten down, secure doors, and shut portholes, before the buyers of scrap and sellers of pornographic sepia photographs of Edwardian ladies — 'Genuine English schoolteachers, mister chief!' — brazen their way aboard. Everything must be 'screwed down', or it will vanish.

One of the first on deck is a conjurer, the Gully Gully man, in his plum-coloured fez and flowing brown robe draped across a capacious belly, with his cry of: 'No Chicken, no Mongoose'. Cheeps, muffled and plaintive, come and go as he sets out his pitch on a cargo hatch. Then, as if by magic, a fluffy yellow chick emerges from his nose, then another from the tip of a thumb. He plucks two others, fluttering, from his mouth, two more from the collar of an Indian engine-room greaser, and one, two, three from the ear of another. Soon, a little flock of chicks are pecking at crumbs around his feet. He performs card tricks, produces tangerines from under empty cups, gives a blast on a police whistle and turns it into a cascade of wristwatches (all for sale). He bows to the applause, then his urchin-apprentice goes around with the fez so we might show our appreciation. Thin pickings for the magician today — our grinning crew have seen this a score of times. But they are impressed enough to flip him a few foreign coins. In hopes of extra income, he offers jewels — genuine treasures from Pharaoh's tomb.

Gully Gully would do much better on the deck of a Union Castle passenger liner on her circumnavigation of Africa, or a Shaw Savill liner bearing emigrants to Australia. Or a troopship crammed with raw National Servicemen, plucked for two years from their jobs as clerks and labourers, bricklayers and house painters, and posted to adventures in foreign parts. But today, only a dozen assorted cargo ships and oil tankers line up for the canal, so we are Gully's only income today.

I wander off in the hope our agent will soon climb the ladder with a briefcase full of airmails care of BOAC's whispering giant, the Bristol Britannia turbo-prop. There will be letters from Beryl.

9

Sovereigns

The canal route south is a thirty-hour, eight-knot amble, with irrigated flatlands to the west and the parched rocks of Sinai to the east. Except for a ploughing camel or two, and the inevitable toiling and beaten donkey, the cultivated bank reveals little amid endless level acres of spring vegetables. Along the barren side, all is weary rock and rubble decorated by the occasional scorched hulk of an Egyptian tank.

Our convoy of thirty-odd assorted ships pauses in the Bitter Lakes to allow the north-bound procession to pass. These ancient salt depressions, flooded by Vicomte de Lesseps' excavation of the canal, prevent most Red Sea creatures from leaking northwards to try out life in the Mediterranean. A few aliens have made it through: venomous nomad jellyfish now sting the tender parts of Israeli bathers as they cavort in the waves off Tel Aviv, and the spine-foot rabbit fish is eating its locust-like way along the coasts of the Levant and as far as Sardinia. Exotic eyes greet Palestinian housewives from fishmongers' slabs and more will come as the brine barrier fades.

Overnight, the pilot aids his navigation with a pair of searchlights mounted on the bows and focussed on either bank. Today he is Egyptian, but he could have been Russian. Pilots from Britain and France are no longer welcome since three years ago when we parachuted in after Colonel Nasser seized control of the canal. Aided by Israel, the Suez invasion was a military triumph, but a political disaster.

President Eisenhower of the USA threatened Britain with financial ruin if she did not withdraw, and Nasser's paymaster, the USSR, muttered about nuclear strikes on London, Paris, and Tel Aviv, so the troops pulled out after a month. It was a humiliation for two old empires in decline.

While comrades Khrushchev and Bulganin blustered, the tanks of their Soviet empire rolled across the plains of Hungary, and along the gracious boulevards of Budapest, to mow down the thousands who had taken to the street in the uprising against Communist rule. Many of Hungary's finest fled their country. Before the Russians closed the border, 180,000 had escaped to the west. One of them, Peter Matkovits, would become a good friend of mine. A decade hence, at Loughborough University, he will be the technician who devises a method of sectioning for microscope slides the fine dust that Neil Armstrong collects on the Moon.

Our north to south movement, which shall continue down the Red Sea, is a blessing for radio watchkeepers. Unlike the rest of the ship's routine, radio watches follow Greenwich Mean Time. The track along the length of the Mediterranean broke through time zones and my duties are now two hours adrift of those of my shipmates. Whilst we steamed from west to east, our shipboard time shifted by thirty minutes per day — the clocks advanced each midnight. These time slips mean I might enjoy a relaxed lunch in the saloon on Monday, but have it piecemeal by a singing transmitter on Tuesday.

22nd March, 1959. Southwards down the Gulf of Suez.

Another Sunday at sea earns us an extra day of leave, for we work seven days a week when not in port.

From the wing of the bridge, with the lowering sun on our backs, the Second Mate and I stare eastwards into the mysteries of Sinai and speculate on the fabled mountains of the Bible. We look for Jabal Musa, the Mountain of Moses, which is said to be the Mount Sinai where Jehovah gave the Ten Commandments. Jabal Musa, surrounded by ranks of lesser peaks, is free of the usual haze. Evening light chisels into the mass so that the ravines and crumbling ridges of the ancient peak are riven black and gold.

'I've read there's a monastery on the top, and a cave where Moses waited to receive the tablets of stone from God.'

Walter Fisk flips open his leather baccy pouch. 'Where did you root out that gem, Sparks?'

'Arthur Mee's Children's Encyclopaedia, where I get a lot of what I spout about.'

'Brought all ten volumes with you? Must weigh a ton.' Walter has a slow, dry wit. He's from Suffolk. Stubby fingers tease and tweak long-strands of Anton Justman's Dutch shag into a limp sausage on a Rizla paper. 'I'll stick with the pilotage book. It reckons those peaks are an eroded volcanic ring of granitic intrusion.'

'Granite? That's a weight! If the finger of God carved the Commandments into slabs of local rock, old Go Down Moses would need a donkey to lug them home.'

Walter runs the glued edge across the tip of his tongue. He rolls it, beds it down, taps the result on the mahogany rail and applies his Zippo. He blows out a blue-grey jet. 'Speaking of equines, do you know what's under our keel just about here?'

I contemplate how the smoke curls and hovers; we have a breeze astern that has about the same speed as our forward motion. 'A drowned branch of the Rift Valley?'

'Apart from that trench, there's the *Shillong*, a P O cargo liner with fourteen thoroughbred race-horses still in their stalls on deck. Like us, she'd not long cleared the canal, but got rammed at night by the *Porofino Congo*, a Belgian tanker who made a navigation error. They had plenty of time to abandon ship — she was slow to fill.'

'They couldn't save the horses?'

'The grooms gave each one a lethal injection — according to standing orders in such circumstances.'

'And the crew?'

'Four dead. The tanker's bow sliced into the accommodation. Killed the chief steward and a cadet asleep in their bunks, and two Asian seamen on duty.'

***Tuesday, 24th March. Jeddah.

Mawana creeps between coral reefs on her approach to a yellow shore behind a narrow strip of dark-green mangroves, and its huddled town of markets and minarets. With a clank, a splash, and a rumble of massive iron links, the starboard anchor hits the water. Chain roars from the locker beneath the fo'c'sle to chase the anchor through a transparent turquoise sea. Her bows into the breeze, the ship drifts astern until the anchor flukes bite and she hovers with thirty-five fathoms of chain laid out in a straight line along a bed of white coral sand. It is sensible to run out chain equal to seven times the depth of water. One anchor plus that weight of chain is enough to hold our eight-thousand tons in quiet waters such as Saudi Arabia's Red Sea coast with its tidal range of a mere thirty inches. The bridge telegraph handle is swung to tell the engine room, 'Finished With Engines'. The throb of turbines dies, the decks cease to tremble. Movement halts and hush pervades, except for the twitch of the blue and white house flag on the foremast, the limp flap of a red ensign at the stern, and the suspended black ball that swings listlessly from the masthead to show we are not under power.

It's the middle of the Muslim holy month of Ramadan. We've arrived off Jeddah, half-way down the Red Sea coast of the Arabian peninsula. The town makes a living as the port of pilgrimage to Mecca. The docks are full, so we must anchor offshore until invited to berth.

My boss strides in. 'Normal watches to be kept while at anchor, but lay off transmissions except where vital — we don't want to agitate the locals. There'll not be much to do, so you can catch up with your correspondence course.' He runs a finger down the last two pages of the watch-keeping log. 'You've got *Mahanada* leaving Aden, homeward bound. You went deep sea on her, I recall.'

'She was my first Brock ship. Chief was Tommy Williams, first trip; then Alex Turner, second trip.'

He nods. 'Both excellent chaps and well thought of. Alex Turner has plenty of technical wit.'

'He's bright. The office sent us to sea with a box of transistors to play with. Alex built a semi-automatic Morse key with them. He was forever fiddling with a bird's nest of wires on the bench.'

Don gives a sigh. 'Transistors! They'll be the next big thing, I suppose. For old hands, the germanium diode and the hot-wire barretter were newfangled enough. I've looked into transistors — they just squat on the baseboard, gangly wires spread out like the legs of a squashed spider. You've not got a clue what's going on inside — not a scrap of emotion. Give me a plump pair of 807 beam-tetrodes in push-pull any day. Sensible ceramic base and a decent top cap. They glow in the dark, warm, friendly, and shaped like a good woman.'

'There's no mention of transistors in the City and Guilds radio course I'm studying. As far as I know, there's no transistor yet that can deliver the output we need, so we should be OK for a few years. How long before we get alongside, Don?'

'It's anybody's guess — could be a while. Not the best time to be here — it being Ramadan. The entire country is on short hours. They eat at night and fast in daylight, so the dockers won't be rushing around full of beans, not that they're inclined to on most days. It's supposed to be the anniversary of Mohammed's first contact with the Angel Gabriel and lasts from first sight of this month's crescent moon to the appearance of next month's.'

'Gabriel? Isn't he one of ours?'

'Don't get me started on all that! Let's hope we're not stuck here for the entire four weeks. Anyway, I'd rather be offshore than alongside. At least at anchor we can have a beer. Once in Jeddah, alcohol must be locked away. There'll be snooping guards. If they catch you imbibing, you're in trouble. Keep your curtains drawn.'

'How far to Mecca?'

'Fifty miles by bus. Some of our crew are pestering for two days' leave to tick off a quick pilgrimage. They can make Umrah at any month. Hajj is the big one, but that's in June. Not thinking of going, are you? They can't abide infidels.'

'They recognise Christians as *People of the Book*. I read that somewhere.'

'And likewise the Jews, but they still knock seven bells out of each other. Anyway, it's forbidden to take a stroll into Jeddah, let alone Mecca. You'll not want to rot in a Saudi gaol.'

The Indian crew waste no time in casting baited lines from the stern into the placid waters of the anchorage. They intend a fish curry tonight, but there are shrieks when someone lands a sea snake. Our Bengalis hop and skip, advance and retreat with yelps as if they stepped out Cooley's Reel, while poisonous jaws sweep round and bright bands of a yard-long body roll and writhe. It seems wrong to drag a serpent from his cool home to be chopped with a cleaver on the hot metal of our deck, only for his bits to be thrown to sharks.

The purser also watches. 'Such a shame. That would have gone down well in a Vindaloo with a few prawns on the side.'

'A sea snake? It's lethal!'

'Nah, squire! Snakes keep out of the Red Sea. Too salty for them. It was only a snake eel. It's a proper fish, and safe enough.'

I wander up to the fo'c'sle and the carpenter's workshop to watch Alf plane lengths of scrap timber for some job or other. This is a great hideout, and has a kettle. A chap can idle away an hour with a cup of tea from Chippy's private brew. It's good to gaze into the shimmering water. A green turtle paddles her leisurely way. I watch her pull at patches of weed on the white sand and note how her shadow undulates as it trails across the sea floor thirty-feet below. Long minutes pass with nothing else significant apart from shoals of baby fish in the shelter of our hull. Those infants are safe next to our steel with its plush fringe of short weed they pick at — tender Red Sea growth, mixed with Mediterranean algae and nibbles of Biscay and Thames. Serenity ends when a ravenous squad of barracuda sweep in and the surface boils with fleeing fish.

After seven such days 'swinging around the hook', serenaded by calls to prayer from the minarets of Jeddah, the port gives us a berth.

On the other side of the jetty is a pilgrim ship in need of a repaint; the two white stripes on her funnel shows she's British India Steam Navigation, one of those who seldom come home, but spend their days in the tropics. She's from Bombay, and steamed in just ahead of us, straight in from the sea without instruction to anchor.

Awnings stretch over her well-decks to shelter a mass of pilgrims. The smell of farmyards and packed humanity wafts our way. Livestock pens hold a few spiral-horned goats, a couple of droop-headed sheep, and crates of poultry — uneaten survivors of those shipped from India for ritual slaughter to feed the pilgrims. I'm sad for hapless animals, dragged from pastures, crammed into pens, to spend their last days staring at the terrible sea. Each morning, a few were lead away to be blessed by the halal butcher and meet his knife.

The pilgrims jostle down the gangways to rush for a line of waiting buses and open lorries. There's bedlam and confusion, and pleadings with dock police when owners of remaining livestock cannot land their animals on Saudi shores. They've come to worship at the sacred Ka'aba of Mecca, the black cube of a mosque said to be built by Abraham and his son Ishmael. Not every pilgrim will make it this far. There's provision for burial at sea for any close to life's end.

I've read that the Ka'aba contains a black meteorite ... experts should investigate.

Farther away, more buses and lorries unload those who return from Mecca. Police herd the crowds into pens while the ship makes ready for her voyage home. Hoses scour the decks free of detritus while buckets of rubbish and forgotten belongings are thrown from the tween-decks.

The returned host is calmer, with a more pious air than that just landed. Many are frail, even stick-like. They shuffle up the gangway, weak and supported. Men have beards dyed red with henna as the mark of a pilgrimage complete. There are women too, all veiled, some who clutch bundles that emit mewing cries. Finally, a new crowd of uncomprehending animals are prodded aboard.

Amid the chaos, an elongated American car arrives. An Arab, white-robed to his ankles, emerges, wearing a headdress chequered red and white. He's bulky and well-fed. Veiled women follow, covered overall in black, grasping the hands of gaily-dressed children. For a minute, he gazes up at our ship, then leads his family up the gangway of *Mawana* as if he owns her. The heat of the day has arrived with them, so I retreat to my air-conditioned cabin to write letters home. I've heard how local sheiks often wander aboard with their families to have a nice day out, but I'm not in the mood to be affable.

In a letter to Beryl, I set out to describe what I've seen when I'm interrupted by a pull on the door curtain. '*As-salaam-alaikum*' (Peace be unto you.) It's a plump, middle-aged, swarthy face beneath a chequered headdress.

I cap the fountain pen, rise from the chair, and respond with: '*Wa alaikum as-salaam* (And unto you be peace).' My pronunciation must be near the mark (I pick it up from our deck crew), for the ocean of white cotton sweeps in and plops down on my settee that doubles as a daybed. There's more than a hint of Old Spice. Two black-robed women follow, with four children in tow. The women join the fellow on the settee while the children stand and stare with luminous eyes the colour of peat water.

The man smiles and holds forth in Arabic. I can only say, 'Welcome to my humble abode', and return the smile while he gazes around my cabin. He picks up the photo of Beryl in the wooden picture frame supported by two carved elephants; I bought it in Port Said a year ago. He raises his eyebrows, points at it, then at me. I nod. The women seize it to examine. They discuss the photograph in a deep and guttural tongue, unlike Beryl's light Durham tones. Some phrases sound as if they are about to expectorate. Even so, I'm gazed upon by seductive, khol-lined orbs. Although I glimpse only a doe-like gaze through the slotted window of the hijab, I sense warmth and interest. They hand back the picture to the husband, who returns it to the desk. The women fondle the porthole curtain with slender fingers. There's a face at the bevelled glass, a policeman in dark glasses and khaki cap. He pulls back, but I sense he still watches. The children play with the taps of the wash basin and pick up my toothbrush, and the safety razor, the one Dad carried in the Great War and gave me when I began to shave. The women make tut-tut sounds and sharp commands until they stop. As they flap their arms, there is the scent of hyacinths, and perhaps almonds.

They stay for ten minutes, inspecting this and that, before caravanning from the cabin with nods and *salaams*. My cabin now has the aroma of harems and boudoirs.

Such experiences aboard ships that call here are not unusual. Those who honour Abraham, revere a code: "Do not neglect to show hospitality to strangers, for thereby some have entertained angels unawares" (Heb 13:2).

The ship's derricks hoist cargo. Hundreds of tons of white sugar, caster and granular, in two-hundred-weight gunny sacks soar skywards in rope slings to descend onto the backs of lorries. The British mills of Tate and Lyle do good trade here — Arabs have a famously sweet tooth. Discharge halts when a vehicle that resembles an armoured car draws up, accompanied by armed outriders. This is interesting.

The first mate (he's in charge of cargo stowage) and Captain Eggleston are at the head of the gangway to greet two men wearing pale Panama suits and matching Fedoras, attended by police. The second mate loiters on the boat-deck, watching.

I'm intrigued. 'What's all this, Walter?'

He winks. 'Hang about and observe. Something special will soon fly from the tween-deck locker.'

After a deal of fuss, a loaded sling rises from the hold. It carries a stack of stout metal crates. Once on the dockside, the boxes are hefted into the armoured vehicle. The men in suits climb in and it drives away at speed, with police escort fore and aft.

I glance at Walter Fisk. 'Bullion?'

'Spot on, Sparks. A king's ransom in sovereigns, fresh from the Royal Mint. The Arab's distrust of nickel coins and paper notes keeps us in business.'

'I had no idea we carry gold.'

'Few do. Secrecy is the best security. Keep an eye out when we get to Massowah.'

10

The Burning Coast

Saturday, 4th April, 1959.
At 1100 hours, once through the coral reefs, *Mawana* drops the pilot and sounds three blasts on her whistle to bid farewell to Jeddah.

Many in the crew nurse sore arms. The company realised we had left London with expired Yellow Fever certificates and saw Jeddah as the first opportunity to put that right. We formed a line in the saloon yesterday where none saw the Saudi doctor change his needle. The injection went deep. One chap fell in a faint; the Saudi seemed amused, unaware of remarks from those who tottered away: 'The bugger's a quack! He's a bloody camel vet!' Tomorrow we'll arrive in a land of Yellow Fever — which is cutting it fine.

Sunday, 5th April. Massowah.
'In Bangkok at twelve-o'clock they foam at the mouth and run.' So chants Alf, our erudite carpenter tenor, as we three march along Massowah's jetty, bareheaded at noon under a glaring dome. We have the first firm ground under our feet for twenty-three days.

'Next line, anyone?'

Henry responds with Noel Coward's, 'But mad dogs and Englishmen go out in the mid-day sun ... Blimey, this is fierce, and I'm getting thin on top.'

'Buy a pith helmet.'

'Pith off! Not worth it. We're only here for twelve hours.'

'Then, cover your bonce with a knotted hanky and pretend you're in Blackpool.'

We stop to gaze up at a flag that shudders a feeble flap above the Port Office, an ornate building that might have flown in from Venice. The banner has three horizontal bands: red, yellow, and green. In the centre, clutching a long sceptre, strides a *lion passant guardant Or* (at school, heraldry was a favourite subject).

Alf raises a palm. 'Behold, the emblem of the Empire of Ethiopia, crowned lion and Coptic crucifix.'

Henry nudges me. 'What'll it take to shut him up?'

I grin. 'If we don't find him a shady spot with cold beer soon, we'll have to stand out here and learn how Haile Selassie, the current Lion of Judah, descends from the lusty loins of Solomon and Sheba, one passionate night in Jerusalem after a hot ragout.'

Alf stands before Henry. 'If you'd been with us last trip, you'd know all about it. Me and Sparks discussed it off Sinai as the sun went down.'

'Well, it's not going down now, and I want shade.'

The town squats on the African shore, a day's steaming south of Jeddah. We arrived at 1000 hours in a port of notorious heat — it enjoys the mid-eighties on cooler days. Despite the barren furnace of this coast, empires have craved to be here. Sixteenth-century Portuguese held the harbour while they fought to wrest the Red Sea spice route from Muslim hands. Next came the Ottoman Turks, then Egypt, then Imperial Italy landed to grab her share during Europe's 'Scramble for Africa'. Italy built a city in the high interior — Asmara, intended to be the Rome of Africa. Once the Suez canal was open, the great powers thought to have a power base in the Red Sea now it was no longer a backwater but a shorter route to the East. Eritrea (from Erythraean — the classical Greek name for the Red Sea) became part of Mussolini's sweaty, Art Deco, East African Empire, until captured by British forces in 1942. The territory is now federated with Abyssinia and so become a province of the Empire of Ethiopia — *plus a change.*

I'm delighted to be in this ancient place. All I know of Massowah comes from a book in the library box of SS *Mahanada* that I read with fascination two years ago. *The Burning Coast* by John Doody, published in 1955, is a memoir of the writer's war service on contraband control along this stretch of coast. He was posted to this port soon after the British Army evicted the Italian forces in 1941. During his time hunting smugglers among the sweltering islands, he was amazed by the sea-faring skill and toughness of the coastal tribes, particularly the dark and slender Danakil. I was touched by how he came to respect the men of the dhows he pursued, and grow fond of them.

We stride through walls of heat across the Italian-built causeway. Old Massowah stands on three islands connected by raised roads to form the safest harbour in the Red Sea, and one able to shelter a fleet. For a thousand years it has been the gateway for traders from Arabia, India, and elsewhere, seeking the produce of the mountainous interior, the fabled Land of Prester John.

The twelve-inch tide of the Red Sea exposes just enough foreshore to hold lines of simple craft, mostly the dug-out canoes of Danakil fishermen. A two-masted Yemeni Zarook creeps into the harbour, her triangular lateen sails almost limp, to join a score of other dhows; there's no telling what mysterious purpose she has. Does she come to buy salt from those glittering white piles in the salt pans, or for rifles? John Doody describes how the high-sterned dhows of Araby have sailed here since the dawn of time, from as far away as Basrah in Iraq. They bring dates, carpets, sandalwood, and the Flower of Gennah (Heaven) — a herb that grows wild in the mountains of Yemen; it makes the invigorating Qu'at that Eritreans delight to chew. They ship out rhinoceros horn to help aged Arabs regain their youth, civet musk for their womenfolk, delicate Abyssinian filigree, salted shark, tree gum, tartar, and evil smelling hides. Doody suspected they still carried, battened below decks, children from the hinterland for the unacknowledged slave markets of Arabia.

A skinny brown dog trots up. 'Scram!' Henry waves an arm.

The timid eyes flinch. 'Oh, leave him be. He's got no scabs and no fleck of foam on his jaws. He's just a poor stray.' We walk on, with the dog trotting alongside, but a safe two yards away.

Before us stands Haile Selassie's Winter Palace. Soldiers guard the bottom of two staircases that sweep up to an arched entrance. They stare at us.

Alf mops his reddening brow. 'This is no place for white folks. Not when we've a hotel in sight.'

Within the mix of Arabic and Venetian styles, all is cool peace. A corner table has a middle-aged fellow deep in a newspaper and a gaunt woman who flips the pages of an illustrated magazine. We plop into capacious armchairs beneath a fan — the long blades rotate without hurry, its job is to swish the air about and keep the flies moving. A portly man wanders over, bearing a tray. White shirt and black coat, he looks like the butler on the Kensitas cigarette packet, except that this fellow boasts a fulsome moustache.

He gives the hint of a bow. '*Buona sera, signores*, welcome to the Dahlak Palace.'

Henry is staring beyond, towards the bar. 'Hiya. What cold beer do you stock?'

'Inglese Worthington IPA. Italiano Birra Peroni, Moretti, and Menabrea. All chilled.'

'Sounds champion! What do you reckon is best?'

'Ah, signore. For me, Menabrea is *bella*.' He pats his lips with closed fingers and flicks them open. 'Bella! From Piedmont, home of my *antenato*.'

'Then we'll sample your excellent Menabrea. *Tre birre, por favore*.'

Mr Kensitas nods, then ambles to the bar. Alf leans across the low table. 'You've Italian in your vest pocket, Henry. That phrase had an authentic ring, coming from a son of Birkenhead.'

'No surprise there, Mister Chips. Picked it up on the short runs to Italy. Docked at Leghorn every autumn, just in time for the spaghetti harvest brought off the hills by lines of donkeys led by sun-kissed nubile girls in headscarves and bright frocks.'

Alf and I fall silent to contemplate Henry's image until the beer arrives in frosted bottles. The Italian lifts the crown corks and pours into stemmed glasses. We can barely restrain ourselves. The sublime heads look succulent enough to require a knife and fork. The Italian hovers while we swallow deep. I lick my lips. '*Bella!* Three more, *por favore*.'

After another three, we pay in Sterling — which pleases our host. The brown dog is outside, asleep in a patch of shade; he wakes to join us. We wander into town with our change in green banknotes that bear the head of the bearded Emperor, and a jumble of strange coins to unload somewhere, such as a shaded pavement table in the souk.

Handsome buildings stand on street corners, the Italians strove to make this a permanent part of empire. We could be in Italy were it not for the heat, the flies, the delicate tenor bells of the Coptic Christian church, and the muezzin's calls from the minarets of Islam. Italians are still here, staying on, running cafes and jewellery shops. Two years from now, a thirty-year separatist war will erupt that brings Eritrea independence from Abyssinia. By then, much we admire today shall be ruined.

Aromatic Mocha coffee, beneath a layer of cool cream, is a rare experience. The beverage in Britain is never like this. We are just emerging from Camp brand, thick chicory in a bottle, and the sludge on the ship is a different species altogether. The Mocha goes well with the Italian pastries. Brown Dog is especially keen on the bombalone. After gulping down the first posh bun, he drools for more.

I give my friends snippets of what I recall from *The Burning Coast*. How crews of a dozen Italian and German cargo ships and passenger liners had scuttled their ships in a line across the entrance to Massowah to deny access to the Allies. How the inner harbour was crippled by thirty sunken small craft and a drydock. The Italians were so convinced that Rommel's panzers would soon roar through the Sudanese desert to drive out the British that the ship's engineers coated their machinery in thick grease before settling the hulls on the bed of the harbour. Montgomery's victory at El Alamein destroyed that dream. The big ships were lifted, sent to Bombay for refit, and pressed into Allied service.

My shipmates sip their coffee, absorbed by the story, only interrupted by Henry, who has sunk several Peronis in bars around the souk, and now declares: 'Those strutting little Eye Ties, in their daft hats, put us to a deal of trouble.' He breaks into song:

> *'Whistle while you work,*
> *Mussolini bought a shirt.*
> *Hitler wore it,*
> *Churchill tore it,*
> *Whistle while you work.'*

Alf leans over and whispers, 'Hush now. Let's not be upsetting mine host, he's Italian.'

Henry gives a burp and slaps a grubby green Ethiopian note on the table. 'They ended up hanging il Duce and his dolly bird by their feet from a lamp post in Milan, so he won't be too bothered. Anyway, if he's a mate of yours, ask him if he'll change this for a silver dollar. I want to take home one of them thalers for our nipper's collection.'

Alf laughs. 'You want a Fat Lady? You'll be lucky! They hoard them against hard times. But you've missed your chance, we are discharging thousands of crated up Maria Theresas today.'

I'm half asleep, but brighten at once. 'Ah! So that's the third mate's mystery of the tween-deck locker. Silver thalers! Doody writes about them. How the Austro-Hungarian empress Maria Theresa died in 1780, just when they'd minted a fresh load of coins with her likeness. Didn't know what to do with them, but the Abyssinian emperor bought the lot. It was his country's first coinage. Until then, the currency was bags of salt. The British mint bought the dies, and churns out Theresa thalers even now.'

Alf butts in, 'And the Habsburg thaler is the only dosh they believe in. Trusted in trade across Africa, it is. To check for forgery, they look to ensure the coin is dated 1780 before totting-up the number of pearls in the old girl's brooch. She looks so well-provisioned they call the coin *The Fat Lady*.'

11

Sheba

I've just opened the wireless station as we steam out of Massowah. The lights of that strange town sweep past the porthole as the Old Man makes a course alteration to head southwards down the Red Sea. My boss has arrived to do his usual evening check that all is well.

'Enjoyed your stroll ashore, young fellow? I saw you supping Mocha outside the souk. I hope you kept away from the local attractions, you being promised an' all.'

'As ever, we were as good as gold, kind sir. That was a strange spot, and long in history. I wonder what tin trunks and saddlebags those Maria Theresas will come to rest in.'

'If history is your thing, take a dekko to starboard. See if you can make out a gap in the hills.'

Few lights show on the Danakil tribal coast, but by moonlight a dark bay is opening. 'I can. Just south of the mountain, Jebel something or other.'

'The Gulf of Zula. Annesley Bay, that was. It's where the British Indian Army landed 13,000 troops from Bombay to free a handful of hostages. The British consul, some missionaries, and other odds and sods, kept in chains for four years in a mountain fortress by King Theodore the Abyssinian. He wanted military aid from Britain and even suggested a joint expedition to liberate Jerusalem from the Turk. But he was ignored and got upset. In 1868, on being overwhelmed, he shot himself through the mouth with the pistol Queen Victoria sent him as a gift.'

'I read about that somewhere. We built a railway to move artillery through the mountains and brought elephants for the hard bits. Must have cost a bomb.'

'Money's no object when it's a matter of national pride. Besides which, have you heard from Gan Island?'

'Not a peep.'

'Should pick him up after Aden. Gan doesn't have much poke on our wavelengths, it's a temporary rig in the back of an RAF truck. Listen out for Djibouti, we'll be there day after tomorrow.' With a glance at the clock: 'Time's getting on, I'm off to my pit. Toodle pip.'

The ship is three hours ahead of Greenwich Mean Time. My watch ends at 0300 hours, when it is midnight in London. At the end of the stint, I visit the bridge to sample, and pass comment on, the second mate's cocoa. Walter Fisk and I lean at the wing of the bridge, admire the Milky Way on its slow rotation overhead, and sip.

The sea is calm tonight, with a hint of undulation, as though Neptune slumbers. Only the breath of our fourteen knots of forward motion stirs the balmy night air. A bright, first sliver of the new moon hangs among the stars. It marks the close of the month of Ramadan. Muslims among our Calcutta crew of sixty-five Indians can now break their daytime fast. I appreciate this time of day: the second mate, a helmsman, and two lookouts on the bridge; one engineer, a greaser, and a fireman below — all is peace. The land of Punt is somewhere in the darkness to starboard. Asleep to port, is ancient Sheba.

'How's the cocoa, Harry? Not too bitter?'

Some pulpy lumps refuse to dissolve. 'It's robust and filling,' is my response. 'Has Jupiter shown yet?'

The second mate points south-eastwards. 'There he is. The white blob. Came up about midnight, heading for Scorpius.'

'Handsome chap. I wonder what midnight is like on Jupiter.'

'It would be queer. A ten-hour day length, so they get two midnights to our one. And Christmas comes but once in twelve years.'

'Be brilliant for keeping down costs — Christmas cards and the like.'

'No it won't. They'll cost more to send, the gravity on Jupiter being twenty-five times ours. Think of the parcel post!'

'I heard on the BBC — might have been *The Brains Trust* — that radio emissions have been picked up from Jupiter. On 22mc/s, which is interesting, because that's one of our transmitter frequencies — the highest we have.'

'Some tramp steamer on the Jovian ocean, no doubt. Call him up. Ask if he knows the meaning of life.' Walter slings the dregs of his cocoa into the Red Sea. 'The Romans called this drop of oggin the Sea of Hercules. Not many know that.'

Phosphorescence flashes and sparkles from the bow wave. As the fiery water rushes along our sides, it illuminates the black hull with an eerie blue and green light. Southwards, beyond the horizon, there are flickers of lightning too remote for thunder to be heard. It's as though battleships are in combat on a distant sea. We watch in companionable silence, each in our own thoughts.

Tuesday, 7th April 1959. Djibouti, French Somaliland.

Last night we navigated the Straits of Bab el Mandeb (The Gates of Weeping) and left the Red Sea. Once into the Gulf of Aden, *Mawana* kept to the African coast and steered southwest, up the Gulf of Tadjoura, to the port of Djibouti.

It will take just six hours to discharge our cargo of machine parts, medicines, whisky, and what not, so it is a quick dash ashore to sample the charms of this fragment of French empire on the Horn of Africa.

Like the Italians up in Eritrea, and the British across the water in Aden, the French are here because it controls the entrance to the Red Sea and the route to Suez. They built coaling stations on such obscure shores so that their trading fleets could refuel. French colonial architecture, banks, barracks, and hotels dominate the town centre, and beyond are huddles of narrow streets that shelter the labourers. The clear, 'back of throat' speech of the Somali fills the alleys, but the nasal tones of French are also on the air. Then sweeter sounds — on a corner, a blind man plucks at a short-necked lute. The hinterland of Djibouti is range after range of scrubby hills, the lands of Somali and Affar herders.

I'm with Tom, the senior apprentice deck officer, sampling coffee and croissants washed down by freshly squeezed orange juice. We lounge like old colonials in the deep shade of the Continental Hotel, beneath French-style Moorish arches, and watch the comings and goings. Government odds and sods meet here, and their wives, and army officers.

Soldiers in baggy uniforms the colour of sand, contrasted by the stark white of kepis on their craggy heads, play at giant chess in the little plaza before us. The chessboard stretches for yards. Pawns are knee high, and bishops the height of a schoolboy. The light and shade echo with laughter and banter. Frosted beer bottles are upturned. There's applause and jeers, and cheroots bouncing in square jaws as rooks and bishops fall to knights.

A black pawn takes a white pawn. There are hoots. Everyone has seen the error. The white queen now threatens the black queen along an undefended diagonal, and the dark lady falls. The black player, a lean lance corporal, lights his dead cheroot while contemplating his predicament.

'*Toropit'sya*!' His opponent is a giant with two stripes.

I whisper to Tom, 'That doesn't sound like French to me.'

'Nor me. Might be Russian.'

The fellow with one stripe is in no rush. 'Leave off! It took you a time to shift yer arse.'

Tom gives me a nudge. 'He's from Belfast — I'd put money on it.'

'The whole crowd look to be hard cases. I wonder who they are.'

'French Foreign Legion. Fancy joining up? It would be an adventure.'

'I'll ponder the matter over a beer. Try to catch the waiter's eye. I've a few Francs left, so might as well get rid before we head back. Sailing time in three hours, don't forget.'

Next afternoon, we slide into the drowned crater of an extinct volcano that is the harbour of Aden. *Mawana* takes up moorings in the British Crown Colony close to a small island of rock and derelict buildings where lepers were once confined. We will take on bunker fuel from a barge, unload a small amount of cargo, and depart tomorrow. So many brief stops. This trip feels like the meanderings of a country bus through the Yorkshire Dales — except that Aden is a bustling port, and not the dusty spot where the British East India company landed Royal Marines in 1839 to suppress pirates.

We have mail from home, delivered by our agents, Messrs Luke, Thomas, and Co. I'm lounging on my day bed, reading letters from Beryl. They smell of sandalwood, patchouli, and honeyed musk. It is Schiaparelli Shocking — she has sprinkled a few drops from the bottle I brought from Antwerp. Beryl has been out with her hiking club on a Sunday ascent of Yorkshire's little Matterhorn, the anvil-shaped Roseberry Topping. She reminds me how we did a spot of courting close to the edge of the precipice. How we looked into each other's eyes on the sheep-nibbled turf a thousand feet above the Valley of Tees and felt we were part of time itself.

To gaze down on the winding lanes and the village of Great Ayton is to watch ants. Great Ayton, known locally as *Canny Yatton,* is where grew a child who became the Pacific navigator, Captain James Cook. We saw no roseberries that day. They have never been seen. The name shifts down a wobbling line of change from Odinsberg, the rock of the Viking god. We could do nothing to offend

Odin that day — he's seen centuries of cloud slide by, and watched forgotten generations kiss on his summit.

Meanwhile, our derricks clatter and squeal as they lower crates into a barge. British delicacies for the troops: HP brown sauce, baked beans, corned beef, Cheddar cheese, bottled beers: Double Diamond, Worthington, Bass — and pickled onions in malt vinegar. That lot should placate hardened regulars and raw national servicemen alike, and stop them going doolally among the blistering rocks.

Aden commands the gates to the Red Sea. Since the Canal opened, its sheltered pool has been a prime spot for steamers to refuel. Why else would anyone want this god-forsaken harbour on the edge of the Yemeni desert? But we must not sniff. It is said to be as old as human history. This is the *Eudaemon* of the classical Greeks, who saw it as happy and prosperous. Cheng Ho, a senior eunuch from 15th century China, landed here with gifts of coats and hats from the Ming emperor. The 16th century Portuguese spilt their blood when they fought the Arabs for the Spice Trade. As for god-forsaken, it is firm local legend that Adam and Eve's sons, Cain and Abel, sleep somewhere beneath those huddled streets, so Eden cannot be far away.

I'll go ashore when the sun goes down. There will be an outing to the salubrious Rock Hotel, to sit beneath languid rotating fans, and quaff lager served by a waiter in a plum-coloured fez. Aden is a duty free emporium — just the place to invest in a radio, a camera, or a wristwatch to smuggle into Calcutta at a profit. They are all at it; Lascar sailors and Europeans alike, hope to eke out their shore-going rupees in India. Buy your Gordon's London Dry Gin here! From our ship's bond it costs a frightening fifteen shillings a bottle, but only a third of that in town. If you can't get ashore, not to worry, the ship chandler will soon be alongside in his launch to offer gin by the crate at a worth-while mark-up.

Eight years from now, gunmen will sneak in from beneath the skirts of the malevolent shadow of the Egyptian dictator Nasser and his brief Pan-Arab dream of empire. They'll terrorise Aden with arson, looting, and murder.

British troops will fight it out with great courage, but their government will deem it high time to grant independence. Prosperous Aden and the British protectorate of tribal Hadhramaut will federate, then soon merge with Yemen into one state, after which comes round after round of strife.

In a Yorkshire pub, in gentle Nidderdale, on our third pint, I'll listen to a retired soldier of the British Special Forces. He will relate how he was part of a team covertly dropped into Yemen to collect tissue samples from dead villagers. What he brought back proved Nasser had tested his latest nerve agents in his efforts to overthrow the Yemeni royal family.

Civil war will continue to curse this ancient land of Sheba, with Iran-supported Shiite rebels pitched against the Saudi-backed Sunni government. Black-robed, scowling priests will wrestle with haughty kings for dominance of the Middle East. They will use Yemen as a killing ground in their proxy war. Violence, famine and disease will ravish the country, already the Arab world's poorest. Aden, where ordinary folk once had a standard of living just behind that of Bermudans, takes the brunt of the conflict. The vibrant commercial heart of Aden will become a bombed-out husk. In shattered homes that line a harbour without ships, the stick-like elderly might tell their starving grandchildren of better times in the twilight of Pax Britannica.

12

South Of Socotra

Thursday, 9th April 1959.

The granite mountains of the primitive and peculiar island of Socotra that often hides from our radar, loom as a sunbaked mass of crags ten miles to port. *Mawana* forges across a glittering swell, through the channel between Cape Guardafui, the eastern extremity of the Horn of Africa, and Socotra. Shipboard yarns tell how infidels landing on that island might find their heads stuck on a spike above the town gate. Even so, it is said that Saint Thomas the Apostle, he who doubted, was shipwrecked there on his missionary voyage to India. While marooned, he converted the magic-obsessed natives. They stayed faithful to Thomas for five-hundred years until Arab conquerors waded ashore.

The North-West Monsoon, with its cargo of dry air from the icy plateau of Tibet, has faded. In a few weeks, the South-West Monsoon will return to lash this sea with warm and sodden winds. Indian ocean rollers will pummel all who pass this way. But this month we are between seasons, bound for the southern end of the Maldive archipelago and Gan Island, one jewel in a necklace of coral outcrops that makes up Addu Atoll. The atoll is the rim of a sunken volcano crowned by coral, a speck in the ocean, sixteen-hundred miles to the south-east and fifty miles beyond the Equator.

I'm rocking the radio receiver tuning control either side of the calling frequency of 500 kc/s (600 metres). The valves of the main transmitter, a Marconi *Oceanspan*, are hot and poised. Captain Eggleston keeps asking if we have contacted the Royal Air Force base on Gan Island. He's eager to alert them of our estimated time of arrival. The signal is on the message pad beside me. He's at the wheelhouse hatch again.

'Any joy, Sparky?'

'Nothing yet, sir.' I pull out the headphone jack to acquaint the Old Man with my difficulty. The loudspeaker erupts with the static roar typical of this sea area. Through the hiss and crackle comes a plaintive signal from a Japanese operator who has spent much of today failing to contact Djibouti.

The captain flinches. 'I don't know how you put up with that racket, young fellow, but I suppose it's a living.'

'Better than working down the pit in Blackhall Colliery, sir.' I shove the jack back in, the loudspeaker mutes, and the din returns to the headphones. I keep one can off my ear so that I can listen to the calling frequency and to Captain Tommy Eggleston at the same time.

'Well, keep trying. And let me know as soon as you have him. We'll be at Gan in five days and I want to know what I'll be dealing with. No doubt you'll have heard they've been having a bit of a rebellion in the southern Maldives these past four months. The islands are in uproar.'

'Aye, sir, I've been keeping up with the news. The rebels took over the post office and are now issuing their own stamps — Maldive Islands postage overprinted with the newly proclaimed Suvadive Republic. I'd like a set for my album — might be worth a bob or two, in years to come.'

'And will it be your first trip to Gan?'

'It will, sir. What's ashore?'

'Not a lot. Gan is part of Addu Atoll. Addu is nowt but a horseshoe of coral islands, coconut palms, and barefoot brown folk who've lived there since the year dot. Every island in the Maldive chain is pancake flat. Not much freeboard, little above three-foot proud of high water, unless you climb a tree. We slip the Maldivian government a tidy rent for the use of Gan as an airstrip. The rebels reckon it should all go to them, rather than the Sultan. Any road up, we got new-laid eggs in Djibouti and I'm told there's Steak Malabar for dinner.' He shuts the hatch.

Our elderly captain likes his grub. He has a stout middle, but keeps in shape by a brisk pacing of the boat-deck for an hour each afternoon. He strides alongside his old shipmate, Don Butterworth, my chief. Their line of march is right above my cabin, but I've grown used to it and can enjoy my afternoon snooze and inspection of the deckhead rivets despite the distant drum of pounding feet.

I give Gan another try: *MEX MEX MEX de GWWZ GWWZ GWWZ MĀWANA QRD GAN FM ADEN QTC1 K* (Royal Air Force Gan from Mawana, bound Gan from Aden. I have one message for you. Over). After a couple of minutes, I try again. Nothing to be heard through the hiss, except for faint cheeps from a Union Castle liner off Zanzibar. I tune the transmitter to short-wave and call on the 4mc/s band where Gan is supposed to listen out for merchant ships. I creep the receiver tuning through clusters of babbling press traffic, past a ranting voice fighting for air beneath the growl of a Russian blocking transmitter, through warbles and squeals from goodness knows where, until I land somewhere near RAF Gan's published transmission frequency of 5695.5 kc/s. I'm startled when Gan replies, fading and returning at the whim of the Kennelly-Heaviside Layer, that belt of sun-generated ionisation eighty miles above us and off which we bounce our signals to extend their range.

I pass the message and ask him to repeat it back, to be sure he has it accurate. He now knows we arrive at Addu Atoll about 1500 hours on the 14th April and that we ask about pilotage and mooring arrangements. The fellow in the air force truck says to come ashore for a look around and a few beers with the lads.

12th April.

It will be better cocoa tonight. That's because the second mate took a short trick at the wheel while the helmsman made the drink. He boiled the chartroom kettle beneath the dim red lightbulb that preserves night vision. The blunt pungency of rough chocolate hangs in the air as Murdo Morrison, a wiry Hebridean quartermaster, gives the cocoa a vigorous stir. In the wheelhouse gloom, he passes me an enamelled mug flecked with froth. I'm entranced by the melodic lilt of his voice. 'There ye are, Sparky lad. Sad tae say, bereft o' the whisky at this hour and in this official situation.' He's off duty in an hour, and like the good Uist man he is, he'll be putting that right before climbing into his pit.

'Thank you, Murdo.' It's scalding hot. 'This'll put hairs on my chest.' My twenty-year-old chest has just seven at present and could do with a few more.

The night is sublime, with the waxing moon of four days a slender curved sail silent among the western stars. I enjoy the casual customs of the dim bridge in the small hours on this empty tropical sea. Low voices and the breath of a breeze. No clatter of galley pans, no chatter of Indian seamen spreading white lead paint along the rails, no shouts and splashes from the little swimming trough, no tread of feet on the bridge gangways, no calls to prayer — only the grey ghost of the ship's young cat on her nightly rounds. She's in the wheelhouse now, tail to one side, raised rump, mewing, rubbing her furry flank against my bare shin. She's the only feline aboard and grows extra affectionate when in season.

The purri-wallah (the bridge lookout man) slides open the wheelhouse door. 'Ship *batti* (ship's lights), Sahib. Port side, she come.' He points ten degrees off the bow. He's a sensible Bengali lad with keen eyes — on his first trip, but safer than a grizzled grandfather with cataracts, regardless of wartime medal ribbons.

'Man the wheel, Murdo, while I take a shufty. He might be looking at a star, likely Canopus.' The second mate, Walter Fisk, secures his cocoa mug in its rack and heads for the wing of the bridge, binoculars in hand. In stark contrast to the dim wheelhouse and its varnished panelling, the Milky Way blazes overhead, the Southern Cross hovers above the horizon to starboard, and Polaris is low on the northern boundary of the sky. Both of these navigator's ancient friends are visible from this equatorial latitude. The sea is so calm, it reflects our home galaxy that encrusts the heavens tonight.

He comes back. 'A ship. Miles off yet. I'll fire up the radar to check his track.'

The purri-wallah watches the scanner leap into rotation. Our Indian crew hold the view that all that moves or flickers on a ship, from winches to electricity light, must be steam powered, and to a degree they are correct, hence they refer to the radar as the *e'steam purri-wallah,* the steam-driven lookout man.

Three minutes later, with the display warmed up and our scanner firing a beam of 3.2cm wavelength electro-magnetic radiation across the inky sea, Walter immerses his face in the radar observer's cowl. I hope the vacuum holds — Merchant Navy college warned us that the pressure on the face of a twelve-inch cathode-ray tube is three-quarters of a ton. He adjusts the range control and makes a note, sips his cocoa for five minutes, watching.

'Ah ha. Interesting. She's on the reverse course to us. What's she doing down here? We'll pass a mile clear at this rate.' He unhooks the Aldis lamp from the bulkhead and plugs it into the 24-volt supply on the wing of the bridge. 'Come on, Sparks. You're supposed to be adept at Morse. Let's call him up. Standby to read while I ask him how he's doing. He'll be as bored as we are.'

Walter works the Aldis lamp to good effect. He's signalling at about six words per minute, which is a plod — I've heard that seasoned hands in the Royal Navy can reach fifteen. Our fleet use it rarely, so the second mate is doing fine. My Morse speed with a telegraph key feels comfortable at twenty words per minute in most traffic conditions. My First Class Post Master General's certificate of competence says that at twenty-five I can keep up well enough. I can send and receive at thirty words-per-minute, but that rate is mainly for show-offs with no respect for accuracy. Walter signals again. I watch the flashes. He's asking: '*What ship? Where bound?*'

Walter chuckles. 'He's probably scrabbling in the locker for his lamp. This could take a while.'

He gasps when there is an immediate response at high speed from a powerful lamp. 'Bloody Hell. What's he saying?'

Visual Morse is a challenge to a brain trained to sound signals, but I got a few letters. As we don't respond, the other vessel repeats at a slower pace. I manage a few more letters. 'It could be he's asking, *Who wants to know?*'

Walter grunts and flashes, '*SS Mawana bound Gan from Aden*'. The response matches Walter's pedestrian speed as it flickers across the starlit sea: '*Then have a pleasant trip, old boy.*'

The penny drops and, from his station at the wheel, Murdo raises his soft Hebridean voice, 'Ye's been flashing the Royal Navy. Gassing tae the Andrew! She'll be a destroyer coming up from Gan, next stop Aden.'

Walter flashes: '*And to you, noble sir.*' On her parallel, but opposite track, the dim shape of a low, sleek vessel, phosphorescence of an electric blue flaring around her stem and stern, grows near, then slides away beneath the stars, with turbines fading.

We return to our sludge of tepid cocoa in the wheelhouse. It's time I was in my bunk, but I turn to Murdo, his lined face dimly illuminated by the pale green light of the steering compass. 'You were in the Royal Navy. Why is it called *The Andrew*?'

'Ah, laddie, some have it as being the name o' some brutal being in charge o' the Press Gang. But that's just blather. It's after the great Victorian engineer, Andrew Clarke. The Admiralty gave him charge of Naval Dockyards when they were in an auld-fashioned run-down mess. Modernised everything after years o' neglect when the ships that fought Bonaparte were rotting on mud in Essex creeks. Andrew Clarke came at the right time. We needed no more aristocratic dandies with scented hankies, but iron ships, iron men, and steam engines. He gave them dry-docks and proper barracks. The man set a new course for the RN, and it's been *The Andrew* ever since.'

13

Gan Island

Tuesday, 14th April 1959.

At dawn, the second mate's navigation gets an approving grunt from the Old Man when the palms of Addu Atoll rise from the eastern horizon off the port bow. Gan, the largest island of Addu, lies at the southern end of a five-hundred-mile double chain of coral atolls running north-south. Ships have trouble finding this speck, easily mistaken for the deposit of some ancient fly that wandered across the chart. Our approach from the north-west, with little else in the ocean to yield a radar bearing, makes it easy to overshoot and steam too far south. Any doubts on the bridge were eased when my chief persuaded the Gan RAF station to send long dashes for DF bearings.

Somewhere beneath our keel, on the dreadful plain that spawned this rampart of submarine volcanoes, lie the remains of a pre-war fruit carrier, a 'banana boat', the Italian auxiliary cruiser *Ramb I*. Whilst we hide from fierce sun, below, in a night as old as the Earth, saucer-eyed eels and lamp-headed fish peer from portholes and rents in her hull. In 1941, she escaped the fall of Massowah with orders from Mussolini to prey on allied shipping. In disguise, she flew the British flag, but challenged by the New Zealand cruiser HMS *Leander* and asked for the secret code, she bravely ran up the Italian ensign and engaged. She hit *Leander* once, but took five salvos in exchange. Ablaze, the *Ramb* blew her scuttling charges. The crew sat out the rest of the conflict as prisoners in Ceylon, which was pleasant enough despite four years of curry and rice instead of spaghetti.

Otherwise, the war here was a subdued affair. The Japanese failed to discover the hastily built base on Gan Island where the RMS *Queen Mary* took on fuel behind anti-torpedo nets. In her wartime paint and loaded with 16,000 Australian troops for North Africa, the *'Grey Ghost'*, with her speed of thirty knots and without escort, outran all attempts to intercept her. Hitler offered a reward of a quarter of a million US dollars and the Iron Cross to any U-boat commander who sent her to the bottom. She was never caught.

Buoys mark the channel into the lagoon. On a full tide, a sprightly RAF launch leads the way through a gap in the reef, and our 8,000 tons follow at a careful creep. The launch steers in a circle to show the anchorage. An officer in khaki drill calls on a loud-hailer, 'Welcome, *Mawana*, the sight of you gladdens our hearts. We are almost out of beer.'

Once the rumble of anchor chains dies and our propeller churns no more, the harbour becomes a palm-fringed mile of turquoise as transparent as gin. All is peace, until a great manta ray leaps from the sea, black wings spread, to perform a booming belly flop. Next, our gangway is lowered. The embarrassing creaks and squeals of pulleys echo around the hushed lagoon, drowning the tonk-tonk of the launch's idling engine as she eases alongside.

Captain Eggleston is smart, though tubby, in his tropical whites. Four bands of gold on each epaulette flare in the glare of a high sun. He has the chief officer at his side. 'Mister Rudge, your gangway mechanism sobs. She pleads for the ministrations of grease.'

'I'll attend to it, sir.' The mate scowls at Tom, the senior apprentice, who gives a freckle-faced nod.

As soon as the lean RAF officer steps onto our deck, the captain takes his salute, shakes his hand, then whisks him away to his air-conditioned cabin for gin and tonics.

My boss points to the shore. 'Here they come. They don't hang about. Must be desperate.'

Three-hundred yards away, a naval landing-craft chugs towards us. The mate organises his team. Hatch covers are stripped away, winches manned, derricks unshipped and lowered in readiness. We are in for a leisurely discharge, there appears to be just one landing-craft to shuttle cargo ashore. There'll be ample time to explore this tiny world.

On the short jetty, a vital part of our freight is manhandled from the landing craft — crates of beer for the NAAFI. A line of military lorries wait to gather up the remaining stores. The main cargo must take its turn. At the landward end of the jetty, I read a smart fingerpost that says:

> London 5750 miles, Malta 4530, Perth (Western Australia) 3522, Cocos Islands 1806.

The beach is white coral sand fringed by palms and backed by yards of tangled scrub, scented creepers, and spindly trees. Hermit crabs trundle about, picking at morsels. I follow a jeep track inland until the vegetation halts. Then, acres of crushed coral being levelled by a pair of bulldozers, and a giant machine that pulverises excavated coral into a size fit for concrete. Another machine, in the livery of Messrs Richard Costain, the building firm, mixes graded coral with poured cement. Most of our cargo for Gan is bagged Blue Circle cement for the Costain company who holds the contract to extend this wartime aerodrome. The island's interior is a blazing white desert, even to squint at it sears the eyes — I forgot my sun-glasses. Acres are cleared of trees and dwellings for a heavy-duty runway capable of taking bombers. They say eleven-thousand trees have gone. Paradise obliterated by the Cold War.

Shaded by a grove of curved palms, at the end of a snaking heavy-duty cable, is the RAF truck I've come to see. Stripped to the waist, two lean young chaps lounge in the shadows, sipping mugs of tea. From the open rear of the truck comes the rattle of a telegraph key.

'Hey up! How do? You Harry, the radio bloke off the latest ship?' The flat vowels could be South Yorkshire.

I stride up and offer my hand. 'That's right. I'm taking up the invite to see your gear.'

'Come int' shade, lad.' His prominent Adam's-apple wobbles up and down. 'We've just brewed up. Sit down. Mind the ants. I'm Fred, from Doncaster, and this here gadgee is Cyril from Cleckheaton, but he can't do owt about that, and the sod's finished his time next month. Where you from?'

'Hartlepool — but I had no choice.'

'Bleedin' Nora, another Monkey Hanger! Take sugar and milk?' He thrusts a mug of tea at me. 'There must be a dozen of the buggers here.'

I sip. 'This tea's welcome.' In truth, it is far too sweet. I turn to Cyril. 'So, you'll be off home soon. How long on Gan?'

'Nearly a year. That's the slot we get. One year among the fruit bat crap on this station counts for two years service time. That's the only consolation.'

'Fruit bats?'

Fred spits. 'As big as pigeons. Come out at night. Kip in the trees all day. Disturb them and they all do a doodle. Best not to walk under the trees. We had to hose Cyril down.' Fred lights one of the Goldflakes I've handed round. 'Posh bank manager's tabs, these. You must have a cushy billet. We've no need for top show, no need for Old Spice, it's a year without women here. That is, apart from the motherly old biddy who runs the NAFFI. But they do keep us stocked with ale.'

'Is there not a village? The chaps working cargo on the jetty look to be locals.'

'Village got cleared away to build the base. Them labourers come from further round the atoll. Here sharp every morning to earn a few bob. There's some fetching lasses in their village, but it's out of bounds. The gaffer gives us big trouble if we sneak across the causeway. Mind you, one has just called her latest nipper by the name of George, him being more than a touch on the pale side.'

Cyril gives a chuckle. 'Some of the blighters stopped fishing once they'd tasted the NAAFI's tinned herring in tomato sauce. Had a craving. They'd spend their wages on it. So they've been barred from buying the stuff.'

I nod in agreement. 'I've seen the rusty cans on the beach. How's the brand new Suvadive Republic doing? The rebellion got a few mentions in the newspapers back home.'

'Delicate. Orders are not to interfere. It blows hot and cold. The sultan's boats come down from Male, the Maldive capital, now and again, to shoot up the locals. They've killed a few fishermen. London tells us to keep out of it, but we're a long way from the Admiralty so the RN frigate sees off the raiders when it can. Swamped the last lot with her wash. Oops! Sorry!'

Cyril comes in: 'We should've refused to be kicked out of Ceylon, three years back. They were great bases, till that creep Solomon Bandaranaike ordered them shut. I reckon he's in the pay of Moscow. The Commies are out to wreck SEATO. That's the only reason we've had to build this bloody base.

(SEATO: Southeast Asia Treaty Organisation — a weaker cousin of NATO. An alliance formed in Manila to resist Communist threat, and one of the 'Domino Theory' justifications for the Vietnam War. A diplomat and naval strategist, Sir James Cable, described SEATO as, "A fig leaf for the nakedness of American policy ... a zoo of paper tigers". It was dissolved in 1977.)

'My ship called into Trincomalee last year. It's empty. The naval base is a rusting ghost. The jungle swallows it up. Saw elephants swimming across the harbour.'

Cyril snorts. 'A bloody shame. Bandy should get the bullet.' (Five months from now, Solomon Bandaranaike will be assassinated with a Webley Mark VI revolver. His widow will succeed as leader of Ceylon and Mrs Sirima Bandaranaike shall become the world's first woman prime minister.)

I nod to the RAF communications truck. 'You won't be running a SEATO base off that old girl.'

Fred laughs. 'Not likely! That's just for the likes of you. She'll soon be pensioned off. We've a brand new station coming into use. Upwards of twenty transmitters, it has. Cost a fortune. Any road, let's show you the antiques in the wagon.'

(The breakaway Suvadive republic of 20,000 people lasted four years. The end came after the 'Massacre of Thinadhoo', when Ibrahim Nasir, the Maldivian Prime Minister, sent armed police. They opened fire on unarmed civilians and killed hundreds.)

Amazed at the rainbow of life, we float in eight feet of transparent warm water above a garden of coral. The friendly RAF chaps loaned us face masks and snorkels. We swim in deck shoes because a graze from coral can be poisonous. Shoals of little fish cruise around us without fear — blue and yellow stripes are in fashion. My skin is kissed and tickled as the clown faces take nibbles. I suppose they assume we are leviathans in need of a clean.

A hundred yards from the shore the coral rises almost to the surface, so that we can wade in our shoes. We stumble across coral lumps the size of cabbages until the bottom collapses into a sudden abyss. This must be the throat of the volcano. The fourth mate and I swim out with the breaststroke. We peer downwards, but have left the company of the little fish. There is only an increasing blue gloom that merges with a dreadful blackness. Shapes rise out of the shadows. Sleek shapes. Sharks! We quail in alarm. No casual breaststroke now, just a fast thrashing crawl until we breathe easier on the reef.

At Gan Island

(After a further seventeen years as a SEATO base, Gan was handed back to the Maldivian Government in 1976. The airfield now has International Airport status. Gan Island is part of the Maldive Islands tourist industry with sumptuous, air-conditioned hotel rooms in 'Equator Village'.)

14

The Grand Oriental Hotel

Wednesday, 22nd April 1959.
We are alongside in Ceylon's capital, Colombo, after two days and six-hundred miles of riding north-eastward, urged along by a glassy heave that lifted our stern all the way from Gan Island. The wind was light, but that swell, born in some remote storm far below the Equator, outpaced our fourteen knots. The ocean was empty. We saw only a scatter of frigate birds, like giant swallows, their deep-forked tails fluttering as they swooped on flying fish.

The mahogany gleam of the bar counter in the Grand Oriental Hotel sets off the amber of three glasses of chilled Lion lager most wonderfully. No one grabs. It is a test. We take time to stare at the creamy froth, time to note how the humid air builds condensation on the pitched sides of the glasses until rivulets form and snake downwards.

Henry, our 3rd engineer, cracks first. 'Sod this for a game of soldiers.' He lifts a glass and pours half the contents down his throat, then utters a cracked burp of appreciation.

Alf, the carpenter, follows, but keeps quaffing until his glass is three-parts drained. They look my way. I take a drink, but soon set down the glass — the lager is tooth-biting cold.

'You two have gullets enough to swallow the Mersey. Don't expect me to complete the trick. The last glass I sank in one go held a pint of Black and Tan in the Custom

House, up Bute Street in Cardiff. It ruined a good night out, but kept me out of hospital.'

Alf catches the eye of the white-jacketed Singhalese bartender who has just served a noisy crowd off a Bank Line boat. To judge by the acrid reek of Burma cheroots, they had come from Rangoon. It's like being alongside a coal-burning tug. The long wooden blades of a languid fan, high in the Victorian moulded ceiling, help to stir the stink. Three more chilled Lions arrive.

This is a favourite watering hole. Not two-hundred yards beyond the hotel's handsome portico is the blue-and-white banded funnel of our ship. Cranes are hoisting sling loads of crates, barrels, and bales out of *Mawana's* holds. We'd steamed out of the Mersey loaded to the Plimsoll marks. Thos. and Jno. Brocklebank of Liverpool, founded at Whitehaven in 1785, is the world's oldest deep-sea shipping line. It's reassuring to watch us make a profit, and keep our name, even though we are now merged with Cunard and have become its money-making cargo arm.

'I know the Custom House,' says Henry. 'Not surprised it ruined your night. That auld boozer serves Baines' ale, as I recall. Greasy glasses don't help South Wales beer, it being a touch shy of showing a head at the best of times. I'm all agog to know how a fancy mix of bitter and stout kept you out of hospital?'

'The black and tan did for me. I was so under the weather, that when we stopped at a late-night pie and pea shop in Tiger Bay, near the docks — right opposite the terrace where Shirley Bassey used to live — they just propped me against a wall in the street while they went inside. Next day, the captain and I were the only Europeans in the crew who were not in hospital getting the stomach pump. We missed the tide. The Old Man wasn't best pleased. The pie shop got raided by the hygiene people.'

'Asian crew, was it?' Alf wipes froth off his top lip — he's growing a coppery moustache.

'Mixed. Lascar deck crew, Chinese greasers and donkeymen. Two Polish engineers — refugees from the Nazis. The Old Man — he had a flinty eye — claimed to be a pure Pict, and nobody dared contradict him. When I announced I'd read how one expert proposed that the Picts might be one of the Lost Tribes of Israel, he choked on his chicken curry. That was on my first day aboard.'

'Not a good start to the trip, then?' Alf seems inclined to know more.

'I'd only just sat down for my first meal aboard. Captain Stuart was at the head of the table. The other officers were seated both sides, with Indian stewards hovering in attendance. I was just off *Dunera*, a big white BI troopship with four in the wireless room. The SS *Hughli* was my first ship as sparks in sole charge, so I'd yet to find my feet. As I took my place at table, I introduced myself as his new radio officer. "And what's your name?" he asked. It's Harry Nicholson, I said. "Sounds like a collier out of the Tyne", says he. "Where are you from?" Hartlepool, says I. "Where they hung the monkey," says he. The whole crowd laughed. They were always careful to laugh at the skipper's jokes.'

Henry lets out a hoot. 'What company?'

'Jimmy Nourse. SS *Hughli* — 6,500 tons of tired rust. I did three weeks coasting, then had to scheme like Billio to get off her, otherwise I was nailed down for two years tramping out East without reprieve. Maybe an interesting time, though. I'd have seen the South Pacific.'

Alf nods. 'You'd come home looking like a character out of *Lord Jim*. Speaking of Conrad, can you get the library swapped over in Calcutta? I'm fed up with Westerns and Marie Stopes. Get us some decent books, like Trollope's *Chronicles of Barsetshire* — and a dollop of poetry while you're about it. Interesting chap, old Trollope. He supposed that the Anglo-Saxon race would eventually become brown.'

'That's what, Mr Dowson, my last schoolteacher at Galley's Field, said — in time, all people would become coffee-coloured. But, I doubt if our average reader would thank me for loading up with poetry. *Half a league, half a league onwards rode the six-hundred*, and all that. I get requests for Hank Janson, *Torment for Trixy*, in particular.'

'Cheap, nasty, and obscene. Banned in Ireland. As for *The Charge of the Light Brigade*, you got it wrong. It's *Half a league, half a league onward. All in the Valley of Death rode the six-hundred.*'

Henry lights his pipe. The aroma of sweet Fair Maid soaked in rum blends with acrid Burma cheroot. He leans back. '*Cannon to the right of them, cannon to the left of them, volleyed and thundered*. Any road up, Marie Stopes, the marriage expert! Alf, you be careful not to let your missus read that woman's *Enduring Passion* or you'll not get any peace in the bedroom.'

'Never fret on that score, Henry. The wife is out of North Wales farming stock. Eyes like peat pools, all of 'em. They need no instruction on what it's about. Now then, let's think on those who slaked their thirsts at this bar in days of yore. There's a brass plate by the door that tells how Anton Chekov stayed here in 1890 on his way home from Vladivostok. He was a touch depressed. But, seems like the dark maids of the Kandy hills lifted his spirits.'

Henry chuckles. 'And I bet that's not all they lifted.'

The bartender has been listening and leans across the bar; he smells of coconut hair oil. 'Yes, sirs. Mister Chekov call our Lankan island a paradise of bronze-skinned women. He liked our animals, also. Took three mongooses home to Moscow.'

Henry raises a finger. 'Shouldn't that be mongeese?' But the barman has slid along to the revellers off the Bank boat. They are singing to the tune of the hymn, *What a Friend We Have in Jesus*:

When this endless trip is over, no more tramping will I see.
I will swear upon the Bible, Bank Line you've seen the last of me.
No more stewing up the Hooghly, no more Rangoon to Baltimore,
Back around the world again to Fiji, Hong Kong Roads and Singapore.

Half the crew have gone doolally, Sparks was like that when we sailed.

Two stewards reckon they are married. The cook thinks he's the Prince of Wales.
Two years on, we've got the Channel fevers — we've got it bad, and that's because
We will pay off in the Mersey, so shove your Bank Line up your arse.

The bartender is waving his palms up and down. 'Please to be quiet. Singing not allowed in GOH. It is rule.'

A glance around the guests at tables shows offended expressions on a couple of haughty matrons, yet others smother degrees of twinkles and smirks. Henry applauds until Alf grabs his hands. 'Behave yourself. This is a posh place. We'll get thrown out.' He turns to me. 'I wonder if Andrew Weir, the 1st Baron Inverforth, knew what he'd started when he founded the Bank Line? Observe the results of two years' Foreign Going, and what you missed by not tramping deep-sea on the *Hughli?*'

I'm subdued for a while. 'Just as well I got off her. Half way through the second year of that stint, I'd be taking down a telegram that said my dad had just died. I wonder if they'd have sent me home from wherever.'

Henry nods. 'Not the best way to find out — through a spray of dots and dashes.'

I'm in a reflective mood. 'Just two years back, I was exchanging Morse with a ship in distress close on seven-hundred miles east-south-east of Mauritius. A lot of empty sea down there. Skipper said to tell him we'd come when we could. We were a day's steaming from her and fighting it out with an Indian Ocean cyclone. Had no option but to keep *Mahanada's* bows into it, otherwise we'd have been over. That chap was tapping out his last. Gone without trace. Fifty-one crew. We'd have been too late, anyway.'

Alf lays a great palm on my shoulder. 'Who was it?'

'*Minocher Cowasjee.* Pakistan flag. Jakarta for Cape Town. Cargo shifted, so she would have capsized in that sea.'

Henry knocks the dottle out of his pipe. 'Terrible to think where they lie now. Could be two or three miles down in that spot. An awful dark place to end your time.'

Our glasses are empty, and it's my round. I order three more Lions. We watch the heads relax while we muse. 'Here's a strange thing. Seven weeks later, we were in Colombo on our way home from Calcutta. I was having a solitary beer at this very bar, just about where we stand right now, when I got talking with another chap. Turns out he was the British mate off the *Minocher Cowasjee*.'

'A ghost?' Henry sits up like a ramrod.

'No, but he would have been if he hadn't left the ship in Jakarta. She'd been badly loaded in Vladivostok. Too much weight in the wrong place. He protested, but the owners would do nowt. The ship had a bad time in the China Sea. She limped into Java, where the mate insisted the cargo was discharged and reloaded to his satisfaction. He was overruled, so he refused to take her any further and walked off. I told him, if there was to be an inquest, he should be called. He said the radio officer was an Anglo-Indian, close to retirement. The chief engineer was German, the other crew were Pakistani. I fancy I still hear those signals ... Sometimes.'

Postscript: In 2006, almost fifty years later, curious about the fate of the lost ship, I made enquiries. The research led to contact with Ardeshir Cowasjee, a journalist for the Pakistan newspaper, *Dawn*. Ardeshir was then the most senior Cowasjee, and patriarch of that family of Parsis (Zoroastrians); Parsis are a much-diminished minority in Pakistan. From him, I learned more of the *Minocher Cowasjee*.

The ship belonged to the East and West Steamship Company founded by Rustom Cowasjee, Ardeshir's father, and named after Rustom's brother, Minocher Cowasjee. I followed his clues to discover that the vessel, launched in 1920 as *Parisiana* for Furness Withy, passed through several owners and changes of name. By 1938, she sailed as the Ben Line steamer, *Benrinnes*. In 1955, she became *Minocher Cowasjee* of the East West S.S. Co. I got goose pimples when I discovered *Parisiana* was built in my home town of Hartlepool; built at Irvine's yard hardly a mile from where I was born eighteen years later, and where my father and his father were ship riveters. Perhaps their hammers drove home her rivets.

Ardeshir had a coincidence to tell of. Only a week before I contacted him, Susan, the granddaughter of the lost ship's radio officer, emailed Ardeshir to ask what he knew about the tragedy, and this was fifty years after the event. I wrote to her home in Brisbane, Australia, to tell her what I remembered of the night of the loss, and sent these poems I'd been moved to write:

Tramp Ship *Minocher Cowasjee*

Fate was stowed crude,
Profit driven, in your holds
At Vladivostok, and your Mate ignored
So that you wallowed in the troughs
And in Jakarta he walked off.

Fifty years are gone
And still I hear your signals
Fill the ether through the howl
Of that terrible rotating storm.

A shaking:
'SOS SOS SOS *Minocher Cowasjee*
25.20 south, 68.00 east,
700 miles south-east of Mauritius,
Bound Capetown from Jakarta.
Severe list, could capsize.'

And my reply:
Reverberating on polished mahogany
Thumped out on a brass, post office pattern key
Heavy, solid, reliable and honest.
Thumped out onto groaning masts:

'SS *Mahanada*

Out of Capetown for Calcutta,
One hundred miles north of you.
Unable to alter course.
Will come when we can.'

That's all I can do,
I'm eighteen, how old are you?
Although I cannot see your face,
You live in a stream of intelligence,
And wireless men can read emotion.

You do not see the grim set
Of our captain's face.
'I have to keep her head into this
or we're over,
Tell him we'll come when we can.'

We have dynamite below.
On deck, two black locomotives strain
At their lashings like captive mastodons.
Our forward hatches are buried.
Astern the screw lifts free –

Spins

Then thuds into the sea again.
You call a few times more until –
In your holds,
Crates of Russian machinery smash
Into sacks of Javan rice.

Topside,
A decorated Serang – steady,
Cropped grey beard – hajji,
Knuckles bloody,
Grapples with the davits.

In the hot oil mist of the engine room,
A clear-eyed engineer
Is mobbed by frightened Lascars

Crying out in Bengali
For mother.

And she goes over –
To be filled, to begin
Her bone-snapping
Five-mile journey down
Into the Mid-Indian Basin.

To lay crumpled in the silence
Of the floor of the abyssal plain
And be gazed upon forever
By lamp-headed fish.

Lost Ship

    We saw nothing on the wind-glazed surface,
    nothing floating in the spume as we steamed
    across her track on the chart;
    no scrap of cargo, no boiler suit,
    nor a crumb of last night's rice.

    In the dark we'd talked
    in bursts of dots and dashes,
    that other man and me.
    We'd clung in chairs chained to the deck,
    one hand on the tuning knob
    chasing each other's warbling signals
    as masts swayed
    and phosphor-bronze aerials swung out
    wild over the troughs;
    the other hand thumping a big brass key,
    in the cyclone.

    It was sixty years ago – she flew the flag of Pakistan,
    a new country. But the *Minocher Cowasjee* was old
    I now discover – launched as *Parisiana*

by Irvine's yard in Hartlepool, where my father,
back from his war with Kaiser Bill, might well
have hammered rivets into her, hard against
his own dad's hammer on the other side of the plate.

Three miles down they're rusted now, those rivets;
strewn about, forgotten, like Asian mother's tears.
She's just another hull – after all
the ocean floors are flung with ships.

Susan replied:

> *'For nearly half a century his son knew only
> a brief written blurb about the incident in
> the local paper. We as grandchildren knew
> little else.*
> *My Grandfather was Anglo Indian, born
> 13/11/1905. His father was Bertram Chadburn (Scottish) who had a tea plantation
> in India. His mother worked in the fields
> and was Nepalese. He was orphaned with
> his sister at a young age, she died soon after.
> His upbringing was English. He married
> 1934, had three children and worked at
> the telegraph, then as a radio officer, and
> was called to war in 1942, then returns in
> 1947. Back working at the telegraph then
> transferred to Burma in 1948 and returns
> again to India in 1951 figuring on retiring
> soon. Apparently, he heard about the radio
> officer's job from a friend and joined the
> crew. That's as far as I go with information
> from my Aunt.'*

A second letter: *'Harry, you have given our family closure as it was my Grandfather, Thomas Chadburn, who was the radio officer on the Minocher Cowasjee, who sent the distress call. Your poems have brought us to tears, and yet a sense of peace overwhelms us. You have taken us through an emotional journey of the last moments of my grandfather's life. Thomas's children never really grieved his death, and by our contact it has enabled them to do this after 50 years.*
I will share these poems with my children, my newborn, my only son, Christopher Thomas, born July 2007, carries his name. Thank you again, Harry.'

Reading the letters once more, I note how Thomas Chadburn was born twelve years after my father (1893), but shared his birthday, the 13th of November.

15

The Miller Of Dee

27th. April.
A humid breeze sweeps off the hills, and the morning scents of India brush the skin as we enter Madras: joss, spices, jasmine, marigolds, and monsoon drains. Elderly cranes creak and clank on both sides of the dock as tugs nurse us past cargo ships. Tall, once noble, funnels from the 1920s slip by — not long to go before they pant their last on their sad trudge to the breaker's yard. Beyond the flared bows of a sleek modern Finn is the low funnel of a spanking new Polish diesel from Gdansk. By a hill of coal, a battered little collier is loaded by lines of men bearing baskets of coal on their heads. The labourers work naked apart from loin cloth, flip-flop sandals, the soles fashioned from old tyres, and a ring of padded rope upon the head to ease the pressure of their burden. The faces are impassive.

'Look at those poor sods, Harry. What a life, eh?' My chief, Don Butterworth, has joined me at the rail. We are in crisp white tropical shirts and starched white shorts with ironed creases.

'Why not load by crane?' I ask a pointless question, for I already know the answer.

'Simple. Mechanise the job and they'd be out of work. How else would the millions feed their families? When the Yanks built them a grain elevator in Calcutta, the Commie trade unions smashed it rather than see their members out of work.'

'I remember that. Was there at the time. There were riots and protest marches around Kidderpore. It wasn't safe to go ashore. Will you be going ashore here, Don?'

'Maybe a quick leg stretch. Don't forget we've just a few cars and tractors to discharge and we'll be off again by nightfall. Been here before?'

'I haven't. What do you recommend?'

'Depends what you want. If you hope for a drink, you'll be disappointed. Madras is a dry state. They've got serious prohibition, so don't try to sneak a bottle ashore, otherwise we'll have to leave you behind, for you'll be in the lock-up. You could always visit the cathedral and pay your respects to the tomb of Saint Thomas the Apostle. It's a decent stroll south of the dock gate.'

'Thomas who doubted and put his finger into the wounds of Christ? The chap who was wrecked on Socotra on his way to India?'

'The same. A crowd of Brahmin priests didn't like the rate at which he was converting the local Hindoos, so they ran him through with lances. They can be a touchy crew, the Brahmins — quick to take umbrage.'

I nod towards the line of dust-blackened, sweating labourers. 'Instead of spearing saints, they should ease the lives of those poor buggers on that coal boat.'

'Nothing to do with the Brahmins, old son, they being top dog. The coal carriers will be Untouchables, so low in the pecking order they don't even have a caste. It's their lot to do the filthy jobs, shovel up Brahmin excrement, etcetera, and keep a low profile as long as they live.'

'I've read if the mere shadow of an Untouchable falls across a Brahmin, he has to take a ritual bath of purification and the Untouchable would get beaten up. Easy to see why Saint Thomas pulled the crowds.'

'The upper castes could never understand how the British Army in India was happy to employ Untouchables as their cooks. But, there again, Europeans don't have a caste. Religion-wise, we are already polluted, so what we get up to is no matter to those born to the sacred thread. Anyhow, if you do get to the shrine of Thomas, remember it's a Catholic church — I don't know what persuasion you are.'

'I'm officially C of E, but was a regular at the Sons of Temperance as a lad — they had free picture shows, cowboys and cartoons. The film was always snapping in the cinematograph and we would cheer and stamp our feet while it was mended.'

'Sounds hilarious.'

'Lately, I've been reading about the Buddha. He makes sense. He even converted a few Brahmins. I once attended Catholic mass in Liverpool. A girl at their mission dance reckoned I was a heathen and should go to midnight mass with her.'

'Did you enjoy it?'

'Our crowd had shifted a load of Guinness, so I had a job to follow what was going on. I do remember a chap waltzing down the aisle with his handbag on fire, then I nodded off.'

Mahanada is nudged alongside, made secure fore and aft, and her gangway lowered. A dapper little chap in a khaki topee, with matching shirt and trousers, is first aboard. He'll be from our shipping agent, Gordon Woodroffe and Co. He carries a Gladstone bag — in it will be mail from home.

I have four letters. Beryl writes of yet more bargains she's acquired for our two rooms upstairs in Warren Road. After we are married, we will have rooms with my mother. She's booked Holy Trinity church at Seaton Carew for Saturday, July 4th, followed by a reception at the Marine Hotel on the seafront. There will be about forty guests sat down to lunch. The bill will be paid by the bride's father, as is the custom. All I have to do is to turn up on time with the best man at my side and a gold ring secure in his pocket.

Mam writes of my mongrel dog, Peter, and his latest escapades. She feeds him every morning with a tin of Chappie and whatever scraps are at hand, then lets him run free.

He barks at the door when he's had enough of chasing cats and searching for bitches. I read how, 'The dogs in the town are looking more and more like your Peter.'

Brian Marsden from Hexham on Tyne, a good friend I studied radar maintenance with in South Shields, is learning Greek. He's gone 'foreign flag'. He's signed up with Stavros Niarchos, who pays him twice the money he earned with Bibby's and Blue Funnel. I read that again. He is now on £90 a month, double what I get. But, next he tells how he went into the wheelhouse on the Greek, and found it empty. The wheel had been lashed while the Hellenic crew had gone below. He found them sat around in the saloon taking coffee.

I slip the letters into my shirt drawer and change into shore gear. I need to find a post office. We'll be on the Indian coast for five weeks, so I'd better stock up on aerogrammes.

As usual in India, there's a throng of beggars outside the dock gate. The kids are a clamouring nuisance. Little brown hands pluck at me as if I am made of gold, and they want a piece. 'Me no mama, no papa,' they cry. I slip through by handing out small coins from the hoard of unspent Indian paisa I keep in a baccy tin — some to an old lady in a faded sari who has no teeth. In former times, I ignored the beggars and pushed my way through. One day, an Anglo-Indian quartermaster told how he: 'Always carried ashore plenty of small coins for the beggars, because, after all, they too are the children of God'. As to the reality of God, I'm unpersuaded, but his words went home.

Turbaned rickshaw pedallers shout for custom, but I press through. This is my fourth trip to India, and I'm becoming an 'old hand'. I've moved on from being appalled at the extremes of poverty and wealth, and all between, to a grudging acceptance of the state of things. Gone are the tensions and twitches that strangeness brings. I can now stroll the crowded lanes and markets with an amount of good humour. It's true that when you relax, you notice more.

A tidy young fellow in ironed trousers, breast pocket loaded with pens, sidles up. He looks more Latin than

Indian. 'Sir, I am student. Please to walk beside you to improve my English?' *Here we go again,* is my immediate thought.

I sigh. 'My English not good. Best find some wallah from Oxford.'

'Oxford person not here today. You like temple? I show you interesting temple. Please, sir.'

'What sort of temple?'

'Jain temple. Sir will like Jain temple — not Hindu. Much better than Hindu. Much to learn. Very old, and it free.'

I've never seen a Jain temple. Fascinating people, the Jains; I've read how their holy men sweep the path before them to avoid stepping on creatures and destroying life. 'How far, this Jain temple?'

He draws me onto the pavement to avoid an approaching ox cart. The humped oxen have lofty upturned horns, painted bright blue. Both beasts have strings of little bells tinkling around their swaying dewlaps. 'Two minute. This way.' He sets off, brushing aside a beggar.

He stops to make sure I'm following. 'After temple, we look at Armenian Church. Six big bells. Famous all over world. Plenty history in Madras. Dutch, Portugal, French wallah, English, come in ships. Much fight for trade.'

'Oh yes? And how did the Armenians get here?'

'They walk, sir. History say walk from Armenia. Buy and sell silk. Make very rich. Moghul kings like them very much. Armenian very honest peoples.'

'Are they still here?'

'Bugger off to America since Independence. All gone.'

'Did you learn that at school? Bugger off, is not good English.'

'Mr Fleming, my teacher say bugger off every day. But he is Anglo-Indian, like me, sir.'

'Really? My headmaster was also called Fleming. A Scotsman from Aberdeen. Made us read Sir Walter Scott. *Marmion* and suchlike.'

The pavement is blocked by a grubby white calf that casually chews a crumpled newspaper, so we step onto the busy road.

'Damn holy cows! You have such bloody cows in England?'

'We keep our cows in green fields, where they eat grass instead of the *Times of India.*'

'Ho, ho! You make good joke, sir. Not far now.' He gives a short skip, and with the attractive lilt of a Hindi speaker using English, recites: '*O young Lochinvar is come out of west. Through all wide Border his steed was best.* That also by Sir Walter Scott. Favourite of my Mister Fleming, also.'

I respond: '*And save his good broadsword, he weapons had none. He rode all unarm'd, and he rode all alone.*'

'Bravo, sir! Do you also know *Miller of Dee?*'

'No, I don't. Not yet, anyway. What's your name?'

'Marmaduke Miller, dealer in pepper and spice, was my remote ancestor. I am humble George Miller, student of literature. And your good name, sir?'

'Michael Nicholson, master builder and knocker-in of nails, is my remote ancestor. I am the humble Harry Nicholson, tapper-out of Morse code.'

He puts his palms together. 'Hari! Hari! Pious Hindu will say you have name of God. But I am only Miller, so what know I?' He chortles. Then, as is a habit among some Indians, with a suck of air through the gap in his front teeth, declaims: '*There dwelt a miller, hale and bold, beside river Dee. He danced and sang from morn till night, no lark so blithe as he.*' He sweeps out his arm. 'Behold, temple.'

I stare up at marble pillars and balconies, with niches that hold painted statues of gods and goddesses. The divinities gaze on the chaos of the street. We join a dribble of devotees and climb the stairs into the shrine to be met by a ten-foot-tall statue. He sits cross-legged on a plinth decorated with the image of a lion. His eyes are downcast.

I'm startled. On either side, carved into the marble, are swastikas. Then, upraised hands with the symbol of a wheel on the palms. Before him are bowls of uncooked rice. A scattering of plump mice feed on the rice. They move aside without terror when a glossy brown rat of exceptional size arrives. The rodents ignore the little group of devotees who kneel before the shrine and make offerings of food. I stare at the vermin in disbelief whilst absorbing the peace of the silent chamber and note how my heart is softening despite the swastikas.

My guide is watching me with twinkling eyes. I whisper, 'Who is it?'

'You are gazed upon by Lord Mahavira. Jain avatar. Live five-hundred years before Jesus.'

'Is he a god?'

'Not God. Great teacher. Mahavira said gods not make world. Gods grow old and die, same as men, but after a long, long time.'

I nod. 'The Buddha said the same, so I've read.'

'True, my friend. Both live in Bihar. Wander forests, meet and discuss best way to live. Agree on many things, except for soul. Mahavira teach soul is real, but Buddha say it all delusion. You like fat rats?'

'I think they are obscene. Why is it allowed?'

'Mahatma Gandhi said, Mahavira first teacher of Ahimsa, precept not to harm living being. So rats and mice come and go, all time.'

'And the swastikas?'

'Ancient symbol of well-being. Thieved by nasty little loosewallah, Hitler. We go tomb of Saint Thomas now?'

'Not today, thank you. I'm off to the post office, then back to the ship. We leave for Calcutta in a few hours.'

In the street, after we shake hands, George Miller looks sorrowfully at his feet. I'm already reaching for my wallet.

'Sir, I am student. Difficult to buy books for study. Can you help me?'

'Just a little. I'm not Nubar Gulbenkian, you know.' I offer a two-rupee note, the best part of half-an-hour's pay for me. I can tell he hoped for more. I'll probably walk away from here with the feeling that I've been conned yet again by an 'impoverished Indian student' on the lookout for an affable European. This latest might be genuine — or not, or somewhere in between — it is hard to tell.

In the unseen years to come, I'll help other students with funds for books, make donations to help pay for a weeping fellow's lost train ticket, and for salve to heal sores on the legs of a teenaged beggar girl. I'll never be sure if such are indeed genuine cases, or just talented actors. But, no matter, I've enjoyed this brief stroll ashore in Madras with the Miller of Dee, and I wish him well.

16

Hooghly

Almost any pilot will tell you that his work is much more difficult than you imagine; but the Pilots of the Hugli know that they have one hundred miles of the most dangerous river on earth running through their hands — the Hugli between Calcutta and the Bay of Bengal, and they say nothing. Their service is picked and sifted as carefully as the bench of the Supreme Court, for a judge can only hang the wrong man, or pass a bad law; but a careless pilot can lose a ten-thousand-ton ship with crew and cargo in less time than it takes to reverse her engines.

So wrote Rudyard Kipling in 1895, in his short story, *An Unqualified Pilot.*

29th April 1959.

A smudge along the rim of the north-eastern sky gives the merest hint of a coast. A smoky sun hangs to starboard and brings a new day to the Sundarbans, the vast delta of the Ganges and jungle home of tigers.

Still many miles offshore, we collect the pilot from the pretty little service vessel at Sandheads anchorage. A well-provendered Indian, with precise moustache, climbs the gangway. In crisp whites, he's as smart as a cricketer striding out to the crease. The pilot's khaki-clad leadsman follows with a valise of overnight gear. Captain Eggleston, and first mate, Mr Rudge, greet him as he steps onto the deck. Our deck officers wear their caps. The captain takes his hand. 'Good morning, sir. You are on time for breakfast, should you require it. Arbroath smokies and poached eggs on the menu.'

'Splendid, Captain. Always a delight to board a Brocklebanker, you are an honourable part of India. Perhaps a pot of Darjeeling, and my usual Haig's whisky with a splash of ginger ale, if it's no trouble.' He turns to the mate. 'The channels are uncertain this season and I expect to be lifted by a fifteen-foot tide. On some stretches, you will attend the fo'c's'le to give supervision to carpenter and crew and be ready to let go with double anchors on my orders.'

The chief officer might be taken aback, it's hard to tell from my viewpoint outside the wireless room door, two decks up. But I note how he nods assent.

The pilot points to a tired Liberty ship with the slow flap of Old Glory at her stern. 'For now, we shall follow the *Dwight D Doodle*, or some such — I forget the name. A Yankee grain ship.'

I squint through the sun at the Sam-boat. She'll be fresh from the mothball fleet in California. The old girl has a list. Maybe she hit a typhoon south of China and the cargo has shifted, her holds stuffed with surplus wheat from the prairie. Food aid from the USA. The cargo a gift to famished India, and they get to keep the ship. Never have there been such days.

Our pilot makes his way to the saloon whilst *Mawana* steams towards the river. Once we have crossed the line of demarcation where the blue waters of the Bay of Bengal give way to the brown sediments of the Hooghly, he will take to the bridge and remain on duty for the entire transit, except for when we must anchor, whereupon he will sleep.

Don Butterworth, my boss, joins me in the wireless room, reads my log, and fusses with paperwork. As chief radio officer, with a mere two hours watchkeeping per day, plus fleet schedules in the small hours, my meal reliefs, direction finding work, and the vital task of keeping the radar in good order, he can become bored. He is forever looking for work, which means I am closely supervised. I respect the man. I heard recently that he was torpedoed twice in the war but, in our seven months together, he has not mentioned it.

He leafs through the latest carbon copies in the message pad and calculates the charges incurred by ship to shore telegrams. He tots up the totals of crew traffic so we can set costs against a fellow's wage. He scrutinises a message to Interflora I sent this morning. 'That's the fourth bunch of flowers the fifth engineer has sent since we left home. One a week! He must be on a promise.'

'Are they all to the same address? I haven't checked.'

He sniffs. 'None of our business, squire. Remember, we sign an undertaking to keep the content of radio traffic strictly confidential.'

'I've never breathed a word.'

'I should think not. I've known there to be ructions among the crew when that trust breaks down. Though, if there's a message about a sudden death at home, sometimes we might want to get the captain to break the news gently, rather than handing the poor blighter a sheet ripped off the message pad.'

I catch his eye. 'In which case, the judgement is down to us. That's a tender responsibility.'

'It is, squire, it is. And it requires maturity and a modicum of common sense. So, if you get one of those, let me know first.'

I'm left pondering my own quantity of wisdom in such matters. My boss will be sending reports about me to head office in Cunard Buildings, Liverpool. I wonder what's in them. I now hold a Postmaster General's Certificate of Competence in Radiotelegraphy and Authority to Operate on a ship, 1st Class, and have passed the Ministry of Transport Radar Maintenance exam. There are no further seagoing 'tickets' to study for. It can't be too long before I'm promoted to Chief Radio Officer and have a ship of my own, with a junior to keep an eye on. But, *be careful what you wish for*, was Mam's caution. It's been an interesting career so far: starting with a pre-war troopship, the *Dunera*; then, in sole charge, a rusty Jimmy Nourse tramp, the *Hughli* — named after the river we are about to enter. Again on my own, a collier out of the Tyne, the little MV *Corburn*, taking Welsh coal to the glue factory in Plymouth. Lastly, a junior's job on the 1943 Brocklebanker, *Mahanada* — hot, sweaty and infested. I now live in comfort on a spanking modern cargo liner with air-conditioning. Promotion would put me right back onto one of our fleet's oldest, where I'd pant among ancient gear, and check my food for cockroaches. Chiefs who have been with this fleet for many years get the latest ships. New chiefs get the primitive wartime and pre-war vessels — which is fair enough, I suppose.

He's been reading my mind. 'Have patience. Take your gin in moderation, and it won't be too long.' He peers through the porthole, open on its chain, so we might catch a breeze. Sometimes the air conditioning intake brings in whiffs of the funnel. 'How many times have you been up the Hooghly, Harry?'

'Twice on *Mahanada*, and twice with you, on this ship. And yourself, Don?'

'I've lost count. It's been every few months for years, except for wartime when we could end up anywhere on the globe. First came here before the end of the Raj, when the pilots were British to a man. Seafarers refer to the Hooghly as the "Arsehole of India", but there's a certain beauty. Look here.'

I unwind from my chair and join him at the porthole. The ship is steady. There's not the slightest roll on the ochre waters of the estuary.

Beyond a scatter of fishing craft, sails limp at this quiet hour, are miles of low shore: glistening mud, and long stretches of dark and light green. The morning grows bright, and the land steams. Layers of pastel shades merge the earth into the sky. 'See that? Sagar Island, start of the river. Flat. No height to its twenty-odd miles. When I first saw it, before the war, there were miles of mangrove and jungle. Now it's mostly rice paddy on river silt. It's sprouted villages, temples, and what not.'

I nod. 'Overpopulation. India needs Marie Stopes and her contraceptives.'

'Ah, well, no doubt Pandit Nehru will sort it all out. Anyway, the south end of Sagar Island is a hot spot of Hindu pilgrimage. They flock to perform ritual ablutions in the Holy Mother Ganga. That's where the river that drains the Gangetic Plain and most of Tibet finally meets the sea. It signifies the merging of human souls with the Creator's consciousness — according to my bit of reading.'

'Each life like a drop of rain on the Himalayas. The drops merging together to form the Ganges. Then all flow into the great ocean. The ocean of Brahma.'

'You are more erudite than you look, being from Hartlepool.'

'Arthur Mee's *Children's Encyclopedia*, chief. I don't recall much from school apart from scraps of Tennyson and how to ridge taties in the school garden.'

He gives a humph. 'Where's the mangroves? There's big gaps along the shore. These days, a cyclone can crash inland and drown thousands in their charpoys. The mangroves used to soak up the storm surge.'

I stand back — it's a struggle for both of us to look through the port hole. The brass is turning green; high time I gave it a polish, 'Folk only learn the hard way.'

'They've built proper roads and a new pilot station. The river mouth gets sounded daily from over there. They say, in the old days, Bengal tigers would swim out, climb aboard a survey craft and snatch one of the crew while he slept. Not so many tigers about in modern times, and what's left has become shy.'

'Never seen a Bengal tiger. Seen plenty of Bombay tigers, though it's only an extra-big cockroach with hairs and stripes.' I shudder. 'The *Mahanada* was wick with them before she was fumigated.'

The pilot service has been guiding vessels up the Hooghly since 1670. A pilot is essential for this river, the western-most outlet of the Ganges. It is one of the world's most treacherous. There are curves and bends, and currents that grab at the hull, and bars which cannot be crossed when the tide is on the ebb. If this were not enough, during extra-high water in the Southwest Monsoon, a tidal bore can charge upstream twice a day as a breaking wave of seven-foot and more. At the worst, mooring ropes snap, anchor chains break, and vessels are carried away; the Hooghly bore respects no works of man.

One hundred and twenty miles of river, from the sea to Calcutta, are constantly monitored. It is rich in navigational aids: buoys with red, green, and white lights flashing and occulting, and multi-armed semaphore posts that signal the water depth across the bars. Vessels face two dangerous bends where fierce currents can swing a ship through 180 degrees. Where the Rupnarayan river flows into the Hooghly, the helm must fight opposing currents. An error on the wheel can cause the vessel to spin out of control and fall foul of the shoals. The conflict of the two streams impedes the Hooghly flow and causes her to drop much of her silt, making stretches of quicksand which lie in wait of a navigator's error. Masters have feared the *Royal James and Mary* shoal since 1694, when a ship of that name was swallowed up. Since then, many others have come to grief and vanished into the graveyard. Should a ship be captured by the shoal when the flow is strongest, she will swing around and topple over into the dreadful void excavated by the current on the downstream side of her hull.

We are a twin-turbine steamship of 8,000 brake horsepower, and yet we must take care not to come to grief in our two-day passage. One can only wonder at the skill of the sailing ship men who came this way. To navigate the river's downward flow or the upstream advance of a flood tide, they would tack their way to Calcutta, anchoring to await favourable winds, and take a week or more to reach safe harbour.

The pilot guides us across the bars at half-speed, taking great interest in the echo sounder. Sometimes we have a mere two feet of clearance beneath the keel. Too much speed would displace enough water to cause the ship to 'squat' — sink lower into the river and risk touching the bottom. In 1892, the British steamer *Anglia* came to grief and rolled over on a Hooghly mud bank. Men drowned that day because they could not squeeze through the portholes. Since then, International law insists on portholes of sufficient size to allow the escape of a full-grown man.

At Hooghly Point, we anchor while the incoming tide arrives, but today the tidal bore is not enough to give us a fright. The pilot times our passage up the Western Gut along the flank of the three-mile length of the James and Mary shoal. We have a flood tide, so there is no risk of us touching bottom. Our captain is close to retirement, and I suppose he might have made this passage eighty times in his career, but he utters a note of relief, 'Nicely done, sir.'

The pilot climbs down from his eyrie on the tall, wooden pilot chair. 'Thank you, Captain. It's good to watch the James and Mary drop astern. That place is a clubhouse sandwich of wrecks. They lie one on top of another, so many slices of iron and timber filling. So many, I wonder why it is not become an island.' He points across the river. 'Sixty years since British India Company lost their pilgrim steamer, *Mahratta*, in the Eastern Gut. It touched the ground and capsized. Brocklebanks have lost two *Mahrattas* since then, both on the same shoal, but not this one. Both foundered on the Goodwin Sands, in your own English Channel. Unfortunate name, *Mahratta*.'

Captain Eggleston gives a grunt. 'I have it on good authority that the company will not be launching any more of that title.'

The jungle ends, and now green fields and huts line the river banks: bright young paddy rice, and villages of simple brick homes roofed with thatch and corrugated iron. Rows of dung cakes adorn every house wall —

close-packed pancakes of cow dung and straw, with stained gaps where some have been lifted as fuel for the cooking fire. Smoothed layers of dung will line the floors and walls within. It sets like cement, but is easy on the feet and cool in summer, and mosquitoes do not linger. The Hindu associates the cow with Shiva and Krishna and declares it holy. Since ancient times, cow urine has been used as medicine, likewise the dung. Rolled into little balls to form pills, it has been swallowed by believers since the Iron Age.

The channel takes us close to the eastern bank. From our great height, we can look down onto streets and bathing spots, and dhobi places where washer women beat wet clothes against the bleached trunks of stranded trees. As our bulk approaches, the women gather up their washing and retreat to safety. Ablutions interrupted, shy girls rise from the shallows and cover themselves. Naked children rush to the water's edge to wave with glee and dive into the river. The bow wave surges ashore, lifting little boats at their moorings and sending the children into shrieks as they ride the wave on their bellies. Older boys have been waiting astride planks of wood. They've paddled out close to our track and now surf inshore on our roaring wash without fear of the huge and churning phosphor-bronze propeller. As we thunder by, a brown dog breaks off his frantic scratching to bark at us.

I've got the chartroom hatch open so I can keep in touch with the rest of the bridge. I'm kept busy with messages to and from the pilot offices, and between the ship and our agents. Everything goes through VWC, the Calcutta marine radio station. The operator at VWC seems to be stilted and without humour today — perhaps he's having trouble at home, or maybe he's under training and his supervisor is listening in.

'Give me *Half Ahead*.' There's a clatter as the pilot slaps his coffee cup into the saucer. 'Bloody idiots. They have no business wandering down the shipping channel.'

The second mate gives the telegraph a double ring by rotating the brass handle to its fullest travel before returning it to the *Half Ahead* position. That will have set the bells clanging in our engine room. The engineer won't miss it among the background whine and hiss.

Three diminutive native craft, bearing domes of straw as tall as bungalows, are scattered across the channel ahead. The cargo of thatch and forage is so piled up that it is hard to discern the boat beneath and, to a casual eye, they appear to be floating haystacks. Earlier, the radar showed them advancing downstream in Indian file. But the lead craft is now in trouble. Her load has slipped to one side, and she proceeds like a drunken matron with her gown trailing in the water. Her companions are now in line abreast, accompanied by much yelling in Bengali. As we go by, screams and wails meet our wash, but all three tottering loads survive.

'Damned river coolies! *Full Ahead*, if you please.' The telegraph rings and we build up a white moustache around the stem.

Now comes the smoke of industry. Brickworks: tall chimneys, stacks of yellow Hooghly bricks, and belching kilns, line the western bank. Hundreds of labourers haul and stack.

Black kites arrive — we must be near Calcutta. The mob takes a few turns around the ship and, with flicks of scimitar wings, twists of long forked tails, and piercing calls, descends on the masts. They'll perch there to watch and wait until a galley steward, bearing a tray of food, risks a journey along the deck. Then they will pounce. If nothing emerges from the galley, they might join some of their kin who feast on the bloated body of that buffalo that slips seaward. The diners hop across the rolling corpse, unaware of their collision course with our bow. Meanwhile it is *Half-Ahead* once again as a ferryboat propelled by great sweep oars and straining muscles, and crammed with humanity, struggles to clear our track.

The dwellings on the eastern bank grow thick as we approach the mooring buoys at Garden Reach. We'll make fast with hefty chains and massive coir rope springs to hold us when the bore arrives. Tomorrow, a different dignified Indian, known as the Mud Pilot, will take us into the foetid waters of Kidderpore Dock, our home for the next three weeks.

17

Chowringhee

30th April 1959.
Kidderpore Dock, Calcutta.
Chants of *'Jumna bordu russi kanara licker jow'* rise from the throats of demob-happy Lascar sailors as they haul on ropes and we draw alongside the old dock walls of Kidderpore. The Bengali sailor's work song says: 'Make fast the starboard ropes and let's all go ashore'. I've heard it many times, and always as we tie up in our Asian crew's home port. They have been away for five months and soon will be with their families.

I've given my steward a goodly sum in rupee notes. It makes a hole in my funds, but he deserves it. The politeness of the stewards, and the tidiness of our cabins, improved with each day we neared India. Even though senior Indian seamen on British articles earn as much as a Calcutta doctor of medicine, each hopes for a decent tip, a good backsheesh, from the officers they served. I have no complaints about the steward who looked after me and my boss this past year. Though he answers to 'Boy', Jamil is a dignified Moslem in his fifties and has been all that we could have wished for. Always clean and upright, his twinkling eyes and cropped salt-and-pepper hajji beard will be missed. With the rest of our Asian crew of sixty-odd, he will sign off ship's articles today and be without a post for twelve months in line with Indian government regulations. With more Lascar sailors than there are berths, each must rotate, one year at sea and one ashore, so all might have employment. If Brocklebank ships wish to continue their old trade with India, the company must abide by the increasingly tight rules of the twelve-year-old independent nation.

A brown envelope slipped to the chief clerk in the Calcutta shipping office will shorten a Lascar's time ashore. Bribery greases much of this country's machinations. Some of our more valued seamen, such as the serang (Indian bosun), might reappear if our agent drops enough rupees into the right hands. An outstanding serang is worth hanging on to, likewise an excellent cook. We all appreciate a Goan in the galley. If we get one, he will have crossed India by train from the Portuguese colony of Goa. He will be a Roman Catholic of mixed blood, perhaps called Antonio or Miguel, (the Portuguese have held the place since 1510), and we shall rejoice at mealtimes. To secure a cook from Goa, a Portuguese enclave that India agitates to subsume, will take a bucket of rupees. Sometimes one of our fleet of twenty-six gains a Goan cook. No questions asked.

After a dinner of mouth-watering curry of huge and succulent prawns fresh from the creeks of the Sundarbans, I investigate the sounds of celebration. A ballad is in full flow. Bearing six cans of chilled beer, and careful not to disturb the slow pluck of guitar strings, I pause outside the blue curtain that covers the entrance to the Fourth Engineer's cabin. Chippy's rich Scouse voice is pitched to baritone tonight. His enunciation is precise, the R handsomely rolled:

The landlord he looks very big
With his high cocked hat and powdered wig;
Methinks he looks both fair and fat,
But he may thank you and me for that.

Then comes the slow chorus in a mix of accents:

*O, Good Ale! thou art my darling,
Thou art my joy both night and morning.*

And back to Alf's Birkenhead tones:

*Thou oft hath made my friends my foes,
And often made me pawn my clothes;
But since thou art so near my nose,
It's bottoms up—and down thee goes.*

As I push through the curtain with my cans, I join the beery chorus:

*O, Good Ale! thou art my darling,
Thou art my joy both night and morning.*

Alf's voice becomes fluting:

*I know my wife doth not despise,
Your beauty with unfavoured eyes.
If she loves me and I love thee,
A happy couple we shall be.*

And the chorus roars out as though to crack the welds in the deckhead. As the songsters turn to their beer, Alf drums his big fingers on the sound-box of the guitar. 'Eighteenth century, that one is.'

There's a hiss from a can of Tennent's lager, and a shout, 'Chuck me the top spanner when you've done, Jimmy.' Another hiss as the tooth of the opener bites into the top of an aluminium can to make two triangular holes from which foam erupts. 'A good old song, Chips. But can we 'ave summat a bit more up to date?'

'You mean, like Lonnie Donegan?' Alf, with calloused thumb and grooved fingers, vamps out *Rock Island Line* in a fierce three-chord tempo. Feet beat out the rhythm on the deck, and voices, Mersey and Clyde, one from the Tyne, and mine from the Tees, roar out the lyrics.

This has the makings of a memorable docking night. We always have a party on reaching Calcutta, for it is our terminus, and every day from now on brings us closer to home. Let it be soon. Two others of our fleet are already in port, at advanced stages of loading bales of jute and chests of tea, so we can expect visitors. All along the alleyways there will be crammed cabins and headaches in the morning.

After last night, which was outstanding, I'm restored by a glass of foaming liver Salts. I take care to carry a tin of Andrew's on a voyage, though today it had set so hard in the tin that I had to chop it out. We rock to the clack of wheels, steel rims on iron lines, the ting, ting, ting, of the bell to clear loiterers off the tracks on our clatter across the vast Maidan park. Then squealing brakes. We hop off the electric tram and push through the throng, dropping small coins into the palm of a beseeching old woman. Fare-dodgers, who have clung to the sides of the tram, have already vanished into the crowds, chased by a policeman with his bamboo staff. Chowringhee Road is all-a-bustle, as usual.

A bride and groom, festooned with garlands of rose and jasmine, pose for photos outside Scheherazade, a swanky open-air restaurant. Gold jewellery drapes the bride, tawdry modern stuff from the bazaar or honoured family heirlooms — who knows? The sun flashes from the chains and bangles. Led by a troop of drums and pipes, another groom, dressed like a rajah, rides a white horse to his own wedding. On all sides, the Gandhi cap is in fashion, upturned little white boats on brown heads, long and thin, round and fat.

Black umbrellas everywhere, carried like a badge of office by bespectacled men in dhotis — their bandy legs without socks end in polished black shoes. A line of them queues outside the magnificent High Court — the Gothic building tries its best to imitate the Houses of Parliament at

Westminster. Fragrant pavement stalls sell hot snacks such as bhajis, pakoras, and dhal and rice wrapped in leaves. A pair of buffaloes with upswept horns pull a cart piled with oil drums. Crows, piebald black and grey, strut along the gutter, picking at scraps. Labourers, under bales of cloth, bend as they trot; the carrying strap bites into their foreheads — what a way to earn a crust. A bicycle strains to pull a loaded trailer. The pedaller has close cropped hair with a bristly tuft at the crown which tells all he is in mourning. Coveys of bicycle rickshaws sail by, propelled by knotted calves; inside each is a fat babu, or a fellow in a khaki topee, or parents with infants on their knees.

Droves of Hindustan Ambassador taxis crunch gears, their horns blaring in impatience. Mustard yellow, they have statuettes of the elephant-headed god, Ganesh, the remover of obstacles, dangling in the windscreens. The Ambassador is a sturdy and thirsty motor car, designed in Britain by Issigonis as the Morris Oxford. Now it is made in India by a firm that bought all rights and machine tools. I shudder at the recall of one night as a passenger in one of those, when something unknown, nasty and hairy, with scrabbling claws, fell from the rear curtain and down the neck of my shirt. I yelped and undressed in haste in the dark.

A bearer trots by with a stack of woven baskets on his head. A woman sweeper squats outside a hotel flicking at dust and leaves with a broom of thin twigs, the sparkle of a cheap jewel in her nose. At Esplanade Crossing, a traffic policeman stands on a plinth beneath an umbrella. The cracked pavements are stained by red spatter expectorated by chewers of betel nut. A flutter of girls, all in white smocks and pigtails tied in red ribbon, march in lines behind teachers across the Maidan, the thousand tree-dotted acres of Calcutta's grassy lungs, towards the statues of Viceroys. The school children are off to the Victoria Memorial where the great marble queen sits on her throne, nursing the orb and sceptre. She reminds all who pass of an Indian empire that ended just twelve years ago. I wonder how long the new India will let the sad Empress, Kipling's *Widow at Windsor*, sit in state.

Box kites dance and whirl on the ends of strings. Excited, ragged boys play at marbles. An ox hauls a huge lawnmower with its dead petrol-engine. Women gather up the mown grass to bear away as forage for milk cows. A lanky blind man holds out his tin cup, white enamel with blue rim, and stares into infinity. A coin tinkles. He smiles and inclines his head.

I'm with Fred, a cadet on his second trip. Damp patterns his shirt, for he is a heavy sweater. I sweat mostly from the forehead and base of my spine. I could use some of Fred's perspiration ability; by the end of this run ashore, my feet will ache and burn through lack of sweat. I say as much.

He responds: 'We are reckoned to have three million sweat glands on our bodies. I've got that many in my armpits. At least your shirt won't get wringing wet. I'll end up in a lather. What do the old India hands say about it? Horses sweat, men perspire, and ladies glow. I'm a horse and you're a lady.'

'You reckon? Ok, if you don't crap in the street, I'll try not to pout.'

'Ok, where to next?'

'We need Dalhousie Square. The post office is on the site of the Black Hole of Calcutta. I'm told there's a plaque. Let's take a dekko.'

On the pavement, next to a row of barbers giving haircuts, and shaves with cut-throat razors, is a fellow who offers to remove our ear wax with slender metal implements. We decline and gaze down at another stall. The vendor is flicking flies off his curios: wooden elephants; snakeskin handbags and purses; soapstone carvings of Krishna standing on one leg, playing a flute; a head of the Buddha in green onyx, I'm taken by his lowered eyes and the hint of a smile that plays around his lips. We inspect a stuffed mongoose in a fight to the death with a stuffed snake. The hooded king-cobra is coiled about the moth-eaten body. Fangs are flashing. The taxidermist has arranged things so that the combatants snarl into each other's glass eyes.

'For you, sahib, only two-hundred rupees.'

We purse our lips, shake our heads, and saunter away. He calls out, 'Special price today, sahib. One hundred rupees only.'

In the dappled shade of a peepul tree, we loiter while Fred opens a flat white tin. The picture on the lid is of two peasant girls among forested mountains. He unfolds the silver wrapping paper. The cigarettes are in a neat row, like infantry. 'Care for a posh tab, Harry. The Mate gave me them after I'd finished a particularly filthy job he set me on.'

'Balkan Sobranie! I've not seen them on the purser's list of bonded stores. Are they out of the cargo?'

He shrugs. 'No names, no pack drills.' He flicks his Zippo and lights mine. 'You know, I reckon we could get that stuffed mongoose down to fifty or less.'

'You'd like to see it on your mam's mantelpiece, would you?'

'Well, it would scare the bloody moggy out of its wits. But it might not look so clever alongside the Staffordshire pot dogs and the picture of Uncle Charlie who died in the trenches.'

The mongoose man is beckoning to us. We give him a cheery wave and stroll on, weaving around beggars, and leaving a fragrant trail of the Balkans to compete with the monsoon drains.

18

The Black Hole

You can't miss the General Post Office and its white dome held up by Corinthian columns. There's a multi-faced clock made by the same firm that made the Big Ben clock in London. Fred and I wonder at such grand statements for a place that sells stamps and postal orders.

The place is thronged, but the queue at the 'Overseas' counter is shortest. It's odd how the many Indian bearers, intent on posting their master's mail, insist on standing so close they leave us without personal space. I keep moving the lad in front of me a few inches forward so he is not stood on my feet. 'Stay there', I tell him, but he just grins and shuffles back into place. Maybe he believes in auras and wants to inhabit mine for a few minutes.

The clerk weighs my three letters to Britain. 'Ninety paise each,' he barks.

I hand over three rupees and get thirty paise in change. Gone is the sweet little anna. India is now decimal. It's now one hundred new paise to the rupee. I watch him dab the stamps on a damp sponge and stick them to the letters. 'Please frank the stamps,' I ask.

He retorts, 'What for you want me frank stamps?'

'I need to see them franked so I know they will not be peeled off and stolen for resale.'

He's not pleased. 'You think Indian postal service is manned by loosewallahs? Thieves?'

'I mean no offence. I can see you are an honest man. But my letters home sometimes go astray. And post from home addressed to Calcutta can arrive with their stamps peeled off.' I could go on and tell him how I advise Beryl and mother not to use showy commemorative British stamps on my mail — India is awash with keen philatelists. But I think better of it. The hand franker thuds down with force to leave a blurred smudge on the little rose-purple stamps, obliterating the map of India. They are now so defaced that I doubt if Beryl will want them for her own collection.

At the side of the great hall is a philatelic bureau. That is the place for collectable specimens. I buy a mint set of thirteen, all in values of annas and old paise. They commemorate the launch of the 1955 Five-Year Plan. They're insipid examples of the stamp designer's art, with poorly defined tractors, locomotives, dams, and malarial mosquitoes. I don't pay for issues beyond one rupee — every hobby has its limits.

'Where is the site of the Black Hole prison?' I ask the friendly chap at the philatelic counter. I do it nervously. It feels as though I'm asking for a pint of black and tan in a Dublin bar.

'In alleyway at side of building. Untidy place these days. Jungly wallahs throw in rubbish.'

Sure enough, the remnant of the Black Hole of Calcutta, made so much of at school, is a neglected spot. Two low walls, with vestiges of iron railings, mark off the sad space. It's become a dumping ground for twigs, discarded newspapers, and other sweepings. Close by, a plaque, set into the wall of the post office, reads:

> THE MARBLE PAVEMENT BELOW
> THIS SPOT WAS PLACED HERE
> BY LORD CURZON, VICEROY AND
> GOVERNOR GENERAL OF INDIA,
> IN 1901 TO MARK THE SITE OF
> THE PRISON IN OLD FORT WILLIAM
> KNOWN AS THE BLACK HOLE IN
> WHICH 146 BRITISH INHABITANTS
> OF CALCUTTA WERE CONFINED ON
> THE NIGHT OF THE 20TH JUNE,

1756, AND FROM WHICH ONLY 23 CAME OUT ALIVE.

Whilst Fred and I peer into the relic, there comes a voice at our rear. 'Not all of this is true, young sahibs.' A tall, pale, elderly Indian leans on a rolled umbrella. Stitched to his black Nehru jacket is an identity label that announces, 'Guide'. He peers at us through thick lenses set in a heavy frame. 'I am Jacob Dutt, historian. I have studied this matter.'

Fred gives me a nudge. 'Watch out. He'll want paying.'

'No, sahib. I do not ask for fee. If my learning is enjoyed, you may donate whatever you wish. You have questions — I can help.'

'You mean the story of the Black Hole is a lie? Back home, it's infamous'. I should have been silent, for my question amounts to an intention to hire.

'Not a lie, sahib. Merely overblown. I am expert on the tragedy. Calcutta has seen much sorrow.' He stands tall and declaims like a Shakespearean actor:

Thus the midday halt of Charnock – more's the pity!
Grew a City.
As the fungus sprouts chaotic from its bed,
So it spread –
Chance-directed, chance-erected, laid and built
On the silt –
Palace, byre, hovel – poverty and pride –
Side by side;
And, above the packed and pestilential town,
Death looked down.'

He inclines his head. 'So wrote Rudyard Kipling, England's witness of India.'

I'm interested. 'Who is Charnock?' Fred gives me another nudge.

'In the city he founded, buried is Job Charnock of London. But not by side of his beloved Maria, his beautiful

Hindu wife. Maria is name he gives after he rescues her from suttee.'

Fred becomes interested. 'Suttee? You mean widow burning?'

'Yes, sahib. Charnock is Company agent in Patna. While travelling through Bihar, he sees a widow, a fifteen-year-old Rajput princess, led out to be burned alive on her husband's funeral pyre. He's smitten by her beauty. At great personal risk, he rescues her. He carries her off, names her Maria, and makes her his wife. She bears him four children. All three of her daughters marry rich Englishmen. Job Charnock and his favourite daughter, Mary, sleep side by side in St John's churchyard, not far away. I can take you there.'

Fred whistles through his teeth. 'Phew! The Rajput princess had a close shave. Why is she not buried alongside her husband?'

'After twenty-five years as Charnock's wife, she was not cremated as Hindu, but buried like Christian, at Barrackpore. He built house there, to be near grave. It is said that each year he would sacrifice a cockerel over her grave. Not a Christian practice, you will agree.'

I glance at my wristwatch; we plan to meet shipmates for a beer in Scheherazade's. The guide notices, and his lilting voice presses on:

'Please to give just few more minutes, sirs. There is more to tell about Black Hole. Nawab tells British to stop building Fort William. They ignore him, so he captures fort. Dungeon of eighteen feet by fourteen was intended for just six men. Only two windows. The Nawab's captives are packed so tightly that strong men must force door shut. The prisoners are mocked. Zephaniah Holwell, tax collector of East India Company, survives. He reports it as night of horrors. The number of 146 people, Holwell claims to be imprisoned in the dungeon, we have only from his account.'

I flinch when my hand is touched by something moist, but it is only a feral Pye dog. She backs away with a droop to her tail. She has mange around her face and the empty udders look sore. I unwrap the packet of milk biscuits I've just bought at a street kiosk. 'I've nowt to give you except these.' She wolfs them down, then fixes her gaze on mine. She wags her tail, but ambles away when two street urchins approach.

'Backsheesh, backsheesh,' they chant. 'Dus paise, dus paise. No mamma, no papa.'

The guide taps the ground three times with the end of his brolly and speaks in a firm torrent. The boys trot off through a shaft of sun that blazes into the alleyway, but the dog creeps back to curl up in a patch of shade.

I glance at Fred. 'That was a mouthful of Hindi. What did he say?'

'Too fast for me. The only bit I caught was *chella jow,* which means clear off, scram, go away.'

The guide gets our attention with a polite cough. 'Not Hindi, sahibs. I address them in Bengali, different to Hindi, although both have Sanskrit as their mother.'

'And now back to the Black Hole.' I prompt.

'You are gracious, sahib. Where was I? Ah! It is peak of hot season. Captives grow delirious and start to die. Plead for water. One guard, less cruel than his fellows, brings water to bars of window. He pours it into hats of nearest men, who pull it back between bars and pass it to others behind, but in frantic struggle to drink, much is spilt. Discipline lost, they climb over dying peoples to reach window. Weakest get trampled or squashed to death. They rave, pray, blaspheme, and collapse to floor in exhaustion, where suffocation brings mercy.

'Britain is outraged. Nation demands vengeance. But, according to calculations by our worthy Professor Gupta, considering dimensions of cell, impossible to pack 146 people into that space. He estimates the total of prisoners shut in Black Hole is probably sixty-four, of which twenty-one come out alive. He claims that Nawab, Siraj-ud-Daulah, does not order prisoners to be shut in Black Hole and knows nothing about it until next day. He is asleep at the time and his officers afraid to wake him — he can be quick to anger. The fools do not know that future of India rests on their decision.' He leans with dignity on his umbrella and pauses for effect now he has our attention. A young woman with a child on her hip sidles closer.

'When Siraj-ud-Daulah awake, he orders door open. The few left alive stagger out, raving, into fresh air. The dead are flung into ditch. Vengeance comes in six months when Robert Clive sets forth from East India Company factory at Madras. He lands at Calcutta and lays siege to Fort William. British warships, anchored in river, bombard with cannon. British take fort in January 1757. After a while, Nawab's army, supported by small French contingent, approach in massed thousands, complete with cannon and war elephants. They intend to drive British into River Hooghly. This will be famous Battle of Plessey. On that day, heavens open and it rains dogs and cats. The British cover their gunpowder, but the foolish Bengalis do not. From his hiding place in mango grove, with tiny army of 900 European soldiers and 1500 Company-trained sepoys, Clive advances and puts to flight Siraj's army of 50,000 — except for one third of Nawab's army, who stand still and watch. Clive has bribed their general with promise of throne when Nawab defeated. At his leisure, Clive attacks Nawab's French allies in their forts on the Hooghly, and drives the blighters out of Bengal for good.'

Fred interrupts. 'What happened to the creepy Nawab?'

'Siraj flees north, to Murshidabad, where he is killed by his own people and dumped in river. After Plessey, your East India Company went from being humble trader to become ruler of Bengal. This dreadful Black Hole affair gives Britain cause to impose rule on all subcontinent, and Burma too, for-goodness'-sake. They do it bit by bit, over one hundred years, by divide and rule, just like Clive did at Plessey. Sikh against Rajput, Mahratta against Moghul, Gurkha against anyone and everyone. Then British make peace and invite everyone to join their army, just like Romans did in Gaul and Galicia, and everywhere else they set foot. To conquer a world, a king must first know his classics.'

We agree that Jacob Dutt is a talented guide. So as not to cause offence to the dear old chap, we offer him far too much. He accepts the three rupees with an inclined head and his palms together. The woman with the infant holds out her palm in hope. But we've had enough by now, for beggars seem without limit. The sun is high. Fred is sweating copiously. We hurry away to Sheherazade's, to relax beneath palms and quaff cold beer bought with what's left of our damp rupee notes.

19

Homeward Bound

21st May 1959, Calcutta.

We are going home. Seven long blasts on the whistle as we are disgorged from the locks of Kidderpore dock announce to any interested party that *Mawana* leaves Calcutta, bound deep sea. We have bales of jute and gunnies for the mills of Dundee, and chests of best Darjeeling for London tea blenders, and we are going home. Not directly; we must pick up extra cargo en route. The tween decks hold most of the tea. One hold is empty, ready to be part-filled at Visakhapatnam with manganese ore for the stainless steel industry. We'll load more quality tea in Ceylon, at Trincomalee and Colombo, thousands of chests of 'first flush' crop Orange Pekoe. At Trinco, barrels of coconut oil for the cosmetics industry will be braced with dunnage timber to keep them safe in wild weather. Last stop is Port Sudan on the Red Sea, where we'll fill remaining space with bales of cotton. A month from now, we should be tied up and paid off in London.

As usual, the Hooghly river teems with craft: ferries, barges, sampans, rafts of fodder that resemble floating haystacks, and a clutch of steamers anchored mid-channel in the southward flow of fertile silt, raw sewage, industrial effluent, and corpses. Not so fair is this arm of goddess Ganga, the Holy Mother Ganges.

I rattle the heavy Post Office-pattern telegraph key. I've not touched it for three weeks and my wrist feels stiff. The key's long brass arm needs a polish and, while I'm about it, I might as well burnish the contacts. Meanwhile, with transmitters switched off, I tap out Morse for the phrase 'best bent wire'. The rhythmic stream of characters makes a chirpy ditty:

Dah dit dit dit, dit, dit dit dit, dah,
Dah dit dit dit, dit, dah dit, dah,
Dit dah dah, dit dit, dit dah dit, dit.

My boss stamps into the wireless room. 'What are you up to now?'

'Not much, Don. Just giving the key a rattle. My fingers are stiff from three weeks in dock. Shall I send a TR to VWC?'

'Yes, and make sure to catch his forecast for the Bay, it's peak cyclone season. I'll wait while you do it, then I'm off to the radar hut to check those grid currents again. Don't want to lose any more EF50s.' He lifts out the radar log from its secure rack. It records faults and how they were fixed, plus our measurements of valve currents. Waxed carbon paper makes duplicates to be pored over by head office. We get through a mass of foolscap carbons.

I slide the starting arm of the inductor alternator and watch the voltmeter needle climb as the machine gathers speed. Our engine room sends 110 volts DC around the ship, hence we must convert the direct current to alternating current (AC) to feed equipment power supplies. Machines with rotating armatures such as inductor alternators and rotary transformers are a simple way to generate the voltages our gear demands.

I enjoy a subdued chorus each time I work the key. It's the song of magneto-striction, of laminated iron plates wound with copper — changing shape under load. They sob and hum through shrouds of waxed insulation. The whine of the rotary transformer rises and falls, valves flicker, and the receiver mutes as I key out 120 watts into the main aerial strung between funnel and mast. It all brings comfort and meaning to lonely watches.

On the international calling frequency of 500 kc/s I send: VWC VWC VWC DE GWWZ GWWZ GWWZ TR K (Calcutta radio from *Mawana*, movement report, over).

After a few repeats, he takes notice and responds with: GWWZ DE VWC UP 434. (*Mawana* from Calcutta Radio, move to 434 kilocycles working frequency).

We meet on 434 and I key: VWC de GWWZ *MAWANA* DEPT CALCUTTA 0950 BND VISAKH ETA 1500 23RD. WX BAY BENGAL? (I've been cheeky enough to ask for a weather report instead of waiting for his scheduled broadcast due in ninety minutes.)

He comes back: GWWZ DEEP LOW ANDAMAN SEA VA.

I reply: R TU VA (Understood. Thank you. End of transmission.)

I'd unplugged my headphones so my boss could hear the traffic. He yields up a grunt. 'That could be a bugger. We need the proper forecast at 11.30.'

At 1140, I open the chartroom hatch and hand over the weather report from VWC: *Depression over Andaman Sea and Nicobars moving north-west. Winds anticyclonic 40 knots. Central Bay of Bengal winds N to NE 20 knots, occasional precipitation, visibility 1 mile, heavy swell. Northern Bay of Bengal and coastal waters Sandheads to Madras precipitation nil, visibility 10 miles, moderate swell.*

The apprentice hands it to the mate. His response carries through from the wheelhouse. 'Shifting our way, is it? Not to worry. Those things feed off warm water, so it could yet wander west. So let's not get our Nicobars in a twist.'

An hour before midnight, *Mawana* lays out anchors half-way down her 120 mile journey to salt water. We now wait for the tide to rise and give clearance across sandbars.

With a full moon high in the eastern sky, the river Hooghly gleams. My parents taught me to see the face of *The Man in the Moon*. But in India, people search for a likeness of the hare of their folklore. Above the Ganges, the hare is clear enough tonight. Bright highlands and dark oceans of frozen lava hint at the arched form of the hare with its elongated ears and gangly legs. I wonder if Beryl can see the hare. We've made a pact to gaze at the moon when it is full, wherever we are. My mind sees her image hovering in the moonlight, and I sense her touch.

The flood of cool light flattens the paddy lands, so they seem like fields of chalk. Rice-straw thatches of country folk shimmer with silver. Shadows grow deep beneath stands of mangoes. Flying foxes, fruit bats as stout as rooks, pass overhead in twos and threes, making for orchards on the far shore. A dog barks into moonglow and is answered from far away. In swirls and eddies, shining as it rolls, a log wanders south. Perhaps it has sailed a thousand miles down the Ganges from the Himalaya.

Craft beneath flaccid square sails drift downstream in scattered silhouettes. Like some ghost, a barge emerges not twenty yards from our anchor chains and hull. A turbaned man leans across the beam of his tiller. I rest my elbows on the cool iron bulwark as he glances up and raises a palm. I lift a hand in salute. When he draws on his cigarette, a spot of red glows in his face. It will be a native sort, a *beedi*, flaked rough tobacco packed into a pale green tube formed from a *tendu* leaf and made fast at the narrow end with knotted cotton. I tried one once and gagged.

Smoke drifts up as the barge slips by, and my nose smarts from the acrid fumes of smouldering cow dung. In her stern, beneath an arched shelter, is a glow that outlines a woman crouched among aluminium pots and pans. All is peace, except for the low mews of a child.

The bargeman hawks and spits into the moonlight. His rattling expectoration hardly dents this enchanted night. The barge and its little family glide downstream, into their futures.

I've no inkling of what is to come. Of a time when grizzled old men will look back and name these long days we live through, *The Golden Age of the British Merchant Navy*. Ships like ours, and the two lovely Blue Funnel steamers anchored astern of us, with their Homeric names and classic lines, will limp into the future to die before their time — doomed to become loss-makers in the face of sparsely crewed giants that bear thousands of cargo containers. Those massive and functional 'box boats', designed without thought of beauty, their crews drawn from any third-world country willing to sign-on for a wage, will make an end of us. Cargo will cross oceans in hulls ten and twenty times our size. They will carry flags of tiny island nations that offer low regulation and light taxation. The port names of Liverpool, Cardiff, Sunderland, and such, will become rare on the sterns of ships. The Marshall Islands, a scatter of tiny Pacific atolls with a population equal to a small English market town, will have more ships under her flag than fly the British red duster.

Vessels like ours will no longer grope their way upstream to Calcutta. Closer to the sea, a deep-draught terminal will grow. Apart from an oil barge or two, Kidderpore Dock falls idle. Bistros and coffee shops line Bristol's ancient harbour, where tourists can admire expensive yachts and floating 'gin palaces'. Across empty water, white wine drinkers shall admire Brunel's *Great Britain* of 1843, and a replica of Cabot's *Matthew* of 1497. Around the world, ancient river ports give way to deep-water harbours where giant, computer-controlled cranes hoist huge containers from the decks of mammoth ships.

I have no sense of our future, of when satellites track across Heaven, when Morse is a footnote to history. No more a cheery glow of thermionic valves in wireless gear, all will be silicon chips that do not speak if they are alive or dead.

Next day, we drop our pilot at Sandheads anchorage in the muddy waters where the Ganges meets salt water. The skirts of the cyclone are upon us, so our gentleman is eager to jump into the cutter and make for the swaying pilot vessel which prepares to weigh anchor and head upriver to shelter.

Circulating storms breed in the Bay of Bengal and this latest has long legs. The Indian meteorological office is uncertain where this fast-moving cyclone will track. It could head for the delta or turn west for Madras and places south.

Either way, the bridge must lay a course for Visakhapatnam, just a day's steaming along the coasts of Orissa and Andhra Pradesh.

The *serangs* (bosuns) and their *kalassis* (deckhands) are making all secure, and rigging safety lines along the deck. Not all sixty-five Indians in our crew are up to the mark yet. Some are youngsters on their first trip, anxious and uncertain, but keen to learn. A few catering and engine-room Lascars are in a sluggish state, the whites of their eyes pink from the effects of some hallucinogen. But, give it a couple of days for the hashish to run out and they'll be fine, or so the purser reckons. Until that comes about, we must rely on a backbone of mature and sober Bengali seamen.

And now, the rain arrives, and with it a 25 knot wind, and an eight-foot sea with foaming crests to hammer at our port side. We know it will get worse. But, there's guinea fowl curry for dinner tonight and none will miss that, whatever the weather. The young Indians, straight from the hills and on their first trip, might have a rotten time of it and turn away their tarka dhal and rice until they grow their sea legs. They'll be told to eat it all up, for it's part of their wages.

I've never been seasick. Mother's family, the Horsleys, were seafarers for generations. I'm lucky she handed on their blood. Six years from now I'll discover those seafarers descend from a mysterious Lancelot Horsley. He wed Isabell Darnell in 1573 at Lanchester in County Durham, where they buried a daughter the next year. He'd settled in Hartlepool by 1576, with loins sturdy enough to beget four hundred years of fishermen and sea pilots.

---

23 May.

That was a wild night. I slept for most of it, wedged in my bunk with my left arm gripped around the Dutch wife, that stiff bolster running the length of the bunk. She doesn't say much, but she keeps a fellow from tumbling to the deck in a mad sea. Don was up in the small hours, changing one of his beloved EF50s in the radar. Then he spent half an hour swapping traffic with others in our fleet within shortwave range. After that, he'd just returned to his bunk when the Auto Alarm went off — a Liberian Greek tramp with a list caused by shifted cargo. She's a hundred miles south. An Indian frigate is standing by her while the cyclone moves on.

I join him in the wireless room an hour before breakfast, to sip muddy coffee sweetened with condensed milk. We dare not set down our cups. I wait for the ship to become upright. That last roll was a touch savage. We'd held our breath whilst *Mawana* decided if she would return to upright for a minute or two. 'Let me do the rest of your watch, Don. You've had a rough night.'

'Thanks, but I'll manage till breakfast. Kedgeree today, then I'll have a kip till twelve. Can't miss my usual pre-lunch gin and tonic with the Old Man.'

'Captain Eggleston might prefer to be on the bridge in this weather.'

'He might well, but he won't miss his traditions. He'll be retiring soon. Been through a lot. Seen all this before. At 0400 he told the second mate this bit of a sea is nowt compared to a torpedo.'

The ship gives a sickening corkscrew and plunges at a scary angle. The man on the wheel must be weary. There's a muffled shout from the wheelhouse. It sounded like, 'Jesus!'

The blast roars loud enough to make us raise our voices. 'What was the last weather report, Don?'

'VWC at 0630 has winds of ninety mph for us. Southwest of here it's expected to be a hundred plus. But the centre will likely make landfall below Madras, so we've dodged the worst. We'll have this on the beam for a few hours yet. Oh, and the wet monsoon will arrive at Cochin on the west coast by next week, or so they hope.'

'Did you chat with any of ours on the fleet schedule?'

'*Maidan* just out of Djibouti for Colombo. *Mandasor* due Sandheads in two days — she'll have had a worse night than us. *Malakand,* Aden for the Seychelles, lucky sods.'

'I've heard all sorts about the Seychelles. About how, if you can't make it back to the ship, you can kip on the beach under the stilt deck of Sharky Clark's bar. The only problem being ... during the night, the land crabs chew your ears.'

There's another sickening motion and green water hits the porthole. Don's knuckles are white as he grips the receiver bench. The doors to the motor cupboard spring open and the whine of the rotary transformer changes note as we roll. I slide to the deck and wedge myself into a corner, feet against an upright.

As the deck swoops upward, my chief yells: 'You don't want to be going anywhere near the bloody Seychelles. Not when you're about to be wed.'

20

Visakhapatnam

Friday, 22nd May 1959.
 The heart of the cyclone missed us. She plunged ashore at Madras and now roars inland to thrash out her fury somewhere among the ridges of the Eastern Ghats, but we still get a wild ride on her coattails. Reverberations pulse through the deck each time the bows plunge into a wall of water. As I key out signals in the faint hope of raising Portishead Radio in Somerset, my chair creaks against its anchor chain. It is screwed into the deck, but I've known chains to break free. Last year, aboard *Mahanada* in a cyclone, my chair escaped and sledged me across the slanting deck to crash into the motor cupboard. The result was a chipped finger bone. That part can still throb.
 It's a five-thousand mile long-shot from the Bay of Bengal. But sometimes GKA, in distant Somerset, will catch our weak signals on 12, 16, or 22mc/s depending on the time of day. The telegram I struggle to send is only an instruction to Interflora to deliver a bunch of red tulips to an engineer's wife — he's not forgotten their wedding anniversary. It's expensive if I can't contact Britain direct and must relay the message through an Indian coast station. Then there's the accounting of extra charges and all the tedium of paperwork. I keep trying.
 To keep down the word count and the cost, the sender can choose code numbers from the Interflora catalogue. The engineer could not decide, so I'd suggested code 7 which would appear on the card with the flowers as: 'Near

or far, I'm with you always'. Being from Bootle, he thought it 'Too bloody toe-curling by half'. Instead, he chose 22, which decodes as, 'I miss you'. It's best to take extra care while keying out these codes. If the wrong figures are sent, or get mangled in transmission, the bouquet might arrive with sad sentiments for a bereavement, or congratulations on the new baby.

Now that the sun sinks in the west, the solar rays decline. High overhead, beginning at eighty miles, the Kennelly-Heaviside and Appleton layers of sun-ionised gas weaken. At the same time, they thicken above the Mediterranean 4,000 miles to the north-west and, for a while, are just right to reflect our radio waves back to Earth instead of shooting through to the stars. There's a thrill when GKA picks me up from a lucky signal bounce off the belt of charged particles. After a couple of repeats, to get through that strange shifting hiss that plagues the frequencies above 16mc/s, the telegram is safe in the hands of those fine operators at Portishead, and I can relax. It is 1830hrs. Night has just crashed down. Even now, I'm astonished at how suddenly the day ends in the tropics. At home, we enjoy a lingering twilight, often grey, but sometimes scarlet and as perfect as watching a schooner dip below the rim of the Earth.

Don arrives to give me dinner relief. 'Have you sent that Interflora?'

'Ten minutes ago, Chief, after a bit of a struggle. Difficult to read Portishead through a hiss that sounds like a frying-pan. Funny how that hiss is at 16 megs and above, whereas 12 megs is pretty quiet.'

'You've been in conflict with Jupiter.'

'Jupiter? Do I know him?'

'It's in December's *Wireless World*. Got the magazine in Kidderpore, off the *Matra*. Scientists reckon all that hiss is radiation from the planet Jupiter. You'd better get away to your dinner. Country Captain tonight — that Goanese cook's a bit too keen on the garlic for my liking. Mouth will be akin to a gorilla's armpit all night, by Jove!'

Paddy, the fourth engineer, is chasing a piece of chicken around his plate. He mutters about it being a lump of Bengali fighting cock that died in the ring last week. 'So, wha' di ye ken, Harry? This bit of a blow dying down, is it?'

I break off from some hard chewing. It's a scraggy bit of old game cock, all right. 'Gone ashore at Madras.'

'It's ashore? That'll put a draught up their dhotis. What else's afoot in the world?'

'A bit of excitement. Jodrell Bank is bouncing signals off the Moon, and Mickey Rooney's getting married for the fifth time. And on Sunday, we've no more Empire Day — it's now to be called Commonwealth Day.'

'Is that a fact? In days to come, how will we recall Queen Victoria's birthday? For that is what the day signifies. And what'll the bairnies sing? We used tae chant, *The twenty-fourth of May is Empire Day, if we don't get a holiday, we'll all gang away.*'

The swell bashes against the high shore. It throws itself across the mole of scuttled ships, decks levelled like aircraft carriers, that guard the way into Visakhapatnam. In the slot beneath steep cliffs, an ancient geological fault, there's an awkward turn to starboard before we creep into the only natural harbour on this coast. An antique, chain driven ferry waits for us to pass. The platform holds a patient audience of thin labourers, plump babus with brollies and pith helmets, an oxcart, some goats, and an elephant. The little port opens to reveal a couple of battered cranes that guard piles of manganese and chromium ore. A steam engine huffs and puffs waggons about the wharves. Figures in ochre-stained clothes stoop under loaded baskets. Visakh is a sleepy place, almost quaint. (But she will become an industrial giant.)

Madras State has banned alcoholic liquor, except for medical need (Mahatma Gandhi declared it to be an invention of the Devil). Three of us off duty take rickshaws to a comfortable bungalow on a point above the harbour. Here we sign the Confirmed Alcoholics Register. We now relax in the sea breeze, high above the harbour, and call for bottles of whatever is on sale. The Indian version of rum is rough, but half-decent when soused with Coke. A comely woman, no longer a girl, hair in a bun, dark eyes lined with kohl, full lipsticked lips, joins our table.

'You boys won't mind me joining you? I'm down from Bombay on holiday, seeing something of my country. I am a professional lady, but am taking a break.' She flutters her eyelids. 'Unless, of course, you might be tempted.'

A good-natured half-hour passes. While chatting in a jovial manner, she's inclined to lay a cool palm on the nearest bare knee. We speak pleasantly about this and that until she floats away in her gorgeous gold and green sari like an ornate galley. After doing a circuit of the bar, she settles at a table of newly arrived Danes. Let's hope they are as gentlemanly as we Britishers.

Time to stroll back, down a street of pavement stalls where we think to bring presents back from the sea. Business is slow today — eyes light up as we show interest in cobra-skin purses, coffee tables in carved Kashmiri walnut inlaid with camel bone (they insist it's ivory), and brass Buddhas. For Beryl, I buy a bracelet of curled leaves fashioned from pierced Indian silver. For Mam, I buy a moirah, a cylindrical cane stool with a nipped-in waist and padded leather seat embossed with the Taj Mahal. Fred bargains for a group of sculpted and painted clay figures, four inches tall: a soldier in a fez, a bearer with his bundle, a haughty Brahmin, and a naked fakir. I bought similar in Calcutta market for fifty pais each. Fred beats him down to a better price. They are skilfully modelled around a wire skeleton. One wonders what the artist earned.

The port side of the ship is now clad in bamboo scaffold and staging. Girls and mature women, in what might have been saris — skirts hitched around bare thighs, move forward in graceful lines with baskets of ore on their heads. The baskets ascend to our deck by stages, hoisted by female muscle. As baskets are tipped into the cavern, there comes the smell of old eggs as dark columns of manganese dust rise from the booming hold. The tippers have noses and mouths masked in cloth. We look for the men. They are in pairs by the manganese heaps. One shovels the black ore while his partner lifts a loaded basket onto the head-pad of the next woman in the queue. In a modern port, there would be cranes with grab buckets or a conveyor belt. Visakh's cranes stand rusted and forlorn. Press them into service, and families of labourers will go hungry.

At the end of their shift, they open their dusty garments to wash demurely at the dockside fire hydrant. The younger women keep an eye on the ship. If an idler on our deck is watching, they might call out, 'Lifebuoy?' The famous soap is a currency here. Throw a bar of unwrapped Lifebuoy, and a brief flash of glistening body is the reward. At first sight, it seems debasing, but there is chatter and giggles. I wonder how many generations the little pantomime has seen. I wonder if Kipling tossed a bar of Lifebuoy to the grandmothers of these sinewy maids, and was the Empress amused? Who knows?

25th. May

From my signals, Visakhapatnam radio knows we have left harbour and are bound for Trincomalee on the island of Ceylon — we'll arrive in two days. I've handed the bridge the weather report for this region of the Bay of Bengal. There's little else to do. The late evening watch promises peace.

I can now dip into a study book. I'm adept at reading while wearing headphones. On the 500kc/s listening and distress frequency, the Morse speaks into my ear, into my brain, and is understood like a mother tongue. If something important is said, it has my attention in an instant. Beneath rasping blasts from a nearby Russian, there comes a weak twittering from *MRSQ* — that is *Maskeliya*, one of our fleet. She is in the Arabian Sea, on the far side of Ceylon, trying to contact Colombo. I put down the book to make an entry in the log, which must be done every ten minutes of the watch to show we are monitoring the distress frequency.

My boss pays his usual call before turning in. He picks up the book. 'Spooner's *Mathematics for Telecommunications*, eh? Clever chappie, that. I have his first edition on the shelf at home.' He flicks through. 'Differentiation, integration, quadratic equations! It brings back memories. I suppose we had to learn this stuff, but I've never had cause to put it to use. Nor will you, I suspect.'

I nod. 'True. Though it's good to know the science behind the gear, if it's not to be a total black art. If we go ashore into circuit design or valve research, we'd not get a job without it.'

'True, Old Son. We are much more than the idle, eccentric, and crazed key-tappers the deck and engine-room reckon us to be. They don't know how clued-up we are. Waveguide propagation, Isaac Newton's calculus of infinitesimals, and the rest. Anyway, good for you for sticking with it. You've an exam coming up. That right?'

'Three days' time. Twenty-eighth of May. We should be on the millpond of Trinco harbour by then. Meanwhile, I keep wading through the equations the BNRS post out.'

'Ah yes, City and Guilds of London, isn't it? The Old Man has the sealed exam papers locked up in his safe. Bet you wished you could take a shufty at them.'

'The founder of The British National Radio School, at his home in leafy Croydon, did well to persuade the C&G people to allow exams at sea. They trust us. If we let him down, the correspondence course will be blown out of the water.'

He shoots a question: 'What's the square root of minus one?'

I straighten in the chair. 'The operator j. It rotates a vector by ninety degrees.'

'In which direction?'

'Anticlockwise.'

'What's the output impedance of a cathode follower?'

'One divided by gm.'

'And what is gm?'

'Gm is the mutual conductance of a triode, which is that change in anode current caused by a given change in grid voltage. It's a ratio that indicates gain.'

'Spot on! I'm off to my pit now. See you tomorrow.' He strides out.

At wireless college, I drilled myself to remember exam-passing formulae and phrases. I can parrot the lines at will, which does not necessarily mean I actually comprehend them.

28th May,

Alongside the simple jetty in the vast tropical pool of Trincomalee. It is the world's second largest natural harbour and, according to William Pitt the Younger, *the most valuable colonial possession on the globe,*

Captain Eggleston has instructed I take the exam in his dayroom.

'Will that surface do you, Sparky? Use the blotter as needs be.'

'Yes, sir. Plenty of space.' A broad oblong of sumptuous green leather stretches across gleaming mahogany. I count the captain's ink blots; there are three in a line. I must take care not to add more. He watches as I rest my bottle of blue ink safely in his capacious, porcelain ash tray — donated by Haig's whisky — fill my fountain pen and glance at the clock on the bulkhead. I lay out a well-thumbed book of logarithm tables and my cherished Faber-Castell slide rule. Ten minutes to go. The steam winches on the foredeck rattle and squeal as they swing in derricks hung with slings of tea chests. There are shouts and yells as the cargo nets rise from the backs of lorries, then muffled clatters and bangs as the chests are stowed in our holds.

'You start on the hour, lad.' With a silver paper knife, he slices open the package and places it on the end of the desk. He's gruff, but kindly in tone. 'There you are. I'll leave you to open it when the time comes. The exam lasts two hours. Good luck.' He plods out, short and stout. Short-sleeved, white tropical shirt heavy with epaulettes of four gold bands. Big buttocks in starched white shorts to the knee. Long white stockings to support the aching knots of varicose veins brought on by forty-five years of legs holding balance on pitching decks.

The minutes tick by as I gaze around the luxury of the Old Man's day room. Spacious, furnished in uncut moquette upholstery, thick fawn carpet, drinks cabinet, easy chairs and curtained windows. I calculate he was born the last years of Queen Victoria. A few years younger than my dad, who died last year, worn out by shipyards and the Somme. The skipper will have started out as a keen cadet on a coal burner in the First War. As master, he took ships through falling bombs, mined harbours, and torpedoes in the tragic convoys of the Second War. Good luck to him.

The clatter of cargo work goes on. Ah, well — time to start. Ten questions, answer any eight, two compulsory. Stomach tense. Calm down. Breathe. Focus. Read the questions through, then read them once more, and decide — like they've taught you. Impedance of tuned circuits, harmonics, and optimal values for inter-stage coupling capacitors, are the themes this year. There's plenty of paper in the envelope — I'll use most of it. I'm soon lost in log tables, nudging the slide rule along its slot to double check the results. I leave the short essay on oscillators until last, and end up writing waffle. Cargo work has paused. It's the crew and docker's time for 'Smoko' (a cup of tea and a 'gasper').

The pen still scratches when the captain ambles in, a couple of minutes beyond the two hours.

'Still at it? Time's up, Sparky. Shame about the din outside. Have you done?'

My mind unhooks from the drying ink. I cap the fountain pen and slip the slide rule into its green case. Time to flex the cramp from my fingers: 'Thanks, sir. Too engrossed to be bothered by the racket. Apart from the last question, I reckon it went well enough.'

'And if it did, what manner of qualification will you get?'

'All being well, I'll have the Intermediate Certificate in Telecommunications Engineering.'

'Oh aye? You'll not be going grey in the wireless room, then. I hear they're crying out for technical folk ashore these days.'

21

Mrs Ferguson's Tea Set

31st May 1959. Alongside in Trincomalee, Ceylon.

Although *Mawana* is the only ship in port, shouts echo from the jungled slopes that pile around this placid blue pool. Slings of crated tea are hoisted from the backs of lorries, winches rumble and derricks creak. Each chest of tea is stencilled with the name of a merchant. Today, Lipton of London is the destination. I'm going ashore to escape the racket.

Trincomalee town squats on the far side of the broad, natural harbour, too far to walk in this fierce sun — it is 85F in the shade. I amble along the jetty towards the shimmering jungle and the shade of palm and mango trees. Tropical forest drapes the hillsides, except where gradients have been bulldozed into terraces punctuated by abandoned storage tanks. Silent army huts, with never a face at a window, are being smothered in creepers. Now the boots of the military have gone, how soon vegetable riot returns in this climate to bury Major Nissen's corrugated half-cylinders. The wild creatures have returned. At night we hear a leopard cough on the hill, and last year I watched an elephant swim across the harbour with her calf close alongside. Hammerhead sharks come here to have their young — droves of their black shapes snake through the brilliant water.

This was a major base for the Royal Navy until Ceylon's leader, Solomon Bandaranaike, demanded the British leave. Our ships gave up the base two years ago, and already camouflage paint peels off guardhouse walls. (Four months from now, Bandaranaike will be assassinated by a monk because of his failure to make good on a promise.)

These parts are famed for spiders and scorpions, so I take care to check for webs and poisonous jaws before I perch on a block of concrete. All is clean this afternoon; the heat has driven all nasties into hiding. A courting tumble of six little butterflies drift by, bronze wings splashed with white. I don't recognise them, but I'll learn they are *Elymnias singhala*, known hereabouts as the palm fly. They are a *Nymphalid*, the same butterfly family as our own red admiral.

Here is shade and space to relax — to stare across the peace of this fabulous harbour. Perhaps the Persians did the same, for they called this island *Serendip*, from which we have *serendipity*, 'a fortunate discovery'. Trinco has seen British iron warships, Portuguese caravels, Arab trading dhows, and Chinese junks. When the Dutch took over from Portugal, they fixed the name *Zeylan* to the ancient island of Lanka. The Dutch hung on for 150 years until their trading posts became forfeit to the British after the Low Countries' enforced alliance with Bonaparte. Then the oaken walls of old England found Trincomalee to be a handy harbour from which to guard the route to India. Ceylon became Britain's 'Jewel in the Crown of Empire'.

The sun tracks across the sky and, after an hour of my idleness, burns into the shade to make the sparse grasses and even the dust appear to pant. I wander deeper into the cool stands of mango, shoes crunching through the litter of leathery dead leaves that blanket the crazed surface of a narrow military track. The trees must be a hundred feet tall, fifty feet of straight trunk and fifty of crown. Within shafts of sunlight that pierce the canopy, tiny flies cavort in mating columns. A few fat hoverflies keep station, and watch. They swing from side to side like sleepy pendulums. Choosing their moment, they take turns to dive into the plume of dancers and grab a meal. From somewhere above comes rustling and chattering. Twigs clatter to the ground. A troop of monkeys swing overhead. Their little faces keep track of my progress. A mango thuds to earth in front of me and explodes in a mass of yellow pulp. And another. They resent amblers under their trees.

The shafts of light fade. Then comes a clap of thunder and a spatter of huge raindrops. I've stayed too long. Every afternoon brings a downpour — about five o'clock. Back to the ship! I run the few hundred yards through the torrent in time to change out of wet clothes and have a gin and tonic before dinner.

Afterwards, as dusk falls, I stroll to the same concrete block. Alf, the ship's carpenter, poet, and folk singer, joins me. After the daily deluge, the shore becomes a stage as life emerges refreshed. The atmosphere teems with insect lights as bright as stars. Luminous points weave and thread through the palms and, for an hour, the shore seems alive with fairies. Anonymous moths, the size of bats, flap by on brown wings. They stir my entomological instincts and the urge to collect almost takes hold. Pinned and drying on a setting board in my cabin is a banded hawkmoth similar to the European bedstraw hawk. Next in row is a slender green cricket, then an ugly Hooghly water beetle. I've a few other insects that fell about our deck lights. Since my shipmates discovered my interest, it amuses them to leave creepy crawlies in my cabin. Even the captain gathers them up from around the bridge and has them sent down, scrabbling around in a beer glass. 'Here's another disgusting jasper for Sparky,' he says. 'Stick it on his desk. He likes bugs. The uglier the better.'

Alf rubs his khaki-clad shoulders against the trunk of a palm.

I look up. 'Chips, you be careful with that itch. Don't go shaking the palms. There might be coconuts up there. This is no time to demonstrate Newton's Law.'

He constructs a roll-up and thumbs the wheel of his Zippo. The tip glows in the dark like one more firefly. He exhales a plume. 'What a place, Harry, eh? Clean and sweet, apart from the odd mozzie. Better than the grot of Calcutta. Never have there been such days. You know, Arthur C. Clarke, science fiction writer, snorkelled here. He found a submerged temple, and a crowd of Hindu statues scattered about. Stone gods, all drowned. Been underwater a long while. I'm partial to a bit of science fiction, takes you out of the daily grind.'

'You enjoy a story, Alf.'

'I do that. Mind you, the best stories are often the true ones. Have you heard the tale of Violet Ferguson's tea set? It took place a few hundred miles east of here. Other side of the Bay of Bengal, a day's steaming from the north tip of Sumatra.'

'Go on, then.'

'You'll know of the *Atlantis*, the German raider?'

'I do. A converted merchant ship, armed to the teeth. She crept about disguised as a neutral, attacking our cargo ships wherever she found them. Caused havoc until a British cruiser tracked her down.'

'True. She chalked up about twenty captures. Well, on Armistice Day 1940 the *Atlantis,* this time masquerading as a Japanese cargo ship — they weren't in the war yet, but were thinking about it — accosts Alfie Holt's Blue Funnel cargo steamer *Automedon* in the Bay of Bengal. I recall Automedon was Achilles' charioteer in Homer's Iliad, but that's beside the point. Anyway, *Atlantis* runs up the German ensign and uncovers her guns. *Automedon's* sparky is in the middle of keying out the distress signal *RRR* that says, UNDER ATTACK BY A RAIDER', when the bridge and just about everybody on it gets blown to bits by four salvos from the raider's guns. It was their way of putting an end to a message that gave away her position.'

'Bastards,' I mutter. Alf pauses while I fill my pipe and get it going.

'*Atlantis* sends across a boarding party to take over her prize. They check out the cargo to see if *Automedon* is worth sending back to the Fatherland with a prize crew. There's machine parts, aircraft in sections, whisky, cigarettes, frozen meat — all handy stuff. But she's in such a mess they decide to scuttle her after helping themselves to supplies. The Krauts organise the survivors into boats ready to be taken prisoner aboard the raider. The one lady passenger, name of Mrs Violet Ferguson — she's on her way to Singapore with her husband — protests that she doesn't want to abandon ship without her tea service.'

I couldn't help butting in. 'Bodies everywhere and she fusses about her bleeding pots!'

'Yes, but the tea set has great sentimental value, you see. That's what she tells the officer in charge of the boarding party. He's a considerate sort of German, so he enquires as to the whereabouts of said tea service. "It's kept in the strongroom for safe keeping," says Mrs Ferguson.

'Our polite German officer narrows his eyes. "Ah! So you have zee secret strongroom? Ver interesting! We will take zee look."

'The Blue Funnel officers who held the keys have been blown to Kingdom Come, so our bold Huns have to smash the door down. They find the tea set and carry it off. They also discover, and bear away, a heap of sealed bags of government mail — papers destined for Singapore, addressed to the British Commander in the Far East. Code books, Naval intelligence reports, details of the strength of Allied forces in the region, etcetera. A treasure trove of secrets, all weighted and ready to be thrown over the side in the event of capture, but the officers charged with that duty are now giving up the ghost on the wrecked bridge.'

I give a grunt. 'What a cock up!'

'The *Atlantis* sends the bags to Japan aboard another captured vessel. From there, they are shipped across the Sea of Japan to Vladivostok in the USSR — at this time, Stalin is still Adolf's dancing partner. From the Siberian coast, the mailbags now trundle to Berlin under guard on the Trans-Siberian Railway. High up in his mountain retreat, in his Berghof, the Great Dictator leaves off patting the heads of little blond children and posing for the camera, and takes to jumping up and down with glee. Iron Crosses and Oak Leaves for everyone concerned. He gives copies of the contents to the Japanese embassy. At first, the Nip intelligence people suspect the papers are a British hoax. But not for long! What they find in those papers gives them the confidence to switch on their plans for war in the Pacific.'

My pipe's gone out. 'Don't tell me Mrs Ferguson's dainty tea set brings about the attack on Pearl Harbour, the fall of Singapore, and all that banzai business?'

'You could say that. Although others reckon what was in the mailbags was so out of date by the time it reached Hitler, and is passed to Tojo, it made no difference at all. Maybe it just brought things forward a few months. Anyway, it makes for a bit of a story.'

'I wonder what became of Violet Ferguson and her tea service?'

'*Atlantis* transfers the gentle lady, along with other survivors from *Automedon*, to a captured Norwegian tanker. Incognito, it sneaks through to occupied France, where Mrs Ferguson and the crew are transported across the Rhine to POW camps, along with the tea set. The Germans repatriate her and her hubby to England some time later, but alas, without the china she'd used when entertaining in the camp. When British soldiers overrun Hamburg, they break into a warehouse. Inside, they discover Violet's belongings in a crate, including the tea service, all in one piece, properly itemised and accounted for in the German manner. We even have a happy ending. Violet Ferguson is eventually reunited with her crockery. She no doubt sips from it, at this very moment, over a breakfast of Melba toast and soft-boiled eggs, behind chintz curtains, up some leafy avenue in Tonbridge Wells.'

My pipe's gone out again. 'What a tail our cat's got!'

'Kapitan Rogge, master of the *Atlantis,* treated his prisoners with a rare humanity. He went on to command the cruiser *Prinz Eugen*. Today, the kapitan is an admiral in the West German navy.

'The *Prinz Eugen*! Now *I* can tell *you* a story. I've seen her dress ensign. Huge flag. Blood red, with a swastika in the centre. Makes your skin crawl.'

'Get away! Where was that?'

'It's in the home of my sweetheart — the girl I shall wed in July. It's part of her dad's spoils of war. He enjoys showing it to visitors.'

'A bit of the *Eugen* in British West Hartlepool! Whatever next in Monkey Town?'

'Beryl's dad was an engineer lieutenant in the RNVR. He was assigned to the German base of Wilhelmshaven after the surrender. *Prinz Eugen* was decommissioned there and Frank Scott came home with her huge ensign, amongst other stuff he packed into his sea trunk.'

'Other stuff?'

'Other things from the *Kriegsmarine* depot. Such as more Nazi flags. Beryl's great-aunt Polly, a maiden lady — there were not enough men to go round after the Great War — seamstress, and teacher of tailoring, cut them up and made them into red blouses for the girls. He also brought home a box of fine German tools, and a bolt of curtain material. And a mysterious onyx vase that he found in an abandoned brief case in a bombed-out school.'

'A mysterious onyx vase. There could be another story there.' Alf is rolling a cigarette from his pouch of Anton Justman's long shag. I pause while he licks along the gum line, and lights up.

'They still have the vase. It makes a handy door stop. But there's more: into his sea chest he packed a sewing box for Beryl, and a clock off a U-boat.'

Alf gives a low whistle.

'He was involved in the scuttling of the U-boat fleet surrendered at Wilhelmshaven. A naval timepiece stared at him from the bulkhead of a U-boat's control room. He rescued it before it sank to the bottom of the North Sea. The case has a bad dent, but the clock keeps good time. His unit searched a German Admiralty warehouse and discovered crates of silver beakers and trays, all ready to be awarded to the officers of U-boats. Each submarine officer was presented with a silver beaker for each successful voyage against Allied shipping. On return from the seventh voyage, they were awarded a silver tray on which to stand their haul of six beakers. Frank Scott's commander made a quick decision. "Whatever is good for Hitler's squad is good enough for my chaps. Distribute that silver among the officers." And now, in Beryl's mam's china cabinet, in British West Hartlepool, there gleams a silver tray that holds a set of silver beakers.'

Alf claps his huge hands. 'I admire the fellow's sense of occasion.'

'He had a haunch of venison in his kitbag; sneaked it past British Customs when they weren't looking. On the front room wall is a watercolour by Baer, of fishing boats drawn up on the shore at Dangast. Baer was an official war artist for the German military. Beryl's dad was in charge of transport. The artist begged Lieutenant Scott to allow him enough fuel to motor to Dangast, on the Friesland coast, to visit his mother, who was ill. When the artist returned, in thanks for kindness shown, he presented Beryl's dad with a picture he'd painted while he was away. It has the place of honour above the fireplace in their council house.'

22

Monsoon Seas

Monday, 3rd June 1959. Arabian Sea.

After loading tea at Trincomalee, we spent two days in Colombo on the western side of the island, where yet more chests of tea were crammed into the holds. We still carry space enough to take 300 tons of baled cotton in Port Sudan, whereupon the ship will be down to her Samuel Plimsoll marks. It makes for another profitable voyage to delight the hearts of our owners.

Another evening begins. Through thick veils of rain, the palms of the western coast of Ceylon drop astern darkly as *Mawana* steers into the squalls of the South-West Monsoon. The pink and amber wash of a sinking sun peeps through rents along a rain-sodden horizon.

Fortified by gin and tonics, those of us off watch gather in the saloon for dinner. In this running sea, the deck climbs and falls away in a predictable rhythm. We keep our balance through instinct until seated. The Indian *boys*, some fresh-faced and on their first trip, others lined and grizzled, draw out the chairs so that we can ease into them. Being fussed over in this manner might be what diners at the Savoy Grill in London's Strand experience, except that chains secure our chairs to a boisterous deck. To prevent crocks and cutlery sliding off the table, the fiddle boards are raised around the edges and the tablecloth is wetted. Despite the plunge of the bows, and the hammer of south-west ramparts that are the Arabian Sea at this time of year, all is bliss, for the wake is straight and we are homeward bound like Noah's dove.

The boys weave their way from the galley hatch with thick fish soup. They tilt the dishes this way and that, trying to counteract the ship's motion, and keep their thumbs out of the soup as it slops to and fro.

I suspect the soup originates from left-over flaked fish from the breakfast spiced kedgeree. Whatever — it is delicious. I turn to the assistant purser. 'Frank, is this the last of the Hooghly *bhetki*?'

'Aye, and the last fish you'll see, apart from tinned pilchards, before we pay off.'

'Your soup is grand. Sometimes bhetki is like chewing bits of old cod. Is it the same sort of fish? Comes from the tidal end of the Ganges, doesn't it?'

'From the Hooghly outlet, but nowt to do with cod. It's a species of barramundi. Bengal's answer to sea bass.'

Henry, third engineer, takes a swig of lime-juice, still obligatory on the tables of British ships — I've yet to hear of a case of scurvy. He swallows two salt tablets and an anti-malaria paludrine pill. He sucks on the gap where he's lost an eye tooth. 'Hope the wife sends out for decent fish and chips when I get home.'

Frank dabs his plump lips with a linen napkin. 'Is that how you judge my catering, Henry? I thought I'd made a special effort.'

'No, no, Frank. Don't get me wrong. There's not been too many weevils in the Weetabix, and your curries are the best yet. And that meat loaf you cobbled together yesterday was something else. I'm just looking forward to plain home grub for a change, that's all. Egg and chips. Yorkshire puddings. Sage and onion gravy. Mebbe a decent lump of cheddar. Tell you what though — I am sick of these bloody pills every day. Do we still have to take them now we're done with India?'

'Daily salt tablets and paludrine are standing orders. Few know this, but should you refuse them, the ship's master can impose a fine. Also, that meat loaf was not *cobbled together* as you so elegantly put it. The recipe is from Les

Flockhart — him from Dundee. Reckoned to be the best feeder in Brocklebanks.'

Henry looks a touch askance, so I deflect the topic. 'I did two trips with Les. His meat loaf was interesting. He bored holes right through, and stuffed them with root vegetables. He'd cook it, then carve it. So we got served a slice of his special meat loaf with little discs of carrot and parsnip dotted about. I poked at one bit of white that looked not strictly vegetable and found a section of a strange fat maggoty thing. It had little bristles on its segments. I gave Les a nudge and showed him. He said to keep quiet lest they'd all want one. Generally though, his grub was brilliant, apart from the time I spat out half a cockroach that was in the China chillao. I'd always loved China chillao up to that point.'

Next comes the braised oxtail — cross-sections of soft bone and gristle surrounded by lobes of brown meat and wedges of yellow fat. Dark and savoury. The bigger the piece, the nearer the bum, so I've heard. I try not to think of that as we tuck in. It's on a bed of mashed potato decorated with tinned carrots. This means that oxtail soup will be on the menu tomorrow. The condiments move along: bright yellow mustard, and pots of salt and pepper. Half the table goes for the second choice — a cutlet wrapped in breadcrumbs. What's within? Who knows? Every purser/steward has a budget of so much per man, and he'll get trouble from head office if he exceeds it. So, he does what he can to stretch his budget, fiddle a bit on the side to boost his wages, and also keep us happy. The provisioning of a ship helps a purser to enjoy the most profitable job aboard. When a purser leaves the sea, he often buys a pub.

There's a crash. The deck shudders and falls away beneath our feet. We grab the edge of the table as she heels to starboard. The square windows of the saloon hiss with the lash of green sea. One breaded cutlet rolls across the tablecloth, leaving a trail of gravy. There's an irritated shout from the captain's table: 'Who is on the wheel, or who is not on the wheel, Mister Mate?'

The chief officer sets down his cutlery. 'Murdo Macleod, sir.'

'Him again? You can tell him to take more water with it. I've no desire to inspect the ocean floor at this juncture in my career. And we are at dinner, for goodness' sake! Take a look, will you?'

Murdo is from Stornoway on the Isle of Lewis, as are the two other quartermasters. Three seamen who have seen every corner and creek of the world, and are close to retirement, along with Captain Eggleston.

'Aye, sir. Will do.' The mate throws aside his napkin, and half-slides from the saloon, grabbing the arms of chairs as he goes. In five minutes, he's back. 'Freak wave, sir. Apparently, a great lump of sea hit us on the port bow. Came out of nowhere.'

'It happens, Mr Rudge. It happens. Now, where's my boy got to?'

'Here, sahib. I help in galley, sahib. Cook fall over. He little bit *jungly wallah* for minute.'

'What's happened to my ice-cream? Has that gone west as well?'

'*Na*, Captain sahib. Ice cream, she come. Cooking now.'

Idris, the junior officers' new steward, taken on to replace Jamil, who signed off in Calcutta, is going round our table asking if we want dessert. The choice is college pudding with custard or fresh guava fruit. Henry and two apprentices go for the pudding. They tuck in with gusto. I'll go for the guava: aromatic, exotic, and unheard of in Hartlepool.

Henry straightens in his chair. 'You can't whack a decent lump of Board of Trade duff. Mind you, this is not the proper stuff. When I was with Hogarth's, it came out of a tin. Stuck the ribs together a treat, it did.'

Frank puts his fork into the dome of his pudding. It crumbles into halves in slow motion. 'Henry — if you crave for stodge contrived from suet and cheap flour, sprinkled with greasy sultanas, and topped with a dollop of molasses, you'll need to go back to Hungry Hogarth's. Here, we hope to improve on Board of Trade minimum rations.'

Henry swallows another spoonful. 'Keep your hair on, Frank. Different ships, different cocoa, as they say in the RN. I've put weight on with your feeding.'

Eldon, fourth mate and peacemaker, speaks: 'Now there's a compliment! But, never mind the duff, who's for a few rounds of carrom tonight?'

There are several short-wave radios among the crew, but we have small hope of picking up European radio in the Arabian Sea. Except for faint stations smothered in static or overwhelmed by rasping blasts from stations in the Soviet Union intent on jamming the Voice of America and the BBC Overseas Service, we are devoid of outside entertainment. The crew gather most evenings in the smoke room for their own amusement. It's darts and the ancient Indian game of carrom tonight. For those who wish to relax with a Zane Grey, or a murder mystery, or a study of comparative religion, I've opened the wooden crate of the ship's library.

The bows climb out of another trough as Paddy Rourke, 4th engineer, dusts the polished surface of the carrom board with chalk as fine as talc. The chalk increases the velocity of the carrom pieces across the surface. He places the red disc of the queen on the star at the centre of the board and surrounds her with alternate black and white wooden carrommen discs, eighteen in all, to form a hexagon. He palms his hands, gives them a shake, then thrusts his knobbly knuckled fists towards Alf, the carpenter.

'Right, Chips. Where's the striker?'

Alf taps the left fist. It opens to reveal a heavier disc. Paddy lays it on the double line at Chips' side of the table. 'You're first to break. Three shots for openers. You're white. No cheating, mind. There's two cans on this match.'

Alf's great thumb and forefinger flicks the striker at the wall of carrommen that hide the queen. It skims across the chalk talc and thuds into the barrier. The wall breaks open and the pieces scatter like scared pigeons. One white piece even vanishes into a pocket. The red queen has crept six inches sideways and stands naked to his next attack. But, to drive her into a pocket, he must first clear away one of his own whites that blocks the best pocket. He replaces the striker on his side of the base line and shoots again, but with less force and more care. The white piece is struck on the side and zips at an angle into a pocket. With extra violence, he attempts to sink another white from a fine angle, but it misses. The flying striker causes chaos. A black piece leaps from the board and rolls across the deck lino. The disarray has left the queen poised on the edge of a pocket. But he scored two points.

Paddy roars, 'Foul shot.' He recovers the escaped piece and puts it on the central star. 'You lose your points and forfeit your go.'

Alf gives a derisory sniff. 'Not enough bleeding drag on the board. You've put too much chalk on it.'

Paddy takes aim. His oil-grimed thumbnail flicks the striker at two black pieces that loiter by a pocket. They both sink. He strikes another black. It cannons into the queen, and she vanishes. Another black follows to *cover the queen*.

'Right then, that's the queen sorted out. Now for the rest.' With bold flourishes, Paddy pockets the remaining five blacks. 'Da, da! Never have there been such days! All cleared, and Chips owes me two beers'.

'Not after I thrash you on the next board, I won't'. He turns to me. 'Any news from the *Malakand*?'

'She's 150 miles south-west of us. Coming up from the Seychelles. She'll have this weather on her tail.'

'And lifting her skirts, no doubt. Pass my salaams across to Chippy Doyle if you get the chance. The *Maidan* gone in yet?'

'Took the Sandheads pilot this morning. She'll be well into the Hooghly by now.'

We brace when the ship climbs another sea. As she drops into the next trough, there's a whoop as someone finds *double top*. At the other end of the smoke room, the darts match is underway with a deal of friendly banter. I'll miss such comradeship if I ever find a shore job. It's warming to be with these fellows — to know the bonding of men that comes from being cooped up for months, bound together by wide horizons.

23

Kitchener Country

15th June, 1959. Port Sudan.
My 21st birthday went by with little fuss last week while we heaved our way through the wet monsoon. Don took my watch so I could have the evening free, and the purser organised a Victoria sponge cake. At dinner, I was treated to, *For He's a Jolly Good Fellow,* followed by, 'Get the beer in', which cost me a crate of beer.

Now, each dusk, the sun boat of Ra sinks in glory across the ovens of Sudan. It lowers into baked hills with a green flash, then dies. The Red Sea sweats mariners on old ships, but *Mawana* is air-conditioned. There's no need to sit in our cabins, naked beneath towels, while the sweat drips. And we are going home. In fifteen days, we shall creep into the river Thames topped out with Sudanese cotton.

It's Port Sudan for five days, mostly idle while we wait for lorry loads of baled cotton. There's little to entertain seafarers bored with the tiny world of a ship. It's a dusty and panting town of crouched buildings — rendered white walls cracked beneath corrugated iron roofs. The place cowers from noon temperatures that touch 100 Fahrenheit. I've heard tell of a grubby bar a mile from the dock, but I shall not go there. Those who venture *up the road* say it makes for an unusual night ashore, it being hard to tell the women from the men, both sexes rangy and muscular. They are kin to the dockers we watch now: Hadendowah tribesmen in grubby white robes and black waistcoats, hair piled in a dome with braided side curtains that cover the ears.

I'm at the rails with a few off-duty idlers from the engine room and bridge. A Scouse voice growls: 'Them Fuzzy-Wuzzies are a rum lot.'

A Glaswegian: 'Best not to stare too long.'

'Or go too close, unless you hold your breath. They ride out of the hills every year for the cotton season. Camel dung holds those massive hairdos together. See how some wear the Sam Browne belt? Seventy years old, those belts must be. Lifted them off British dead when they broke the square, and a Black Watch square at that! A shock to the country. None of our squares broke at Waterloo.'

Alf comes in with a verse:

'So ere's to you, Fuzzy Wuzzy, at your 'ome in the Soudan;
You're a poor benighted 'eathen but a first-class fightin' man;
An' 'ere's to you, Fuzzy-Wuzzy, with your 'ayrick 'ead of 'air —
You're a big black boundin' beggar and you broke a British square!

The Scouse engineer responds, 'Got any more?'

Alf scratches his stubble. 'Not a lot. Though some bits stick. Kipling pays respect to wild men with spears and teases the cocksure British Army of the time:

We took our chanst among the Khyber 'ills,
The Boers knocked us silly at a mile,
The Burman give us Irriwaddy chills,
And a Zulu impi dished us up in style:
But all we ever got from such as they
Was pop to what the Fuzzy made us swaller ...

And there's a fair bit more, but I forget. Though, I have it in a book.'

Eldon, our well-educated fourth mate, adds his piece: 'We were too late to save Gordon at Khartoum. They chopped the general's head off. Kitchener got the job of putting down the Mahdi and his Dervishes. By the time he got here, the new prophet had died of typhus. That was the end of his vow to found a caliphate and have the world bend the knee. Kitchener shelled the Mahdi's tomb to stop it from becoming a rallying point. He had the Mahdi's body beheaded and chucked into the Nile. Queen Victoria was not amused, and Kitchener had to write her an apology.'

'Why were we here, anyway? There's nowt but camel shite.'

'Only to keep out the French, who thought they had the right to Egypt. The Mahdi had his sights on the Suez Canal, so that was Kitchener's main job, but the folks at home were told he'd only invaded to avenge Chinese Gordon.'

I've not added to the discussion until now. 'Kitchener? Him of the finger-pointing poster, *Your Country Needs You*? My dad and his mates signed up for it.'

Alf grunts. 'Your dad was in the Great War? When was he born?'

'Eighteen-ninety-three.'

'So he was a Victorian, like Kitchener.'

'Yes. And Mam, likewise — 1899. She had me late, after she thought it was all over. Said I was a gift from God.'

Alf slaps me on the back. 'So you are, Harry. So you are!'

'If he's a gift from God, he can shout for six cold beers. I'm parched.'

On the quay-side, a car draws up by the gangway. All interest in me is wrenched away as our agent steps out. He carries a briefcase. Mail for the crew! Letters are our oxygen, the only contact with home.

I've three letters. One has chased *Mawana* since Calcutta. A letter can wander the seaports from agent to agent until it finds us. One letter took two months to reach me. It clearly stated: Georgetown, Madras, India, but some sleepy postal sorter had dispatched it to another Georgetown, the capital of British Guiana, on the other side of the world.

Beryl tells how she makes progress with dresses for her bridesmaids. It's a lot of work. She's sewing her own wedding dress and spends an amount of time on the floor cutting out fabric. Then she stands on the kitchen table while her dad, who is a skilled draughtsman, measures the hem. She says I'm not to know any more. The design is a secret.

Mother writes of her latest visit to the fish quay to buy a couple of gurnards for teatime. She knows how I enjoy the little cylindrical fish with the dragon face and says she hopes the drifters will land more in time for my leave. She's bought a pair of kippers from the smokehouse, because they will keep — she has no means of stopping food going off in summer except for the cold slab in the pantry. It'll be a few years before we have a refrigerator. She's often at the Fish House to hunt for a wing of skate: 'You'll remember how much your dad liked that,' she writes. And I won't believe what they want for fresh salmon this week: 'A pound for a pound it is now! Terrible! I'll stick to the Co-op's sockeye from a tin.'

Mam keeps busy. She trained as a tailoress through the Great War and now makes a few shillings by altering dresses for women who come to the door. Clothes shops in town send alteration work. She spends hours on the floor, a row of pins between her lips, pinning out the garments. Then, foot on the treadle of her sewing machine, she worries she might ruin the garment. For all that, she earns a pittance.

Eva, her neighbour, pops in and out. The back door will open and she'll breeze in with: 'Can I borrow a cup of sugar for Sammy's tea, Dorothy honey?' Eva will plonk herself in a chair and have Mam shake with laughter at her ribald tales of the latest night out at the Brus Arms, a cavernous ale house at the end of Winterbottom Avenue. I've never taken Beryl to that pub — it's a rough place.

Reading between the lines, I think Mam finds life as a widow a lonely business. As the ambulance men lifted him from his bed, Dad's last words to me were, 'Look after your mother, Son.' It's only eighteen months since he died, and here I am, about to be married. I'm cheered to see she writes: 'Folk tell me I'll not be losing a son, I'll be gaining a daughter.'

Father was born in 1893, so he was a true Victorian. Many years hence, I take up creative writing and, based on his service records and the sparse fragments he revealed, will attempt to imagine my father, Charles William Nicholson, speaking of his war with the Kaiser:

'I volunteered in August 1914, nearly a month after it started. Joined up at Gateshead — I was in the yards there, hammering hot rivets into ships with my dad. Everyone was keen, so I went along. I'd be away from the yards for a few months, that's all. Me being from Hartlepool, I asked for my local regiment, the Durham Light Infantry.

When I'd gone through the system, had my private parts looked at, had my arms and legs counted, coughed for them, and suchlike, I found they'd put me in the artillery along with my mates because we were clever with hammers and hot iron. They had me down as Roman Catholic instead of Wesleyan, but that's the army for you.

Next thing, I was down in Devon at training camp near Dawlish, where I had to learn to ride a horse. That was a job and a half. Still got the bump on my head from when I was thrown. Sergeant was a swine. Took a dislike to me. Said I was an idiot.

"You're an idiot, Nicholson. What are you?"

I'm not an idiot, so I didn't answer. He asked me the question three times in all. I kept quiet. So he put me on a charge. I ended up in front of a court martial. They stuck me in an army prison for the crime of feigning dumbness.

That was hard. When I got out, my unit and my mates were already in Belgium. They shipped me with another outfit. I knew none of them.

I was a driver now. Before my charge, I was supposed to be a gunner.

Ypres — now there's a place. Wipers, we called it. By the time I got there in 1915, the place was in bits. Most of it just piles of rubble with a wall here and there. The tower of the big Cloth Hall stood like a broken old man bent over his stick. We had to hold Wipers, otherwise Fritz had a clear route to Calais.

My battery was part of 70th Brigade RFA attached to the 15th Scottish division. They went about in kilts. With no drawers on, they said. The battery was at the battle of Loos in 1915. Then came the Somme in 1916, with us supporting at places like Pozieres and Flers-Courcelette. Our job was to dig pits, bed in the guns, and build parapets of sandbags.

I got my wound stripe at Flers. I was driving a waggon down from the line to load up with more ammunition when a German shell landed close. The blast tossed us all over the shop — the wagon, the horses, and me. I came down with a bump and shrapnel in the head. Had damaged knees and wrists. Horses were not so lucky.

I was trundled out of the line, down to the Canadian medics at Etaples — that's a whole town of hospital tents and huts near Boulogne. I had such terrible headaches they sent me back to Blighty. I went home on the hospital ship *Salta*. (Six months later, the HS *Salta* hit a mine and went down with the loss of fifty.)

I had a month's treatment in Edinburgh War Hospital. Then afterwards to KLMCH — that's the King's Lancs Military Hospital, built on the old racecourse at Blackpool — for six weeks convalescence with massage and exercises until I was fit enough for sending back.

This time they shipped me to Salonika — that's in Greece, on the Serbian and Bulgarian borders. The chaps stuck on the Western Front thought a posting to Salonika was a picnic. The Bay of Biscay was rough that late January 1917. The horses had a bad time of it. I was down below — someone had to clean up the mess. We didn't get any visits from the officers while that went on.

In Salonika, it was so hot, we fried our eggs on the rocks. There was a lot of sickness. Salonika water stinks, and the mosquitoes are a plague. Like everyone, I got malaria and dysentery. Forever in and out of Field Ambulance we were. I was put into hospital four times in that fifteen months. My section was part of the Small Arms Ammunition Column, which involved long, sweaty slogs nursing loaded ammunition mules through ravines like ovens and across bare mountain sides, or through blizzards, depending on the time of year. To our left, the Serbs and French were dug in. The Greeks covered our right flank. We all faced the Bulgars, who held a line of Macedonian crags with artillery. If they spotted us bringing up the mules, we could expect a half-dozen shells. But, if they saw we were having a cricket or football match on a bit of level ground, they would never shell us — Johnny Bulgar could be a decent sort when he felt like it. German aircraft flew over to shoot down our observation balloons and drop bombs on us. It was a job to keep the mules calm when that was going on. In winter we came down with piles on account of too much time astride wet saddles.

I was there a twelve-month until Britain was short of ships and they sent me home to work in the Hartlepool yards for the last six months of the war. That was me out of it.

If I learned one thing from the Great War, it was always look after your horses before you see to yourself. Just as well I missed out on the DLI — thousands of them are asleep along the Somme.

24

July Wedding

Thursday, 25 June, 1959. On the train from King's Cross.

The European crew of twenty signed off ship's articles in the London docks and promptly dispersed from *Mawana;* she's been our home these past five months. Many shipmates, though they will pass unseen beneath the stars on the world's oceans, will never meet again.

The steam engine hurtles north. I brace in the corner of a swaying buffet car, to drown chilled pork pie in Worthington Indian Pale Ale, and reflect on how I've come to inhabit a world of men, to grow up among them thousands of miles from the world of women. My pals on shore have grown through their acne and teenage years in factories, shops, shipyards, and coal mines. After their shifts, they went home each night to mothers and sisters. They supped beer at weekends in the Volunteer's Arms, then tottered off to the Queen's Rink where they eyed-up girls of all shapes and sizes: rivet-catchers, shop workers, shorthand typists, clerks, and comptometer operators. Girls by the hundred, sprinkled around the dance-hall walls like blooms in a cottage garden. Girls bold, with knowing eyes. Girls demure, nursing handbags, nervous of beery breath. Lines and clusters of hopeful print frocks and hooped skirts. My mates cavorted in wild jives to the latest skiffle, and their thick suede soles crunched many a tender toe. Sunday morning, they would crawl out of bed to gather at the milk-bar and compare hangovers.

Except for occasional leave, I've not known that sort of maturation through the teenage years. It is beyond the young seafarer's experience. I've seen only fluttering Chinese and Japanese maidens, and in the streets of Indian ports, shy women in saris, sometimes with heart-stopping dark eyes above a veil. The haughty and unapproachable daughters of British tea planters, sipping gin around the pool at the Calcutta Swimming Club, do not count. I've danced with quaint, mixed-race, Anglo-Indian girls at the Calcutta Missions to Seamen — they have surnames like Hardcastle and Morgan from unions long ago. For them we are potential husbands, and some succeed, like the lovely Enid Clump, and go 'home' to Blighty as brides. At the other extreme is the rocking Gulf of Mexico dame who might exclaim: 'Gee, wise guy, ya'll are so old-fashioned!'

I'm here because I failed the grammar school entrance exam, and so left Galley's Field school for boys, at a vague and dreamy fifteen. Then came a year as an errand boy peddling a cumbersome Co-op grocery bike. I made sixteen, whereupon I took fright at, but overcame, algebra and trigonometry when my brain woke up among grown men at South Shields Merchant Navy College. My mongrel dog, the childhood stamp album, and the insect collection, were left at home one cold Southampton January in 1956, when I joined my first vessel, the HMT *Dunera*. She was a great white ship, a trooper, crammed with famous battalions bound for Singapore, Hong Kong, and Japan. I survived the first few days of the embarrassments and humiliations of the novice to become competent at my job. After *Dunera*, the Marconi company sent me to the *Hughli,* a veteran James Nourse tramp steamer, followed by *Corburn*, a tiny modern Cory collier out of the Tyne. Between four long trips to India with Brocklebank general cargo steamers, I returned to college twice for more qualifications. It's been an interesting life so far, and here I am, at twenty-one, going home for the tenth time. On this leave, in nine days' time, I'm to be wed.

Saturday, 4th July, 1959. Seaton Carew, County Durham.

Arnold's little green Morris Minor hums like a sewing machine across the Steelworks bridge, passed the Prop Yard with its myriad stacks of Baltic pine quietly seasoning to support the workings of Durham coal pits. To our left, the North Sea, gentle today, sparkles as the incoming tide breaks over Langscar reef and swirls through the water-worn stumps of a fossilised Ice Age forest. In the bay, colliers and cargo ships stand off-shore waiting for high water and their turn to enter Hartlepool or the River Tees. Southwards, beyond waving banks of blue-green marram grass, where larks rise bubbling above the dunes, is the salt marsh. There squats the Zinc Works and its sulphuric acid plant. Behind that brutish, rusted wonder of the Industrial Revolution soars the Tees Transporter bridge, and the massed chimneys of the Imperial Chemical Industry, each with a noxious white plume set against the violet hills of Cleveland. Like a little Matterhorn, the anvil summit of Roseberry Topping rises out of the moorland haze, a place of our courtship. With a breeze from the Pennines driving the belch of industry across the German Ocean to Heligoland, we have a fine blue morning for a wedding, and the start of a heat wave.

Inshore sailing and rowing cobles no longer line the yellow sands here; those clinker-built North Sea craft were almost unchanged since Danish Vikings settled this shore. In the days of Henry the First, Seaton was the fief of the Norman-French Robert De Carrowe. Seaton Carew is now a holiday place for boisterous families of steel and chemical workers, miners and shipbuilders. We are here because it's the parish of Beryl's childhood.

Brother-in-law steers past quaint cottages of forgotten fisherfolk; those that have not been cleared away to make space for a brash fun-palace stuffed with slot machines are now ice-cream parlours and gift shops. A few yards beyond the old house where Beryl's grandmother keeps a lady's hairdressers, we take a right turn off Front Street. With a jolt, I see, at the end of Church Street, the Victorian tower of Holy Trinity. Not far now! I've a slight pain behind the eyes from a jolly session at last night's stag party in the public bar of the Volunteer's Arms.

Arnold slows the car to a trundle, then brakes by the door of the Seaton Hotel. 'How are you feeling? As your best man, and husband of your sister, I believe it's my duty to inform you that there's still time to change your mind, should you so wish.'

I roll my tongue around a mouth like the floor of a parrot cage. Is it fright? The words come cracked and slow: 'I'm parched.'

'Then we'd best have a swift livener. Come on. We're too early, anyway.'

The landlord pulls two pints of frothing Nimmo's bitter from the beer engine. I down half of mine in one swallow. The last drink as a single man. Ah! Now I can speak. I glance at my wristwatch. The luminous green hands of the self-winder come into focus. The Felca is one of the few choice things I own, and cost me a week's wages in Aden. Twenty minutes to go. I stare into the froth.

'We don't get many Merchant Navy uniforms in here these days — except for certain Saturday mornings, that is.' The landlord squints at the hat under my arm, at the unfouled anchor beneath the crown of sails on the cap badge, then at the brass-buttoned uniform, and takes in the single stripe of gold braid backed by green on the cuff of a navy-blue sleeve. I've had the uniform cleaned of Guinness stains. It is quality stuff, handed down to me when Arnold gave up the sea. The landlord grins and gives a sideways wink. 'Looks to be a nice bit of barathea. Are those church bells for you?'

'Most likely.' I turn to Arnold, who drains his glass. He can soon shift a pint.

Arnold adjusts the white carnation in his lapel, then slaps me on the back. 'Feeling better, Harry? Time to move. Sup up, and steady as she goes.'

In sunshine, beneath the clamour of church bells and the squabbles of rooks in the ash trees, a happy throng chatters around the church door. To one side is a cluster of grinning young chaps in the latest gear: Slim Jim ties, draped jackets, and drain-pipe trousers — the cycling mates I'd road-raced and learned to drink with. Stout men in middle age, uncles from both sides, converse in freshly pressed suits, some a bit shiny. Watch-chains drape across well-provendered waistcoat stomachs. Wives of various sizes sport festive hats — grey curls peeping from under. Bent elderly folk exchange ailments. Clusters of widows lean on sticks. Many of these people I don't know. Conversation dies as we are appraised.

The two sidesmen, my cousin Norman Fields, and Edwin Scott, my soon-to-be brother-in-law, shake our hands and usher us into the cool church. We stand before the altar where Canon Maughan, in white vestments, waits with an open book. The organist is bent over his keyboard. The tune sounds familiar, but I'm unaware it is Bach's *Jesu, Joy of Man's Desiring,* that swims to the rafters. Behind us, the pews fill with whispers and the rustles of frocks as the music flows into *Sheep May Safely Graze*. Long minutes drag while I try not to fidget. The organ drones on. There are occasional coughs from the congregation. She's late!

At last, the purr of a Rolls-Royce limousine is heard. The organ fades, then strikes up with Wagner's *Bridal Procession*. Here comes the bride! At one with the assembly, I turn. On the arm of her father, Beryl floats in sunlight through the door. A golden halo shimmers around her ivory wedding gown and bouffant head-dress. She carries a spray of yellow roses. Two little page boys, Arnold's sons, walk behind in white suits and blue cummerbunds. Next come three bridesmaids: two sisters of the bride and a cousin, pale blue gowns shot with silver, heads topped by circlets of white flowers. They dip out of the sunbeams, into the cool aisle of the church, like a cavalcade of fairy folk from under the hill.

I blink, and assume I'm not supposed to peep, so turn to face the grey-haired priest. The hiss of satin grows close and in moments she is beside me. We smile, our fingers touch, and the church is hushed.

After a hymn, the clergyman peers over the top of his glasses, and begins:

'Dearly beloved, we are gathered together here in the sight of God, and in the face of this congregation, to join together this man and this woman in holy matrimony...'

Beryl is concentrating on the canon's words. Perhaps I should do the same. I've already missed some bits. I focus when he reaches an important part. My mouth has dried again.

'Wilt thou have this woman to thy wedded wife, to live together after God's ordinance in the holy estate of matrimony? Wilt thou love her, comfort her, honour, and keep her, in sickness and in health; and, forsaking all other, keep thee only unto her, so long as ye both shall live?'

'I will.' The words leap out. In a reasonably manly manner, I hope.

Beryl's response is confident and clear. I'm impressed. All sense that I've a headache is gone. There are glances at each other, and sometimes our eyes meet. A feeling of ease comes. The ring is blessed. I slip it onto Beryl's finger, pleased that I do not tremble. The priest declares us man and wife, and invites us to ascend the stairs to sign the register.

We kneel before the altar while the priest takes us through the Lord's Prayer. Amid the holy words, random thoughts drift through my mind, thoughts of short trousers and of childhood, of rolling decks and sputtering Morse, until I'm aware of: 'O God of Abraham, God of Isaac, God of Jacob, bless these thy servants...' And we float from the church to the throb of organ pipes.

Outside the church

Our 1930s wedding car has running boards. White ribbons drape the bonnet from the wings of the kneeling *Spirit of Ecstasy*. It's one of a pair of hired Mason's taxis I'm to pay for, bought from the Queen's fleet of redundant Rolls-Royce Phantoms when she had new. To the sound of bells, and dotted with confetti, we climb aboard this luxury to be whisked away to our wedding reception at the Marine Hotel.

How young we are! Years will pass before the poet in me will emerge, so my speech at the table is halting and formal. But I manage to thank Beryl's parents for producing a lovely and vivacious daughter, and promise I'll cherish her. I thank both my parents, though only one remains alive, for their sacrifices in setting me on the road to an interesting life. I tell them how my father had said: 'I don't care what you do, Son, as long as you get a trade — if you have a trade, you'll never go hungry.' Mam is dabbing her eyes. Some wedding gifts get a mention: a wondrous device — a pressure cooker from Beryl's employer. A tea service from Aunt Marion — all are invited to call in for tea. A pair of flannelette bed sheets in a shocking purple, from my pal Harvey Blogg (Those sheets will last thirty years before Nell, the Labrador, has them for her bed. They last longer than Aunt Myrtle's dinner service, which hits the deck with a shattering crash one inebriated Christmas Day in Leeds).

After the best man's speech, as soon as Arnold sits down, Uncle Henry stands before the fifty guests. Henry, a twinkling-eyed member of the Hartlepool Fire Brigade, and husband of Dad's sister, Margaret, is a powerful tenor. Adam's apple quivering, gaze unfocussed on the far corner of the ceiling, he begins *I'll Walk beside You*. He's every bit as good as Josef Locke. By the time he reaches the final lines: *And when the great call comes, the sunset gleams, I'll walk beside you to the land of dreams,* elderly widows have fished out their handkerchiefs. With a photographer hovering close by, the cake is cut. Beryl's mother had baked the three tiers. She hired her coalman, a skilled amateur, to craft the layers of icing sugar surmounted by the figure of Eros. Despite his normal trade of delivering coal round the houses of the town, he's made a splendid job. There's not a trace of a black thumbprint on the white icing.

Beryl looks lovely in her fashionable coffee and cream 'going away' outfit. We sit side by side, holding hands in the rear of the little car. By the steelworks, Arnold stops the engine. With a clasp knife, he severs the strings of tin cans and old boots that have clattered and bounced behind the Morris Minor for the last mile. He slings the collection into a waste bin and we set off for Newcastle-on-Tyne. Beryl has booked our honeymoon night at the majestic Royal Station Hotel, next to the railway.

I squeeze her hand. 'Why were you late at the altar? I thought perhaps you'd changed your mind.'

'Oh, it was Dad. He sent the Rolls away because the white ribbons on the bonnet were untidy. He told the driver not to come back until the car had been decorated in the proper manner. Don't forget, during the War he was a Royal Navy lieutenant and does insist on things being shipshape.'

At Newcastle, Arnold takes Beryl's blue suitcase and leads the way up the steps to the grand entrance. He nods at the sign by the door. 'Look here! Opened by Queen Victoria in 1850 for the York, Newcastle and Berwick Railway Company. Let's hope they've changed the sheets.'

The spotty bell boy takes my battered sea-going case. 'We had no complaints from Vera Lynn.'

He'd grabbed the case before I could avoid him. I wonder if sixpence will do as a tip.

Beryl has booked us one night in a chamber with a private bathroom. Tomorrow we shall catch the London train. Arnold bids farewell with a married man's words of advice: 'Be kind to each other. And never go to bed on an argument.'

The mainline express roars south on the line of the old LNER (London and North-Eastern Railway). Nationalised by the Labour government under Clement Attlee, it's been British Railways for eleven years. We are all owners now.

We have a table seat. Opposite are two black-clad, middle-aged nuns who appear to be under vows of silence. They look at Beryl's left hand, then treat us to benign smiles. Perhaps we look like newlyweds. The apple cheeks beam at intervals, but are mostly intent on their books or nibbling at sandwiches while one hand covers the mouth. We entwine contented fingers under the table and settle into the journey to King's Cross. It might be unseemly to drink beer and sherry in front of the nuns, so we make trips to the buffet car. It's always worth swapping hearty yarns with the buffet stewards, so many of them have served at sea.

We stop at Darlington, and at York, Doncaster, Grantham, and Peterborough. On every platform, amid the panting steam and barrows of London mail, are flowered hats and confetti.

25

Drydock

A week after honeymoon, we begin to wonder if I'll be recalled soon, and how long will be our parting. If the next trip is India and straight back, it could be just five months. If we get diverted from India to the USA, as one in four of Brocklebank's voyages are, it will be seven months.

The red telephone box at the top of our road is engaged. There's a woman inside. She must be going out tonight — she has her hair in curlers. She's not using the phone, but has the heavy iron door ajar while she has a smoke. 'I won't be long, Flower,' she sings out. 'I'm waiting for a call from me husband at three. He's a sergeant at Catterick Camp. Shan't be long.' The phone rings and she closes the door.

Even though I've backed away a pace, I discover she's worried about her mother. I must not step back too far because a stout man has just wheezed up. A young lass hurries towards us. We now have a queue. It takes only ten minutes for the husband to run out of coins, and the telephone is mine. The box reeks of stale vinegar. Among the spent matches and Woodbine packets on the floor, there's a crunched up newspaper from someone's fish and chip supper. I lift the heavy bakelite receiver off its cradle, dial 'O', and ask the operator for a reverse charge long-distance call to the number of the Brocklebank office in Liverpool. In Cunard Buildings, the radio superintendent comes on the line.

Arthur Orum gives a throaty chortle. 'What's up, Harry? You ready for another ship? Had enough of wedded bliss?'

I bring to mind the strong features, the irregular teeth, the heavy jaw, at the other end of the line — the 'seen-it-all' kind eyes of a man who went to sea in 1939, at the outbreak of war. 'No, Arthur. I'm happy to be stuck on leave come the Crack of Doom. It's just that folk at home keep asking when I'll ship out again. Do I need to keep a bag packed?'

'Let's see. As of today, you've had sixteen days of your due leave.' Behind the crackle of the line, I detect the rustle of paper. 'You've a few days owing. Here we are … Ah, yes. I'm about to send you a wire with instructions to join the *Matra* in six days' time.'

I sigh. 'For deep sea?'

There's a chuckle. 'No, no. Not to fret. Just on standby. You'll sign Home Trade articles ready for a bit of rock-dodging round the UK coast.'

'Where is she?' I imagine I'll meet her in the Thames or the Mersey.

'Graythorp drydock. Not a million miles from you, if I'm not far wrong.'

'Just a half-hour on the bus, Arthur. How long in drydock?'

'Roughly two weeks. Then London, where you can sign off and nip home for a few more days. After which, all being well, I've got you down for foreign-going on *Mahronda*. Does the plan suit a newly married man?'

I make a mental calculation. Arthur has organised things so I'll have another month at home before shipping out for India. 'That's champion, Arthur! Thank you indeed. Beryl will be over the moon. It's very thoughtful of you.'

'We like to do what we can for our people. You take good care of each other. Cheerio!'

I've gone soft after two trips on a brand new, air-conditioned vessel. Now it's back to rattling electric fans and cockroaches that parade across my damp chest at night. But the steamship *Matra* is not too antiquated. She's only ten years old (she will live for thirteen more years before she dies at the breakers at Gandia, in Spain).

Like many another of the Brocklebank fleet of twenty-five, she was Clyde-built at Port Glasgow by William Hamilton & Co. I find her clean lines, her 10,000 tons deadweight, and 508 feet of steel hull slumbering in drydock. Here, she'll be fumigated to rid her of rodents and sundry entomological vermin. The three steam turbines, geared to a single screw shaft, will be overhauled. With the hull cleared of fouling weed and rust, she will have a total repaint, and once more be worthy of her lovely sister, the *Mahseer*. This vessel honours the *Matra* of 1926, mined and sunk in the Thames Estuary near the Tongue lightship in 1939, and the sixteen Indian seamen, mostly of the engine room, who did not go home to grow old.

Matra is named after a village in India, but here she rests high and dry, chocked up by timbers, next to tiny Graythorp, a dockyard workers' village on the north shore of Tees Bay in County Durham. The Gujarati village of Matra is seventy miles from the sea and the great salt marsh of the Rann of Kutch, but the two-hundred British souls of Graythorp can take a mere ten-minute squelch across the ooze of the Tees saltmarsh to wade in the North Sea.

All is flat and featureless here. Except for black cattle and wild geese, not much moves of man apart from drydock cranes. The skies are wide and level and throb with larks. Along tidal creeks, grey seals haul out on mud banks. Overhead, the bleating peewit soars and tumbles with lonely joy. (Sixty years later, this empty wet land will have become a thriving bird sanctuary, with a visitor centre where people relax over coffee and cake while they look out for bittern and avocet.)

An isolated pair of cabins, just astern of the funnel, house the deck apprentices. It's an unusual feature, known as 'the dog house'. I've not seen such an arrangement before, but there's been no invitation to visit. It has a secret. 'Ginger', the senior apprentice, seems a furtive young fellow. I notice him bearing covered plates and dishes to the dog house. Sometimes, he creeps down the gangway with a slop bucket. In drydock, the ship's sanitary discharges are closed off; instead, there's a line of basic lavatories ashore, for the use of.

After dinner, on the third day of drydock, I'm climbing into shore clothes, ready to catch the bus home for the night, when there's a knock. Ginger's red head pokes around my door curtain. He looks harassed.

'Sparks, can I come in? I've got a problem.' He is whispering.

I hang up my uniform in the locker. 'I'll be catching the bus in an hour, but sit down and tell me more.'

He fidgets on the edge of my little settee-cum-daybed. 'I've sneaked my girlfriend aboard. She's from London. Three days now, but the mate is getting suspicious.'

'Then you'd best send her home. Plenty of good trains from West Hartlepool to King's Cross.'

'It's not so simple. She's run away and is afraid to go back. But you live here, don't you? You sleep ashore every night. Is there any chance she could stay with you and your missus — just for a little while?'

I close the door, so we can split a can of Guinness in private, while we ponder the matter.

The red, double-decker Leyland bus is crowded with shipyard workers from Smith's Dock, on the Tees at Port Clarence. I stand with Ginger in the lower deck aisle while the lanky conductress squeezes through the crowd to take our fare. The clippy is Maggie, a casual girlfriend from long ago — a full five years back. She's handsome in her uniform, and winds the handle of her silver ticket dispenser with a touch of flair. 'Back again, are we? There you are, Harry. Three singles. Who's the third one for?'

I point to the seated girl huddled in Ginger's warm navy-blue coat. Her dark locks and angular elfin features peep from beneath the duffle-coat hood. 'For my friend's girl.'

'Fancy you being married now! To Beryl Scott, I hear. And you at sea, too. I hope you behave yourself in those foreign parts.' She grins and squeezes to the nearest bell-push. 'Head Wrightson's,' she yells.

A dozen dungarees and flat caps clamber aboard. A few climb the stairs. Maggie shouts, 'We're full up there. No standing on the top deck. Sit on the floor if you must. And you put that pipe out. No smoking downstairs.' She's on the rear access platform now — thrusting out a palm at three panting workmen. 'Sorry, luvs! Full up. There's another one behind.'

Such confidence she has! Where is the timid lass I waltzed around the Queen's Rink ballroom? Where's the girl with flour on her hands by her parent's winter fireside? The lass who kept her pinny on, the only time we were alone and out of the lashing rain.

At my mother's house, where Beryl and I have two rooms upstairs — a bedroom and a lounge with new wallpaper and tidy second-hand furniture, Ginger and his girl are greeted with wide eyes. Mam fusses around, laying extra places for supper. Tonight, it's corned beef and potato fritters, fried with bacon. Peter, my mongrel, is stretched out on the clip mat, watching the food arrive. Beryl has tried to persuade the girl to speak of her background, but she seems shy.

While passing the HP sauce bottle, Mam fixes the girl with a steady gaze. 'Flo, hunney, how long have you been away from home?'

Florence is a dainty eater and will not speak whilst chewing. The slender features flush a girlish pink. 'This will be the sixth night.'

'And are you in touch with your parents?'

Ginger breaks the tension. 'Florence is nearly eighteen. She's followed my ship. She doesn't want to go home yet. But her picture's all over the national newspapers. Girl runs away! Missing! And such.'

Mam tut-tuts a few times. 'Oh, dear. Your mam and dad will be worried sick. Do they have the telephone in?'

There's a whispered, 'Yes'.

'You can stay here for two nights at most. But only if you ring them tonight. Straight after this supper. There's a telephone box up the road. Tell them you're safe and well. Put their minds at rest. Then we'll make sure you're on the train home.'

Beryl speaks: 'Florence can sleep on the settee in our lounge upstairs. I don't mind for two nights, if you don't, Mrs Nicholson.'

Mam strokes Peter's head. The supper is savoury. He rests a hopeful muzzle on her knee. 'Two nights, then. But Flo's young man shall sleep down here, under a warm blanket in the armchair — if he's not gone back to his ship tonight, that is.'

Even so, Mam fusses over our visitors and regales them with stories of the town. I hear again how her mother stood, wrapped in her shawl, on the headland cliffs in December 1914 when a squadron of German battle-cruisers loomed out of the morning fret and opened fire on the town. This was after taking down the British flag and running up the German ensign. I've heard the story so many times I'll never forget how the women of Hartlepool ran from the town with children at their heels, and pushed prams loaded with babies and Christmas cakes not long out of the oven. How my dad had already volunteered for the army, and how his friend, Charlie Hudson, did not take the King's shilling. Mrs Hudson had pleaded with Charlie not to go — he was her only child. One of the German shells killed Charlie on his bike in the street as he was hurrying home from the shipyards that were under attack. Another shell crashed through his bedroom. Straight in one wall and out the other, without exploding. That nasty Kaiser Bill was out to get Charlie; but Dad came home safe, and only a bit knocked about.

The stories go on until Mam gets up to wind the luminous mantelpiece clock. Dad died eighteen months ago, but she keeps up with his rituals. This is the signal for bedtime.

26

Cliff Land

My sea time on the *Matra* will be brief. It's but one day's steaming to London while we keep sight of the headlands that jut into the North Sea from England's east coast. After leaving the Tees, we turn south along the coast of Cleveland, or 'Cliff Land' as it was known to the Danes of the Ninth Century, who settled here from their low heaths of Jutland. Mariners whose motive power was wind, dreaded this coast in an onshore gale. Below our wake sleeps a graveyard of luggers, brigs, and barques; their cargoes of Durham coal for the hearths of London still stain the shore after a storm.

From last night's rain, the morning air is gin clear. We have the slightest swell beneath us, and a dome of blue overhead hung with a few mare's tails of cirrus. A pod of dolphins race across to take station around the bows and ride the breaking wave. White fulmars, small cousins of the albatross, skim the water alongside, stiff-winged and hopeful. Their reward comes when a galley boy empties a bucket of slops over the side. They gorge on toast, bacon rind, and bits of breakfast kipper.

From the bridge, I imagine a trace on the southern horizon to be Flamborough Head. Not possible, given the curvature of the Earth — Flamborough's four-hundred-foot chalk cliffs are sixty miles away. From my height above the sea surface, on a day like this, I should not see that headland until we are forty miles off. They'll be the cliffs of Whitby.

Ramparts march south, bursting into the North Sea like heads of terrible giants. Huntcliff Nab, by the Victorian town of Saltburn, is the first. Over three-hundred feet of strata. On one of my leaves, Beryl and I sunbathed there, unaware the level pastures behind us covered the grave of a 7th century 'pagan princess' buried in her bed, surrounded by a ring of graves of her kindred. It will be forty years before she and her golden jewels are excavated. The grave goods will show they were Saxons from Kent. Why had they moved north to dwell among their cousins, the Angles of this coast?

Next come twin headlands sheltering the tiny harbour of Skinningrove with its steelworks that supplied iron work for Sydney Harbour Bridge. The village keeps the legend of a merman who crawled onto the shingle beach one day, was captured and held for a while. It's said he had a courteous manner and enjoyed meals of raw fish in his prison, a fisherman's shed. Local women were much interested. But he escaped. Perhaps the ladies pestered him.

Hummersea looms. Its black Jurassic mass rich in alum-bearing shale. Lewis Hunton, the inspired geologist, was born in Hummersea Farmhouse in 1814, above that growling cliff, to a father who managed the local alum works. For hundreds of years, smoke smothered this coast as the shale was roasted for nine months. Then came awful stinks when the result, aluminium sulphate ash, was slaked in stale urine. The vital ingredient was shipped here in the holds of luggers, in barrels collected from the ale houses of London and Sunderland. The humble urinations of thousands kept the industry going. The terms 'piss poor' and 'taking the piss' arise from this. When the heated liquor was dense enough to float a hen's egg, they deemed the mixture ready to crystallise into alum, a mordant vital for the fixing of dyed cloth.

The six-hundred-foot twin bastions of Boulby now appear. They shelter the fishing village of Staithes, a harbour cursed by two offended mermaids. But no matter, mermaids might be a fiction. Staithes is where an apprentice boy, the future Captain James Cook, worked for a draper. He watched the local luggers come and go. The filled sails of blue-water ships swept by like migrating swans and called to him.

Runswick Bay cliff is where I took a tumble trying to win a kittiwake's egg. As the bay opens, I make out the steep road where I crashed off my bike into a mass of brambles, just after the cliff fall. Dad put me in the bath, picked out the thorns, and washed away the blood.

My chief, a Yorkshireman I've not met before, and will never meet again — such is seagoing — joins me at the rails outside the wireless room as we come abreast of Whitby Abbey.

'A fine, bright morning, Harry.'

'Yes, Jim. Rare to pass this shore in such light, so I thought to hang about and take it in.'

He grunts. 'But nasty in squalls. The bridge is cautious. They've had the radar running since we dropped the Tees pilot. Maybe this master doesn't care for rock-dodging on the Holy Ghost.'

I glance at him. 'Holy Ghost? I've not heard that term since I sailed out of the Tyne on a two-thousand ton Cory collier, the *Corburn*.'

He laughs. 'Cockney rhyming slang for UK Coast. I've done time on smaller than that. Reardon Smith's little flatirons are no joke in winter. I was glad to get deep sea again where decks are drier and the feeding better. I'd had enough of tripe and onions stewed in milk.'

'Yuk!' I say. 'It was plain pickings on *Corburn*, but never tripe. When we came alongside Battersea power station to discharge coal, the cook sent the cabin boy ashore to buy a dozen cut loaves and fish and chip suppers all round. I can see that cook now, at the galley hatch, scratching his fat hairy chest through his string vest while he served our dinner. It was a comedown after my first ship, the trooper *Dunera*. We shared a saloon with brigadiers, admirals, and their formidable wives. We dined posh, on Dover sole and poached salmon, with Baked Alaska to follow. Ice cream served in flames — amazing! And me not sure which cutlery to use. I had my first curry on that ship. I'd no idea what it was. Never heard the word before that day.'

The chief laughs. 'And now we get it morning, noon, and night. Whether we like it or not.'

I nod. 'Can't get enough now. With our Indian crews, we must have the best curries on Earth. I take it steady though, and poke about. It's hard to tell apart a strand of crisp onion from an over-done cockroach.'

'Sometimes it's best to keep your eyes shut.' He squints up at the monkey island. The radar scanner has stopped turning. 'Thank goodness for that. I don't care for being slow-boiled in microwave radiation hour after hour. Deep sea navigators can grow nervous inshore. You'll have heard the story of the P&O liner at Tilbury, sharing the lock with a little coaster?'

'No. Go on.'

'While the lock is filling up, the captain of the great white ship, in his posh doeskin uniform, leans over the bridge wing and peers down onto one of Fred Everard's tiny rust-bucket coasters, many, many yards below, and hails its captain. "I say, old boy, what do you do when you lose sight of land?" The coaster's skipper, in his moth-eaten gansey, bellows back, "When I lose sight of land, I do exactly the same as you do when you CATCH sight of land. I experience a loosening of the bowels!"'

I snort with laughter. 'That's priceless!'

Jim goes on: 'But we do well to stand clear of the Whitby cliffs. See the tall lump of black rock offshore with broken water round its foot?'

'The one just south-east of the abbey? Like a church steeple?'

'That's Saltwick Nab. On the west side of it, where there's a lot of foam, is the wreck of the *Rohilla*, or what's left of her.'

'*Rohilla*. A BI ship?'

'Right. She was a passenger liner built for the British India company. In the first war she became a hospital ship and in 1914 was on her way to France to collect wounded. Blinded by a full onshore gale she was too close in, but didn't know it — the lighthouses were blacked out for the duration. She scraped across a reef off Whitby piers, then struck the Nab full on and broke her back. It took three days to bring off survivors by rocket line and lifeboat. All the nurses were saved. One of the rescued women had survived the Titanic. About eighty others didn't make it.'

We stay quiet for a while until a thought comes. 'A lot of drowned to find on the shore in the morning.'

27

Mahronda

5 August 1959. London Docks.

It's a strange business, this itinerant life of coasting ships around the Irish Sea and North Sea ports, discharging and loading, while the deep-water men take their leave. There's hardly time to get to know shipmates and form the bonds which bind a ship's company as brothers for months in foreign parts. Coast relief fellows travel with light luggage. We hand over our charges to crew who clamber up the gangway with suitcases and kitbags crammed for distant seas. Then, the temporary crew signs off and scurries down the gangway to waiting taxis, clutching their grips.

We sign off *Matra* and dash to London's railway terminals. For me it's King's Cross for two-hundred miles on the mainline express in hope of a few days at home before the next ship. My pale leather holdall is no weight. Embossed with camel and pyramid, I'd bought it off a bum boat in Port Said on my first trip — the vendor claimed it was camel leather and would last a lifetime — so far, it's holding up.

For my first ship, I'd heaved a venerable wooden sea-trunk that might be large enough to double as a life raft should we sink. A concerned dad bought it off an old salt in West Hartlepool. Sea-trunks were the thing in the days of the open fo'c's'le. Now we have homely cabins with drawers for storage of clothes, toothpaste, stationary, Brylcreem and bottle opener, there's no need for a sea-chest.

The trunk was cumbersome to manoeuvre onto buses and London Underground trains. Perhaps it was faithless of me when, half-way down the Red Sea, I chucked it over the side of the troopship *Dunera*. The trunk drifted astern, forlorn and abandoned — undulating on a sea of mazarine. In my fancy, I imagine it gathered a shoal of pretty coral fishes in the shelter beneath, until it washed ashore on the coast of the Sudan to become a beachcomber's prized possession. Even now, it might be the bed space of a couple of sloe-eyed children.

My next ship will be SS *Mahronda*. Hamilton's yard on the Clyde built her in 1947. She's 8,500 tons and a 15 knot steam turbine. This *Mahronda* replaces a vessel of that name lost to a Japanese torpedo off Portuguese East Africa in 1942. She'd carried a perilous cargo of depth charges and fifteen-inch shells, but most of her crew made it ashore in lifeboats. German agents living incognito on the neutral coast of Portuguese Mozambique tracked and reported her to the Japanese navy.

I sign *Mahronda's* articles as 2nd Radio Officer on 12th August 1959, once more at Middlesbrough, just a couple of bus rides from home. Loading might take a week. This could not be better. I'll sleep at home every night, have an early breakfast, then Beryl and I will join the queue of working folk for the red double-decker bus at the draughty bus shelter in Winterbottom Avenue. At West Hartlepool bus station, we'll kiss before she rushes off to her job as a bookkeeper at Pounder's the plumbers and electricians. Then I'll hop onto a bus crammed with chemical and shipyard workers bound for Port Clarence and the Tees Transporter river crossing. Brocklebanks are indeed good to the newly wed.

SS Mahronda

Just downriver of the steel lattices of the Transporter Bridge, *Mahronda* leans against the wharf. The ship fills for foreign parts to the shouts of dockers and the rattle of cranes as she takes on the exports of Middlesbrough. Loads are slung into her echoing holds: iron castings; railway track; girders; rolls of sheet steel. Each day she'll settle deeper into the river, weighed down by general cargo: sacks of fertiliser; bales of Terylene fibre, drums of pesticides and paint, acids, alkalis, dyes — all from the ICI (Imperial Chemical Industries) complex. Battalions of metal chimneys sprout from both sides of the river and pour nose-biting vapours into the air.

In less polluted days, 'Bass' and 'Smokey' Horsley, my mother's uncles, netted salmon off this estuary. Few of the noble fish risk a migration today. They'll struggle to scent their way into the mucky river. Even so, each season, a rare one wins through to leap the sweet cascades of Upper Teesdale in search of a mate. Fifty years will pass before the Tees is clean enough for Beryl and me to watch scores of salmon queue for their turn to leap the weir at Stockton.

This is the industrial giant Gladstone declared *an infant Hercules*. Just a cluster of farms made up Middlesbrough in 1801, but, when Queen Victoria was a lass, Henry Bolckow, an immigrant from Pomerania, paid a visit. With his partner, Vaughan, he gazed across the level pastures and deep river, to hills rich in iron ore, and thought of the seams of coal in nearby Durham. The place was perfect for an iron industry. Today, the products of the Tees smelting works are in every corner of the globe. Welsh ironworkers brought their skills, the Irish and Scots brought their muscle, the hungry of Europe came from the sea. They settled to earn wages, make homes, have families, until they made a bustling town of 160,000. Forgotten now, the ancient wetlands are drained and concreted. Where thousands of bleating wildfowl were netted for the London markets, all was smoke and the thump of steam-hammers.

Mahronda is fresh from Graythorp drydock and gleams with new paint. I push open the teak storm door into the accommodation, and step over the weather combing that keeps out the flood when we ship a steep sea. I lug my gear along an internal alleyway on the port side, past the cabins of engineers and a communal bathroom complete with a stout Servis washing machine. Each berth opens into a weatherproof corridor. Although Brocklebanks trade through the Red Sea, across the Arabian, and into the Bay of Bengal, our ships might spend weeks in Atlantic storms and North Sea gales. True tropical cargo ships, those which rarely come home, such as the *Hughli* (I coasted her three years ago), have cabins which open straight onto the deck to catch any breeze in sweltering climes.

Linoleum covers the alleyway, beige coloured and varnished. By a cross alley, I find my cabin and pull back the dark-blue patterned curtain. The room is rectangular, decked with the same sensible lino. A washbasin with chromed hot and cold taps hangs on the left bulkhead, with a mirrored cabinet over. There's a glass tumbler in a bracket; another bracket holds the usual Brocklebank chilled-water flask in pale cream printed with the company's blue and white flag. Beyond is a dark mahogany wardrobe. To the right, my daybed, covered in blue moquette, with two long drawers beneath. Above the daybed-cum-settee, a porthole of gleaming brass peeps from behind a blue curtain. A desk, with drawers and chair, occupies the forward bulkhead. A bookshelf hangs above. It has a thin rail to keep the books in place. Nearby is a reciprocating fan. I switch it on — it rattles and whirs and pans from side to side as is standard. I sometimes wonder about those carbon brushes grinding away at the commutator and how much black dust we ingest at night. But, compared to those chaps who sweat in the oil mist of the engine room, we deck officers breathe pure sea air — when not up the Ganges.

Ventilation trunking above the door feeds adjustable nozzles intended to keep the air moving with whatever flow of warm or cool the engine room might send. The inner bulkhead holds my bunk; deep, long drawers beneath, and a wooden partition at the foot to give privacy from the doorway. A raised wooden edge keeps the sleeper in place in wild weather. Behind the fiddly board is a long bolster to hold one snug when the ship moves with violence. The bolster makes a comfort known to sailors as the *Dutch Wife;* she speaks not, but keeps you in place.

The distress bell is prominent just above where my head will lie. I bring to mind those pulses of roaring static in the Red Sea. Sometimes, they can resemble the four-second dashes of the distress signal closely enough to set off the auto-alarm and break my sleep. To make it less shrill, it's best to wrap a sock around the bell. This is my home for at least the next five months. It will do well enough — I've seen worse, and I've not spotted a cockroach so far. The Indian steward who looks after us must be conscientious — every bit of woodwork glows with polish. I dump my bags, and lock the door — it's time to make myself known.

The mates' cabins are above, also the wireless room, so at least this cabin won't roast overmuch in equatorial parts. Next to mine is that of my boss. His name is John Dee, but I've yet to meet him. Beyond my chief's locked cabin is the officer's smoke room, with ping-pong table, dartboard and easy chairs. I spot a crate on the deck. It's marked *Missions to Seamen* and is the ship's library. My boss will be in nominal charge of it, but I expect to be delegated librarian.

Glazed doors separate the smoke room from the saloon. They'll slide open to make a bigger space for betting on the *Calcutta Races* when little wooden horses and jockeys race round a track spurred on by a pair of huge dice thrown from a bucket. The Purser/Chief Steward will supervise, keep order, and hold stakes. It's much looked forward to and helps while away the months. Ale will be swilled and there'll be uproar.

I discover the 1st Radio Officer in the wireless room. My boss looks to be forty, average height, a roundish face, and going thin on top. He peers at me over horn-rimmed specs, then grasps my hand.

'Welcome aboard, Harry. I'm John. I've been expecting you.' He glances at the bulkhead clock. 'A bit early for coffee, and you'll not want to crack a can before eleven?' I get a quizzical look. 'You're coming deep sea with us, right? And you've got the MOT radar ticket, I'm told. What did you train on?'

'At South Shields, we had the 268 wartime radar, a grey grumbling monster. Canadian Marconi built. It had queer devices I've not seen since. A quaint wheel-turned carbon pile voltage control, a row of gas-filled iron-wire barretters for current control. It was a right palaver to tune up.'

'You'll not find any such archaic stuff on this lady. But it's what I like to hear — a sound background on difficult gear. You did two trips on the new *Mawana* with Don Butterworth, so you'll be familiar with the BTH radar.'

'I am. It was hardly any trouble.'

'*Mahronda* is twelve-year-old and into middle age. The radar is post-war Marconi. It works, but needs a careful nurse.'

The door opens to the clank of a crane and the lilt of Bengali. 'Sahib, coffee time.' He's lean and elderly, with a close-cropped white beard. He sets a tray on the work bench and points a long finger at a parcel of sandwiches wrapped in a paper napkin decorated with our house flag, 'Tabnab come, she sardine, Sahib. I *dekko* (see) *chota* (little) Marconi sahib come, so I bring for two men.'

John's eyes twinkle at the steward. '*Atchaa* (good), Hamid. Thanks.' He nods at me. '*Chota* Marconi come Calcutta with us. He good man, so must have good steward. His beer must always be *boht tunda* (very cold).'

The Indian grins and wags his head sideways twice. '*Atchaa*, Sahib. Hamid, best cabin boy on ship.' He wags his head again, and leaves.

John lifts his coffee. 'Hamid's a great steward — never any cheek. This might be his last trip. As you, a denizen of County Durham, might put it, he's a *canny auld lad*. Now then, let's have this tabnab before I show you round the gear.'

28

Pickled Egg

31 Aug 1959.

The miscellaneous cargo is slow to arrive and *Mahronda* takes seven days to load at Middlesbrough; I sleep at home every night and have no complaints. Beryl sometimes visits the ship to join us in the saloon for dinner. One evening, the ship is alive with local girls. Who organised the party, and where he found a dozen pretty women, I never discover. Beryl knows one of the young ladies.

Meanwhile, John and I, with little to do, have to search for work around the radio station. We remove casings and peer inside. With a paintbrush, the innards of transmitters and receivers are freed of felted dust and the husks of shrivelled cockroaches. Components get a suspicious eye — wherever a rolled paper capacitor appears a touch swollen, we solder in a new one; they can leak, grow fat, then exude wax before they die and take a few neighbours with them. Critical valve currents of the radar are recorded and watched for decline. Waveguides have their joints tightened. John has me scrape paint off the insulators of the Bellini-Tosi direction finder loops wherever the Indian deck crew has plastered them with lead paint — Bengalis will slap it on anything that does not wriggle. As junior, it is my job to bring a shine to the porthole brass, cupboard doors, and anything else that looks dull. This is all to the good, for before we sail, we expect a visit from a General Post Office surveyor of marine radio stations. If he finds fault, he can stop us from putting to sea. We go through the spares yet again, counting valves and components, laying them out in neat rows like toy soldiers. Do we have the correct tools: the regulation screwdrivers, pliers, tin-smith's snips, soldering iron complete with spare bit, solder, and a two-pound ball-pein hammer?

'Hey, John, this ball-pein hammer. I've often wondered why we need to carry one?'

'You might well ask, Harry, old son. I imagine some long-forgotten operator, in the days of spark transmitters, got a nasty burn around the groin that brought on a testicular malaise, such that his Morse became erratic and a ball-pein hammer was the only cure.'

I heft the hammer. It has a flat face on one side and a domed, egg-shaped face on the reverse. It looks unblemished. 'The engine-room uses these for knocking out dents and freeing-up stuck valves. I suppose we might have to do a bit of panel beating and riveting.'

'Have you never met the giant cockroach of myth and legend? The ball-pein hammer comes in handy whenever you encounter a monster Bombay Tiger who wants to fight.' He croons a ditty: 'It's in the evening, after dark, when the Bombay Tiger runs berserk. With his hairy legs and his greasy dirt, here comes the Bombay tiger.' He opens and inspects the essential tin of petroleum jelly. 'Now then, this tin of grease is incomplete, and it's speckled with grit from the last mucky devil who coated it on the battery terminals. The surveyor could fail the station if he opens this. You'd best nip ashore to a chemist and buy a two-ounce tin of Vaseline.' He looks at the clock on the bulkhead. 'They're open. I'll come with you. We can have a swift pint before lunch.'

On a corner, beyond the railway bridge, is Winterschladen, the wine importer. I'll buy Beryl and Mam a present. They rarely see the inside of a bar; North-eastern public houses are not places for decent women.

It's an ornate building, with pointed arched windows like a Norman abbey, but crusted with sixty-five years of industrial grime. A bell tinkles as we push open the ornate Victorian door. Behind the counter there's a plump man with slicked-down hair, in suit and tie. He looks up from a ledger. He reminds me of Jenkyn, the butler on the Kensitas cigarette packet.

'Good morning, sirs. How may I help?'

I lean on the handsome mahogany counter. 'A half-bottle of Benedictine liqueur and two bottles of Babycham, please.'

'Certainly, sir. Happy to oblige.'

While the man wraps the bottles and lowers them into a stout brown-paper carrier bag, we admire the shop fittings. There are gleaming cabinets, embossed and chamfered glass and, on a top shelf, a row of rare whiskies I've never heard of.

John seems intrigued at finding such a place in Middlesbrough. 'This must be the most sumptuous off-licence I've ever been in. The name ,Winterschladen, has a foreign ring to it.'

'Indeed it does, sir. Our founder was born in Cologne in 1842. Herr Winterschladen, a successful wine importer, settled in Middlesbrough and opened this business in 1885. His full name was Henry Joseph Balthasar Hubert Winterschladen.'

John whistles. 'Just as well he didn't start up a shipping company. Can you imagine a coal boat out of the Tyne — the SS *Henry Joseph Balthasar Hubert Winterschladen*?'

The man frowns. 'I am quite unable to, sir.' He passes me the carrier bag. 'Your liqueur and two bottles of perry. That will be five-shillings-and-sixpence, sir.'

I fish out my tired wallet and pass over a red, equally tired, ten-shilling note. The drawer of the ornate black and gold till slides out with a chime, and I receive two florins and a sixpence in change. 'Thanks. We now need to locate a chemist.'

John adds: 'And we crave your advice as to which public house is noted for the quality of its ales at present.'

'You'll find a chemist in the square, and along Corporation Road is the Lord Raglan. I'm informed he keeps a clean cellar.'

We don't venture as far as the Lord Raglan, but end up in a pub close to the Transporter, along the cracked pavements of Durham Street. There's a pleasant smell from the thin layer of fresh sawdust on the floor. I assume it's there to soak up spillage, unless it's what's left of last night's furniture. The customers wear lived-in cloth caps. The house serves potent Cameron's bitter, and bags of potato crisps. On a shelf, by a half-empty bottle of cheap port, stands a two-pound jam jar of pickled eggs in malt vinegar. Some are at the bottom, others float mid-way, and one has risen to the surface as if in an attempt to escape. Through the brown fluid gloom, the peeled eggs stare at us like the vacant eyes of dead dogs.

John buys the beer. We watch the capable hands draw the pump handle of the beer engine until the sleever glasses are brim-full and topped by a handsome head. 'And two packets of crisps, landlord, if you please.' He turns to me. 'Unless you'd prefer a pickled egg? They look interesting.'

The landlord carries massive shoulders and a robust face. He has the look of a steelworker. The blue pits in his cheeks might be the gift of the blast furnace. 'Made by the wife's mother, they are. They wash down well with a pint. Fourpence apiece, same as a bag of crisps.'

I look into the forlorn eyes of the dogs. 'I'll stick with the crisps. No disrespect to your mother-in-law, but just in case it's curried eggs for lunch on the ship.'

John squares his shoulders. 'I'm tempted.'

At a corner table, in a veil of pipe smoke, and to the clack of dominoes, John sips the cream off his pint. 'This is to be taken gently, methinks. There's a bite to it. Cameron's is brewed in your town — is that right?'

'Next door to Stranton church in West Hartlepool. There's a pong of malted barley all along Stockton Street.

That beer made Colonel Cameron enough money for his family to build the town a hospital as his memorial.'

John nods. 'It's said that beer drinkers keep the gentry in fine wine.'

He lifts the pickled egg from its saucer, the glaze crazed by time, and bites the egg in half. While he chews, he inspects the remaining half. The white is the colour of an old man's eye, and the dark orange yolk sports a rim of grey. He masticates, and that's the best word for it, the other half.

'How's the egg, John?'

He's still chewing. His Adam's apple swivels as he gulps and swallows. After a long pull on his beer, he removes his specs to wipe a drop of moisture from one eye. 'A bit like chewing on a whelk. Like with a whelk, it's best to forget what it is, and just get it down. Let's have a couple of your crisps to kill the memory.'

I open the bag, root around for the tiny blue twist of waxed paper that holds the salt, toss in the salt, shake it up, and offer the potato crisps to John. With two fingers, he extracts a third of the contents.

'What ship you gaffers off, like?' It's one of the domino players on the next table. He's scraping the bowl of his pipe. I wait until he's knocked out the dottle into the big pot ashtray marked 'Bass'.

'*Mahronda*. She's under the cranes up the road.' The watery eyes turn to their pals. 'There you are. Didn't I tell ya? It's the way they walk.'

John snorts. 'We'll have to watch that. I was hoping to come across as a doctor of medicine.'

The old chap lifts a stumpy finger. 'Even a quack wouldn't take a chance on one of yon's pickled eggs. Ship's officers, Ah'll bet. Navy-blue bridge coats wi'out a mark on 'em. Dead give away. Me and me mates were deckies on colliers in the hard times.' He lifts his buttoned-down cloth cap to scratch his head. It reveals the ridge left by the front of the cap — my father had the same across his forehead.

'During the war?' I ask.

'Coal from Shields, Sunderland, Seaham Harbour, then down to the Thames power stations. In sight of land all the way. Rock-dodging, we called it. But it chewed at the nerves. Mostly, I was with Stevie Clarke's. Walter here, was with Cory's. Up and down we went, day in, day out, in convoy. Mines, bombs, torpedoes, U-boats, E-boats, bloody Stukas. They chucked everything at us. But we kept going. Kept London warm.'

Somewhere in the distance a hooter sounds, and then another. 'There she blows,' the old chap says. 'Any minute now and they'll be pouring in here.' He opens a square tin of Ogden's Walnut Flake, rubs half a slice between his palms, loads his pipe, tamps it down, then strikes a Swan Vesta. The baccy comes alive. A beam of rare sun from the window brightens the billow of smoke; it becomes a shade of light lavender, the colour of the lustrous fur of the Blue Beveren rabbits my father used to breed. I do miss him.

29

Malta

27 August, 1959

Mahronda slips out of the Tees to head east across the North Sea and into the navigation waters of South Holland. She spends a few hours in Rotterdam (the dam by the river Rotte) to load crates of Mercedes Benz engines for the newly rich of lands served by ox-carts and donkeys.

We cannot know that eleven years on, our ship will end her career in this port. In 1968, our owners will sell her for £110,000 to a Cypriot shipowner who will name her SS *Lucky*. The new owner's optimism is crushed when she's severely damaged in 1970 by fire. A few months later, she'll be towed to Yugoslavia to be dismembered by the Croatian ship-breakers of Split. Months before I joined her, *Mahronda* had a narrow escape. In February, she collided off Lowestoft with a ship one seventh her size. She was merely bruised, but she holed the MV *Sleaford* below the waterline and the little coaster had to be tugged in haste to drydock.

With no time to stretch our legs in Rotterdam, we are off again. London is next. Then, after a week loading a cornucopia of small goods in the Thames, on 8th September, it's deep-sea for us. We are bound for Calcutta, with stops along the way.

All goes well until the 13th of September. The Mediterranean has been sparkling, with none of the nastiness that can brew-up in the Gulf of Lyons and charge south to hammer this shipping lane. As we pass ancient Carthage, our bow wave shrinks and the rhythmic thump of the propeller slows. The chief engineer and Captain Ross huddle in conference. A forced-draught fan has squealed, screeched, stopped, and no longer feeds its boiler with pressurised air. The engineers dismantled the fan and discovered the shattered remains of a long-handled sweeping brush. There's damage to the commutator and other moving parts. Our engine, built by D Rowan of Glasgow, has twin steam-turbines geared to a single shaft. The loss of one forced-draught fan reduces the ship to half power. Who left the broom inside the giant fan? It is not the sort we carry, so the culprit is assumed to be some feckless labourer in Graythorp drydock.

Until now, we've kept our position in a strung-out cavalcade of vessels bound for the Suez Canal. Since the Straits of Gibraltar, miles of eastbound ships have been our wireless companions. Ships flying the Red Ensign: Stricks, Ellermans, Bibby — and sundry foreigners: Swedes, Finns, Danes, West Germans — our Morse chatter formed us into a straggling family. Now, an empty oil tanker, bound for the Persian Gulf, ploughs past. A rust-streaked Liberian draws close and overtakes. An old coal-burning tramp, flying an illegible tattered ensign, overhauls as we plod at seven knots towards Malta and repairs. 'Need assistance?' they ask. We are embarrassed.

It's my first visit. I'm keen to see the island that was awarded the George Cross. King George VI gave it for the population's courage under siege by the bombers of Hitler and Mussolini. For two years, while ancient Malta was pulverised, and the inhabitants survived in tunnels and caves, the islands did not break. One after another, supply convoys were massacred in the Mediterranean by torpedo and bomb. The fuel tanks of the RAF defending Malta were almost dry when the loaded *Ohio,* of a mere 11,000 tons, then the largest tanker afloat, wallowed broken-backed towards port with half her crew dead. As the sea washed across her decks, a Royal Navy destroyer on either side held her above water with cables stretched beneath her keel. On the Feast of Santa Maria, with a shot-down Junkers 88 on her foredeck, a Junkers 87 complete with unexploded bomb, in her starboard side, and a torpedoed stern, in she came. She passed beneath the bastions of Valetta's Grand Harbour to a welcome from cheering crowds and a brass band. Once safe within, the two destroyers held her as the weary keel touched ground. There she took her last sleep while her cargo of vital aviation fuel for hurricanes and spitfires, and diesel for Malta's fleet, was pumped out.

Ohio supported by destroyers.

Ohio enters Valetta with support.

The Cornish poet Charles Causley knew this place from his time in the Royal Navy during WW2. He writes of how clear is the water. And how, by leaning over the side of his warship, he saw wrecks, and tins, and tiny explosions of fish. He tells how he returns from Malta more brown than Alexander. And indeed, though the wrecks have gone, the water in the harbour is clear enough for us to watch sparkles of little fish among the beer bottles and tin cans.

Mahronda moors between two buoys. In a lowering sun, the giant limestone ramparts of Grand Harbour flush with pink. The stones are pock-marked by bomb blast and shrapnel. Some damage might be from the cannons of Napoleon, or the Ottoman Turks, but most is from Fascist bombers as they reduced Valetta to rubble.

Those of us off duty are already spruced-up to go ashore. Three of us loiter by the gangway, waving to the jetty in hope of a water taxi.

Our 3rd engineer, Brian Buckle from Hull, slaps Stan, the 5th, on the back (he's from Formby). 'Hey up! They've seen us. Here comes a *luzza*.'

Stan shades his eyes and peers into the evening glow. 'What's a luzza when it's at home?'

Brian hoots, and I see the gap in his front teeth. 'What's a luzza? There you are, Sparks. Once again, we Yorkshiremen must educate the Lancastrian.'

Stan digs a squashed packet of Senior Service from his top pocket and pulls one out. 'And a fat lot you know, Brian, me bucko. Harry's no Yorkshireman — he's from County Durham. And anyway, he reckons Yorkshiremen are bugger-all but Scotsmen bereft of generosity.'

Brian squints at me. He has a turn in his eye, so I'm never sure who he's looking at. 'You traitor! You stood with us in the Wars of the Roses — some of the time, anyway. White agin red it were. If yer forebears were alive today, they'd be spinning in their graves.' He spins the wheel of his Zippo and lights Stan's cigarette. 'Now then, you of indifferent schooling, a luzza is a carvel-built Maltese craft of ancient days. Here she comes. See that high bow and stern? She'd put any gondolier to shame.'

The craft is vivid. A bright blue hull with yellow and red bands, and two staring eyes painted on her bows. 'What's the eyes for?'

'To see off evil. The eyes of Osiris. Goes back to the Phoenicians, they say.'

The luzza noses up to the foot of the gangway. She's lovely, though her diesel engine smokes a bit. The rotund and swarthy boatman, adorned with splendid moustache, cranes his neck. 'You want for go shore-side?'

We waste no time clambering into the boat. It rocks and sways as Brian sits astride a bench — he's a hefty man. I'm still thinking about Phoenicians. 'The eyes of Osiris, you reckon? I thought Malta was Roman Catholic.'

Stan flicks his cigarette end into the water. 'We're a broad church, so we are. If them creepy eyes scare off Satan, the Holy Father will likely make that Osiris geezer into a saint.'

Brian offers the boatman a Pall Mall. 'Not much in port today. How's business?'

The boatman wedges the cigarette behind his ear for later. 'No Good! Navy gone to sea for Cyprus exercise. Business bad till ships come back.'

Our 3rd engineer slaps the gunwale. 'Then we'll have a few up *The Gut*. It's a den of iniquity, but it'll be nice and quiet for a change. We'll have no aggravation from half-cut matelots. In one bar, there's a bloke dressed up as Carmen Miranda. Hat loaded with fruit. The works. He packs the place to the rafters.'

First stop is a pavement table in the elegance of St George's Square. The waiter plonks three empty glasses and three bottles of Simonds 'Hopleaf' pale ale onto our table. I pay with a ten-bob note and receive a mix of British coins in change. Stan's eyes are everywhere as raven-haired girls promenade with their families. Many women could be from any fashionable British street, but a few are tripping along with heads enveloped in elegant mantillas that only tempt our stares. Is the face that peeps from those rustling folds, pretty or plain? Whatever they look like, the frequent glimpse of a coquettish dark eye can raise the pulse. Street urchins hover around our table, their eyes like burning sloes. Deep in conversation or scurrying past is the occasional black-robed priest in wide-brimmed hat.

Brian drains his glass. 'Sailormen know Malta as *The Place of Three Ps*': Pubs, Priests, and Prostitutes. Right! Sup up! Let's get you two droolers to The Gut to meet Carmen Miranda.' He waltzes down the street singing: *I, yi, yi, yi, yi, I like you very much...*'

Stan and I trail behind as he strides by expensive shops, turns corner after corner, and stops by a narrow lane about ten feet wide that seems endless until dim-lit doors fade into twilight. 'Here it is, lads. Try to keep out of mischief.'

I loiter to read a rusted metal sign bolted to a tenement wall. It says, *Strada Stretta — Strait Street*. Brian stops his striding rush. 'That's right, Harry. Very long and very thin, that's why it's called The Gut — even though there's not a wiggle in it. Follow me. I know the best spots.'

It's a canyon of patched and decayed limestone buildings five stories tall, festooned with balconies. Behind the tempting neons, the bars, clubs, and tiny dance halls are dimly lit and forlorn, with just a couple of patrons here and there, shadowy figures at gloomy tables, and no sign of Carmen Miranda. The narrow lane undulates for 500 yards. Almost at the end is a bar on the left. Brian dives in. 'Come on, then. This was a great joint last time I was here.'

The only customers are three mature women at one table. Like the flash of a lighthouse beam, their gaze sweeps on us as we order a round. We've hardly got the froth of our beer before they're at our table.

'It's so quiet tonight. You boys won't mind us joining you.' They ease matronly thighs, in flowered skirts, under the table.

Stan is an affable fellow after a couple of ales. 'That's fine, ladies. I'm Stan. What'll you have?'

There are homely smiles. 'Port and lemon is our favourite. Thank you, sailor. I'm Ruby, and this is Margot and Mila.'

Brian swallows half his beer. 'I'm Brian, and I'm sorry to say that I'm already spoken for, as are my two splendid shipmates here.'

Ruby puts a bejewelled hand on Brian's. 'Your sweethearts are very lucky girls. Never mind though, we might retire soon, anyway. We three did our best to ease the troubles of those brave boys who flew the spitfires, you know.'

I nod. 'It all helped. You should have been given a medal for your service.'

'We did get a medal, my dear. We got the George Cross.'

Brian is keen to show us another 'lively spot'. After more gentle banter while the bored barman polishes glasses, we leave the ladies to their port and lemons.

Even though they play Jazz and Swing on a record player, the Blue Peter and the New York bars are subdued. The Union Jack bar shows more promise. Three of our shipmates are already at a table. Otherwise, it's empty apart from a cluster of morose Norwegians quietly sinking beer while listening to a Maltese knock out a thin tune on an upright piano.

Our fellows: Two apprentices and Chips the carpenter are pleased to see us. They've had a few and soon have us singing.

Stan leads with *Maggie May*, then I have a go at *Cushy Butterfield*, followed by the *Lambton Worm*. Brian does Harry Belafonte's *Banana Boat Song*. Chips follows with *Brown Skin Girl*. The pianist picks out chords as best he can, and the Norwegians thump their table and call for more. At one point, we must stay quiet while they drone out a morose Norwegian whaling song. The beer keeps coming, and I begin to worry about the bill.

We'd been dimly aware of customers drifting in from the quiet street, attracted by the noise. Now, every table is taken. Americans, Dutch, Chinese, all sorts. More squeeze in. Men lean against the bar and join in the singing. It must be an Italian who keeps shouting out, 'Bravissimo.'

The barman plonks down another tray of Maltese beer. 'On the house! While you sing, the beer is free.'

It goes on till late.

We sway, rattle, and clip-clop back to the docks, content with life, in a pair of horse-drawn gharries.

30

Equator

The voyage is brisk once more. Four days out of Malta, with the Suez Canal transit complete, we steam down the roasting Red Sea.

It's a one day stop at Jeddah, half-way along the sun-baked Saudi Arabian coast. Time enough to offload a few hundred tons of Tate and Lyle granulated sugar and carefully counted crates of Royal Mint 1957 British sovereigns. Those glorious gold coins are craved by the Saudis. The bullion is lugged ashore in strong-boxes under armed guard.

Jeddah is unpopular with sailors. It's my second visit and I've still not ventured through the dock gate. In the country of the Prophet, evil alcohol must be locked away. Guards peep through portholes to check if we keep the law.

---

23 September 1959. *Mahronda* leaves Jeddah.

Three more days of the Red Sea before we escape through the sun-tortured rocks of the Bab el Mandeb (the Gates of Weeping), the old slave route from Africa to Arabia. Then, a day into the Gulf of Aden, and we are alongside in the colonial port of Djibouti on the Horn of Africa. We have but one day in French Somaliland, unloading fancy goods and Dutch machine tools. This strolling itinerary reminds me of grocery-boy days when I packed and unpacked shelves on the Co-op mobile shop while swaying around the country lanes of Durham.

In Djibouti, there's just enough time for a quiet hour in the shade of palms; to lounge in the plaza, sample chilled local beer, admire the architecture, listen to French, Arabic, and snatches of Afar, and watch a game of chess played with giant pieces. Only six months ago, I sat in this same spot, sipped fabulous Mocha coffee while fierce soldiers of the French Foreign Legion played chess. The coffee here has no kinship with the bittersweet mud served on the ship.

'Kilroy was here' announces his ego from the wall of a French urinal, as it did in April. Where hasn't he been, that man? I've seen 'Kilroy was here' and 'Kilroy woz ere' scrawled on lavatory walls in Galveston, Cardiff, Bremerhaven, Tilbury, draughty bus shelters in Hartlepool, dockside cranes in Birkenhead — he gets everywhere. Who is the fellow?

Then comes a day's jaunt across the Gulf of Aden to discharge stores for the British Army, and load bunker oil for the extended voyage to Bengal; extended because we must now turn south for six days across an empty ocean for the island of Gan, thirty miles below the Equator.

We are hardly free of the cliffs of the drowned volcano that is Aden's harbour when Captain Ross enters the wireless room.

'Any contact with Gan yet, Sparky?'

'No, sir. We've tried since Djibouti. RAF Gan has plenty of power for military use, but there's not much clout on the rig dedicated to us. It's only a mobile lash-up in the back of a truck. He's supposed to call and listen out for merchant ships at scheduled times. But nothing yet. The static's bad hereabouts.'

'Keep trying, lad. I want to know the pilotage and what moorings to expect. While you're at it, find out what other vessels are there.' The captain glances around, eyeing up the transmitters, the copper and brass fittings, the ship's cat snoozing on top of the main receiver. 'Tiddles likes it in here, does she?'

'Seems to, sir. She used to shoot off when I wound up the motor-alternator, but it's become her second home this past week.'

'Ah well. They've a queer old life, do ship's cats.' He scrapes out his pipe dottle into our ashtray and wanders back to the wheelhouse.

Next day, at the scheduled time, I tune the receiver to what I hope is Gan's frequency of 5695.5 kc/s, and listen. There's nothing. I rock the tuning from side to side, through splatters of coded traffic, and strangled wails from goodness knows where.

Our main transmitter is a Siemens SB186X. She'll soon be antique (there's talk of changing her for the latest IMR), so we treat her as a fiend with an evil bite. It's a capacious grey box with three conical insulators on top. Inside is an array of simple electronics: a transformer, a bunch of chunky resistors and condensers, a Westinghouse rectifier, seven barretter stabilisers and one stabilovolt tube that feed the three valves: two minor pentodes and a massive pentode power tube, all complete with top-cap anode connectors. In the North Atlantic, the cockroaches come to warm their toes around that power pentode. The front carries four graduated brass knobs, one in each corner, and a vertical row of four meters to show transmitter voltage and current. One instrument is a thermocouple ammeter in series with the aerial, it has our full attention. We tune the beast by sliding a metal coupling rod through the front of the cabinet. The bar moves across the turns of a big air-spaced coil, altering its inductance. That, together with adjusting the aerial tuning capacitor to locate a dip in the anode current on the ammeter, brings the aerial circuit into resonance. Tuning for best output is done with the key held down, but woe-betide if you still hold that sliding rod, it stings like a scorpion and zaps with a radio-frequency burn. Dip the current, slide the rod in and out, and repeat until you find optimum.

Someone's had the bright idea of fitting a large neon bulb to the bulkhead by the aerial buss-bars. The Neon gas glows when the transmitter is powered, and a strange pinkish-violet flame licks the inside of the glass bulb. The excited neon gas flicks and dances as we key out Morse. It's handy for tuning the SB186X — hold the key down and tune for 'maximum smoke and flame', as they say.

I start the inductor alternator in stages and watch the voltage rise. The grey cat stirs and stretches. The gear tunes up on the 4mc/s band. I key out:

MEX MEX MEX de GDNB GDNB GDNB MAHRONDA QRD GAN FM ADEN QTC1 K (Royal Air Force Gan Island from *Mahronda* bound Gan from Aden. I have one message for you. Over).

As the signal races to the aerial strung between our masts, Tiddles reaches up and dabs at the neon bulb with her paw. It's her favourite game. She's determined to catch that dancing light one of these days.

Siemens SB186X main transmitter.

GDNB is a sweet call sign that lends a lovely rhythm to the sending wrist, as well as to the ear (dah dah dit - dah dit dit - dah dit - dah dit dit dit). I enjoy the feel. It looks splendid, pulsing on the neon. I call a few more times. There's no response. Now for a re-tune to 500kc/s, the international calling frequency. Out goes the call again, and again, with Tiddles dabbing furiously throughout. Apart from faint chirrups from distant ships, I hear nothing amongst the background hiss. The course we steer is through a lonely stretch of the Indian Ocean. I'll try again tomorrow, when we are 300 miles nearer the atoll. The radio watch proceeds in a hum-drum way, apart from the Portishead traffic list (nothing for us) and a Brocklebank fleet schedule where we keep in touch with our sisters. Two are trudging the Bay of Bengal, and another has just entered Suez bound for the States.

In a spotless white tunic, except for a scatter of dhobi rust stains, Hamid enters with sandwiches and the evening cup of tea. The napkin-wrapped sandwiches are for later, when I'll yawn my way on watch in the small hours of the morning.

'What's in them tonight, Hamid? No cockroach, I hope. Two lots of feelers waved at me from the folds of the napkin last night. It put me off the sardines.'

'Ah, Sahib, not Hamid mishtake. Plenty cockroach in galley. She come after sandwich put in napkin.'

'Maybe put dish over sandwich, Hamid. Keep cockroach out.'

'Atchaa, Sahib. I tell cook. Tonight special sandwich. Pilchard from tin. Sahib like pilchard fishy?'

'I do. But best to watch out for bones.'

Hamid waggles his lean, grizzled head. 'No bones, Sahib. I take out. Cat like pilchard for tiffin.'

We have six days of steaming through the dying days of the South-West Monsoon. With the sun climbing ever higher as we approach the Equator, noon temperatures hover around 85F, and drop by only ten degrees at night. Even the sea temperature is 85F. Night and day become of equal length. Daybreak and nightfall in these low latitudes are sudden, without the drawn-out pink dawns and magical slow dusks of home. Though we sweat, it does little to make us cool; there's poor evaporation in this moisture-laden wind. The sun beats down, interspersed by bank after bank of dark cloud marching up from desolate parts of the Indian Ocean. Every ten seconds, a long swell meets us broad on the starboard bow and she lifts, rolls, and twists to port. Every ten seconds, the helmsman must compensate to hold course south. Rainstorms pulse across, followed by searing overhead sun that makes our decks steam.

As we are still heavy laden, the ship sometimes rolls deep enough to take a surge of water across her deck, and with it come the flying fish. On fin-wings, they skim along the troughs or launch from the peaks of the swell to escape swordfish and marlin. The silvery shapes glide like javelins for a hundred yards and more, flicking the sea with their tails to keep going. A few flop onto our decks where they struggle and gasp. They're attracted to lights and land on the ship at night. In the morning, our Asian sailors search the decks and gather up the expired creatures in buckets. They make a fine fried breakfast, though the bones are sharp.

At the whim of the marching monsoon clouds, the nights can be rain sodden, or else glorious, as we rock beneath the spangled Milky Way. On this crystal-clear night, the barest sliver of the new Moon hangs like a brooch pinned to Heaven's sable cloak.

Radio wave propagation improves at night, and so our first contact with RAF Gan comes late one evening. Now that we have him, we can ask the operator to send a series of long dashes for a D/F bearing. John leaps to the Bellini-Tosi direction finder, locates the signal from MEX, rocks the goniometer dial from side to side until the signal is null, and takes a bearing relative to ship's head. He takes three bearings through static before he calculates the average, then plots and corrects it against our calibration chart. The bridge officers welcome the figure with huge satisfaction, and compliment us. Our D/F bearings always meet with praise when they confirm the chartroom's navigation by sextant or dead-reckoning. In foul weather, when days pass without a sextant sight of sun or stars, there can be tension when the radio room disagrees with the bridge. But, today we are happily on course for Addu Atoll, a speck on the chart of the vast Indian Ocean. A ship of our fleet once missed it and wasted sea-miles before they realised the error and turned back. Gan is just one of a ring of coral islands that make up Addu atoll, the southernmost of the Maldive Islands, a 600-mile double chain of atolls with an altitude of a mere few feet above sea-level, and easily missed in steep swell by our radar at its extreme range of forty miles.

6th Oct. 1959.

The seabed here is one-and-a-half miles below our keel; enough depth to drown Ben Nevis twice over, and if the Eiffel Tower were added, its viewing platform might just break surface. It's an awful abyss, unnerving to contemplate. I find it best not to think about it, but in years to come, I'll write:

Looking Over the Side
Sometimes, when you lean,
beer in hand against the bulwarks,
you might contemplate the abyssal plain
two dreadful miles beneath the keel.

An iron-stained, rivet-strewn
floor of ooze where, across a scatter
of bunker coal, archaic crabs walk
like prima ballerinas on points,
picking over the crumbs of sailors.

Here, an anchor flaking rust,
there, a brass-bound port
that looks, wall-eyed, at an upturned hull.
A tramp with all her ghosts attending,

*who wait, together with the giant worm,
decked overall in ruffs of bridal voile,
asleep within the chain locker;
anticipating down these busy years
that you will someday come to bed.*

Sixty million years ago, when India collided with Asia, a bit before Abraham moved his tents, this abyss sprouted a vast mountain range of volcanoes which broke surface to belch above the ocean for a million years or so. After an epoch, they sighed their last and, by increments, sank. As they subsided, coral colonised the sea-washed calderas and built a series of precarious atolls. Ancient seafarers found them and stayed because of the fishing and the peace. Thus we have the Maldives, a five-hundred mile chain of atolls that peep above sea level.

Coconut palms grow taller as we make what we hope is the right approach. *Mahronda* slows to a crawl; the echo-sounder works overtime in the wheelhouse — reefs haunt these parts. If we have it right, we should soon see buoys that mark the channel into the lagoon.

A sparkling RAF launch zips from behind a wooded sand-spit and soon circles us.

The smart officer in spotless ironed whites, lifts a loud hailer. 'You are welcome, sir. We trust you've brought the beer! Follow me into the moorings. We have launches waiting to make you fast.'

We creep behind the launch through a gap in the reef, and into a vast lagoon. There's only one other ship, a Royal Navy frigate. Along with military paraphernalia, we have good things for the NAAFI stores (the Navy Army Air Force Institute). But mostly we bring bagged cement for Costains. That construction company has the contract to build the new British base and airfield on this coral island. We'll be out of here in two days. Enough time for a leg-stretch along the white shore beneath the palms, and a swim behind the shark nets.

Britain has leased the coral outcrop from the Sultan of the Maldive Islands, whose fief has been a British Protectorate since the 19th century. Before Britain became dominant in these waters, the French, Dutch, and Portuguese had their own sessions at controlling local affairs.

Maldivian politics have not moved on since I was here in April. In January, these islands at the very south of the archipelago declared independence from the Sultan in the north. They still defy the capital and the Sultan's government, and declare themselves *The Suvadive Republic*. They agitate for the rent the British Government pays for the lease of Gan Island, to not go to the Sultan, but be paid instead to them. It's a tricky situation in which our military tries not to take sides, but the Royal Navy does what it can to disrupt armed raiding parties the Sultan sends this way.

31

Tuticorin

9th Oct. 1959

The last hint of Gan Island sinks below the rim of the sea. *Mahronda* steers north-by-east on a two-day course for the Laccadive Sea — a fragment of the immense Indian Ocean. Tracked by a squadron of scattered white cumulus, we head for the Gulf of Manaar, a triangle cradled between the southern tip of India and North-East Ceylon. We have cargo for Tuticorin. Anciently known as the City of Pearls, 'Tuti' is one of those trading towns that, since Vasco da Gama adventured this way in 1498, has shuffled ownership from Portugal, to France, to Britain, and back to India.

In the lee of the Maldive Islands we have some shelter from the thrust of a South-West Monsoon that weakens by the day. The ship rides a swell that lifts her stern and sweeps along the port side. There's a steady motion — nothing unpleasant, but you can't leave a mug of tea unattended. I'm loitering in the chartroom, in the first hour of the afternoon 4-to-8 watch, leafing through a volume of *Admiralty Sailing Directions* concerned with the Indian Coast. The description of the Gulf of Manaar is spiced with nuggets. There's a bit about Adam's Bridge and how it closes off the head of the gulf.

The 1st mate/chief officer lays parallel rulers across a chart. 'You find those books interesting, do you, Sparks? You'll have your work cut out if you want to read the lot.

It takes seventy volumes to cover the whole globe. Maybe you're in the wrong job.'

I'm in awe of the chief officer, a big bluff man who, but for waiting on 'dead men's shoes', might have his own command. His beard gives him the look of King George V. I assume nonchalance and turn a page. 'I've enough to be going on with, thanks, Arthur. Though I do find charts fascinating. Have you one that shows Adam's Bridge?'

The top chart is slid aside to uncover another. 'A lot of the Gulf is hardly above three fathoms, so it needs care.' He plants a thick finger on a string of islands and shoals that connect Ceylon with India. 'Here's Adam's Bridge. Starts with Manaar Island and runs across to Rameshwaram. Thirty miles long and a bloody nuisance. Only half a fathom at the deepest. There's been talk of dredging a seaway since Victoria's day, but nowt happens. A channel through would save us over a day's steaming round Ceylon to make Madras after Tuti.'

'Why's it not been done?'

'Because the bloody priests roll their eyes and their turbans catch fire, that's why. Hindus say Rama built it. Moslems say Adam and Eve waded across when they got chucked out of Eden. Either way, it's a hindrance to navigation.'

That rings a bell for me — something I'd read in one of Arthur Mee's mighty tomes. 'Ah, yes. There's a mountain in Ceylon called Adam's Peak. It's got a sacred footprint on top made by Adam. It's the place he touched down after the Fall. But some say it's the Buddha's footprint.'

Arthur snorts. 'For the Hindu, it's Shiva's foot that made it. Some bugger with a hammer and chisel, more like. I know a chap who's been there. Says it's covered with a fancy roof. Shrines and trinket stalls all over the shop. Pilgrims flock to make offerings. It all adds up to a pretty income for the priests. Woe-betide anyone who threatens their fat livings.'

That was the longest conversation I've had so far with the chief officer. The voyage is shaking down well.

Dinner is Singapore Curry: mutton and pineapple — a sweet dish with a bite. The mutton is stringy, and a touch ripe, but it's well camouflaged by hot pepper, fenugreek, and cardamom. The purpose of spice is to mask the stink of meat on the turn, says the cynic.

Table conversation ranges across politics. On the day we sailed from London, Prime Minister Macmillan announced he was ready to face an election a month hence. A few fellows have forgotten that people at home went to the polling booths yesterday to cast their ballots for a new government. But I'm able to report morsels. In between rasping bursts from the Soviet Union's jamming transmitters, John and I have been tuning into the BBC Overseas Service and jotting down the results. For the third time in a row, voters return the Conservatives to office.

A newsreader claims it to be the first occasion the Tories have formed three consecutive governments since Bonaparte was a nuisance. Now that Britain emerges from the dark days of rationing, we've enjoyed a spending spree on credit: TVs, fridges, washing machines, even motor cars. The country has drifted right. Harold — *You've never had it so good* — Macmillan is to be Prime Minister again, and this time he pulls in a landslide majority. The journalist calls him, 'Supermac'.

Hugh Gaitskell, the Labour leader who expected to be Prime Minister, watched his party lose. The Liberal leader, the honourable and most reasonable, Joe Grimond, MP for Orkney and Shetland, and his vanishing Liberals, came home with the usual half-dozen Members of Parliament. Among the fresh faces in the House of Commons are a suave Liberal gent, Jeremy Thorpe, and a grocer's daughter from Grantham, one Margaret Thatcher, who has no interest in the Front Bench, but claims to enjoy cooking and shopping.

Amazing that the socialist bastion of my home town has elected a Tory. The new MP for The Hartlepools is to be

Lt. Commander Kerans. But not so surprising, for he is the hero of the 'Yangtze Incident'.

Just ten years ago, in 1949, during the Chinese civil war, the battered British frigate, HMS *Amethyst,* with her commander slain, spent 101 days trapped two-hundred miles upstream, among the shoals of the Yangtze river. She had been mauled by the field guns of Mao's Communists. Lt. Kerans, a naval attache from our embassy at Nanking, took command, extricated *Amethyst* from the sandbanks, and sneaked her to sea under cover of a typhoon. His crew had twenty-two dead. Simon, the plucky ship's cat, had shrapnel wounds and burns about his black and white body.

Lt. Commander John Simon Kerans earned the DSO for acts of gallantry. The crew promoted Simon the cat to Able-Seaman for his efforts at driving vermin from the shrunken food stores, and for killing a giant rat known as *Moa Tse-tung*. In his bandages, he'd kept up the spirits of all ranks and became the only feline to be honoured with the Dicken medal — the animal Victoria Cross. He survived his war with Chairman Mao, only to die soon after Amethyst reached home at Devonport.

The Gulf of Manaar opens up in the watery light of morning. Off the port side, the low Coromandel coast stretches green and yellow beneath the brown haze of breakfast-time cow dung fires. There's little to see on either hand except clusters of humble fishing craft — wedge-shaped catamarans with lateen sails. Some get out of our way, others laugh as the wake from 8.000 tons sends them plunging. Spinner dolphins ride with us. They dance and acrobat around the bow waves. With upright leaps from crests, they twist their torpedo shapes into a flashing spin: three, four, and even five times they rotate, then crash back on their sides into the sea. It might be the sheer bliss of play or to shake off parasites. We watch, but don't enquire.

Later, in the radio room, John and I discuss the spinners. I offer: 'They're so fast it's hard to count the number of spins. I saw one do six revolutions before he flopped.'

John finishes checking my recent log pages, and signs them off. 'Stranger things than spinners live in the Manaar. Close in, by the mangroves, there be dugongs. Fat aquatic mammals that graze on seaweed, like bovines on grass. Sea cows, they're called. They look human when they stick their heads above water. Old sailors thought them mermaids.'

I take a few seconds to absorb that. 'One of our fleet is called *Manaar*. I've worked her on the key.'

'That's right. Built 1950, she's still fit. But it's her predecessor who radio men should remember. The old *Manaar* sleeps on the seabed off Portugal. The first ship the company lost and the first British merchantman to open fire on a U-boat. Bound for India in thirty-nine, she was blown to bits by a U-boat. The chief sparks, Jim Turner, got the Empire Gallantry Medal, and the Lloyds Medal.'

'What for?'

'He ignored the order to abandon ship and stayed at his post, calling for help. When he'd had enough, he was delayed getting off when he found two wounded Lascar sailors who'd been left behind in the rush. The skipper yelled up from his boat and told him to jump into the sea and be picked up, but he refused to leave the wounded. The U-boat was scoring hits all around him as he tried to launch the last boat. Just as he got one badly injured man into the lifeboat, a shell blew it away. He ended up in the drink, swam to a waterlogged boat, pulled it alongside and got the other seaman into it. All under fire.'

'Blimey! Is he still at sea?'

'No. He was torpedoed on another ship and lost half a leg. Spent time in a German prison camp. Didn't go back to sea after that. Good-looking chap. There's an oil painting of him. Hangs in the MOD in Whitehall.'

There's no berth for us in Tuticorin, the 'City of Pearl Fishers'. Apart from the steeple of a blue-and-white cathedral, and the tall wedge of a Hindu temple poking above the low roofs, I can only wonder what's ashore in this ancient town. We anchor in shallows, with barges alongside which rock as our derricks lower Middlesbrough chemicals in sling-loads of drums. There are few letters from home. None for me, but my chief has one. John has worn a blank face since the letter came, and rarely speaks. Tomorrow we leave, circumnavigate Ceylon, and head for Madras, where there should be lots of mail.

32

Madras

15 October, 1959.

On rounding the south of the island of Ceylon, we find the Bay of Bengal in smiles. To port, the tea-terraced hills of Lanka hang with gloom where the soggy southwest monsoon has finally run aground. Eastwards, a molten sun peeps from the rim of the sky. It slicks the undersides of high cirrus with pink. Southwards, rooted below the horizon, stands a cumulonimbus, a towering anvil of white cloud perched atop an ominous dark column. The rain-laden, supercharged trunk flickers with electrical discharge as the monster builds power enough to hurl down thunderbolts. Farther off, other thunderheads build, but we are well clear.

The sea heaves slow and oily. Our world is hushed except for the dull beat of the propellor, the quiver of halyards, the whisper of water along the hull. Tropical daybreak can make a fellow *half afraid to speak* as Kipling writes when *the dawn comes up like thunder outer China 'crost the Bay.*

Mahronda steers north by two points west as we make for Madras. I'm looking forward to breakfast, followed by a couple of hours of sleep. I've taken over John's radio watches and schedules, his direction-finding work, and radar maintenance. As we departed Tuticorin, the second mate found John in the washroom. He was perched on the edge of the iron bath with a rope around his neck while making fast the other end to an overhead steampipe. He was persuaded down, escorted to his cabin, and put to bed. That letter at Tuti was from his wife. She's leaving him.

But his shipmates won't leave him. There's always someone in his cabin, ready to chat if he's inclined. Our purser is the medical man. He has no qualifications except years of sea experience with day-to-day emergencies, and he holds the key to the medicine locker. He gave John some pills and a comradely talking to. I call in when I can and sit with my chief. It's been decided the best treatment for now is to bring a bottle, keep him company, give sympathy, and be cheerful whenever there are signs of brooding. The instruction is: try not to let him get sober.

Late last night, he insisted on climbing from his bunk to make me a gin and tonic, and another. The Gordon's bottle was soon empty and John set about defacing the label with his penknife.

He peered at me. 'You know why there's a boar's head on the bottle?'

'Not a clue, John.'

'Once upon a time, long, long ago, the King of Scotland was attacked by a wild boar on a hunt. A gadgie from the Gordon Clan rescued him.' He scratched away more of the image. Empty European bottles are sought after in India so they can be refilled with cheap local spirits. If we order a decent gin and tonic in Sheherazade's nightclub in Calcutta, after a few drinks, when they hope we won't notice, we might be served Bengali-made Carew's from a Gordon's bottle.

'Let's not turn our nose up at Carew's. It's usually half-decent,' John said. 'Been around for at least a hundred years. In the Mutiny, the distillery was attacked by maddened sepoys. They killed the manager, Carew's younger brother.'

We continued to talk of this and that, until he stared at me and recited:

'For I remember stopping by the way
To watch a potter thumping his wet clay:
And with its all-obliterated tongue
It murmur'd — 'Gently, Brother, gently, pray!'

'Is that Kipling?' I asked, knowing it couldn't be.

'Nay, lad. It's the Rubaiyat. We'll get you educated yet.'

He climbed back into bed, turned to face the bulkhead, and was soon lost in snores.

Any more toast, Hamid?'

'Atchaa, Sahib. Toast, she cooking.'

Frank, the senior apprentice, takes a seat, and signals for coffee. 'Milky.' He picks up the menu from its silver stand. 'Papaya. And I'll have the kedgeree. Don't have much time.'

Ginger Ellis, the 2nd apprentice, chomps on a lump of toast and marmalade. His freckled cheeks bulge, and he swallows. 'Are we in sight already?'

Frank slides the linen napkin from its silver ring. 'Soon be in the offing. You can just make out the twin towers of the Law Courts and that pyramid-shaped temple thingy. Probably pick up the pilot inside the hour.' He leans back as the papaya comes in from his right-hand side. 'Word has it that John's a touch more cheerful.'

I nod. 'He's showing a bit more sparkle. Been teasing me with scraps of verse.'

I slide butter across hot toast and contemplate the two starved lads as they take on more fuel. Like me, they are from industrial working-class homes, reared through wartime food rationing and the thin years that followed. No anxious mother watches today to see we don't spread our allowance of pale whale-oil margarine too thick. No hungry father with tired muscles is here to pass you the top of his soft-boiled, one per week, rationed egg as a treat. That's all in the past for us young adventurers. Here we are, with silver napkin rings and a breakfast menu with choices: fresh papaya or juice to start, fish kedgeree or bacon and eggs for mains, with, if there's space, syrupy pancakes to finish. All with lashings of toast and marmalade. Older chaps, those with rotund middles, tend to be moderate at the table. But we are lean, agile, and still filling into maturity, and the sea air makes us ravenous.

The Madras pilot is aboard. I've informed Madras Radio (VUM) of our arrival and am preparing to close the station when John totters through the door. He gives a cheery grin and slides across the deck linoleum a cardboard crate of twenty-four cans of Tennent's lager.

'These are for you, Harry. A token of esteem for keeping my watches. The black dog's gone — I'm fine now.'

Madras is a scented city, ripe with jasmine and drains. The coastal plain and the low hills beyond, steam from a soaking and now exhale vapours onto the town. The tail of the wet monsoon still flushes the gutters free of debris. And it's hot.

By coffee time, Mahronda's decks slap and clap with flip-flopped feet as hatch boards are lifted and our innards exposed. By noon, it's close to 100F. The ship sweats beneath cranes while second-hand Grey Ferguson tractors and drums of chemicals emerge from our holds. Crates of this and that pile onto the dockside in a bedlam of Tamil yells. It strikes me that we resemble a floating mobile shop, or an Argosy. We drop off good things here and there, in between days of steaming. Where is the profit in this? But a thousand tons of coconut oil, collected from Ceylon on the way home, could pay our expenses for the entire trip. For the time being, the rattle of machines and the racket of dockers is a numbing contrast to the sublime ocean of yesterday. Today is Saturday. We leave on Monday. Oh, where is our agent, and where is our mail?

With perfect timing, an immaculate Indian from Gordon Woodroffe and Co. arrives, clutching a bulging Gladstone bag, just as the captain considers it time for his pre-lunch gin and tonic. A small crowd gathers in the saloon in hope of letters from home.

There's none for me, and only one for my chief. John holds the thin airmail up to the light, grunts, and wanders away.

Despite the lack of mail, our agent brings good news. I write to Beryl:

(I can quote from correspondence between us. For sixty-four years, Beryl has kept safe two boxes of our letters. The sentimental bits are excised):

> *"We are for a home sailing (instead of the USA) which I had almost given up hope of, but didn't like to tell you. We will dock at Calcutta next week and complete discharging in four days. After this, we leave Calcutta for good and head for East Pakistan (Chalna and Chittagong) about two days away. There we take a full cargo of jute, and gunny sacking, and sail from East Pakistan for home about November 20th. With normal speed and a decent schedule, we should be home about Dec. 20/22nd, I reckon, and if we meet a bad spot, we should be certain of at least New Year at home. As we are loading jute (from which sacks and rough cloth is made) it is likely that we put into Dublin, Eire, before the UK, and our first port in the UK will probably be Dundee in Scotland. So I may be coming home on the Edinburgh train and not the King's Cross Special.*
> *I do hope nothing happens to spoil this, but everyone is convinced that they'll be playing Santa Claus with their kids this year. I'm over the moon about it.*

Thurs. Oct 22nd. We docked (in Calcutta) *this morning and I received your Madras letter. I must have lost four of your letters — I see you've written ten, but I've only had six.*
We are in a completely new berth for me — Calcutta Jetties, the original sailing ship dock of many years in age. It is in the heart of Calcutta and we don't need taxis to get to town. Chowringhee, the main street, is right around the corner.
Our Indians are leaving the ship here, and we are shipping almost a complete new crew. But the chief cook is a Pakistani and, as he can go home from Chittagong, we are hoping he can sail with us again. He is an excellent cook. His pastry is a dream compared to his countrymen's usual standard.
John's sent in for me twice, and threatened me if I don't honour his request to join him in a pre-lunch beer. So please excuse me for about an hour, darling...

Hello again, sweetheart. This won't be as long as usual as I must get some sleep. I had only four hours last night and not much the previous. I'll post this today. I'm just awaiting the 'Ghost' (Mr Ghosh) *who posts our letters. Do you know, I'm happier today than I've been all trip. Think of it — only six days and we'll be loading for home. We should be in East Pakistan about next Thursday..."*

At last a few letters have caught up with the ship. I read how 'monstrous' black spiders have invaded the house now that cold weather has arrived. My mother is busy disposing of them with a rolled-up copy of *The Northern Daily Mail*. My dog Peter has returned after two days missing. He'd caught the scent of a bitch and went off courting again. I have missed my cousin Norman's wedding. Beryl says I must keep the beard I've been growing. I'd described how it was brown, but flecked with shiny coppery bits around the point of the chin. She wants to see it. And I'm in my mother's prayers.

33

Chittagong

30th October 1959,
It's a sultry Friday noon when *Mahronda* sights a yellow shore fringed by coconut palms. There's not a scrap of high ground — this is a flat and killer coast. When a cyclone sweeps in from the Bay of Bengal, hundreds of thousands can drown here, but still the paddy farmers return to rebuild their villages on the fertile silt.

The estuary opens. We gather up a pilot and enter the Karnaphuli river for the East Pakistan port of Chittagong. The chart shows how the river sweeps inland to form a giant *S*. Ancient Arabs traded this way. They sailed their dhows to the interior on the tide and gave the flow its name from the cloves they sought — the Arabic for clove is *qarnaful* and has become today's Karnaphuli. It drains the jungled hills of Assam, from forests once inhabited by headhunters. But the brown folk toiling in the rice paddy are not almond-eyed Assamese, but are Bengalis, doe-eyed and slender. They were Buddhists and Hindus for a thousand years before Islam ruled.

Already, the crafty black kites have swooped on the ship. A dozen of the scavengers ride on our masts and aerials. No edible thing is safe. They watch every movement on deck, particularly the opening of the galley door. A pair of sage-green pigeons perch on the rails of the monkey island. Now, they are a novelty! But dotted along the river's edge are birds I know well: redshank and greenshank, come out of the north for winter. They probe the ooze. Dapper ringed plovers dressed as diminutive butlers in black and white, trip about, picking at morsels. They flee in piping flocks as our bow wave sweeps the margins. The land is so low, the wash from our 8,000 tons overtops the banks, and spills into the rice paddy.

Chittagong is a sweaty place in the afternoon. Like Spaniards, it makes sense to labour in the morning and take a siesta after lunch. John and I are out of our bunks by 4.30am, and by five o'clock are drinking tea outside the wireless room. In the last coolness of night, we have the best hour to start work. We lean on the starboard rail to watch the sunrise. A chortle of brown mynah birds with yellow eye stripes perch among the derricks waiting for a breakfast of those moths, crickets, cockchafers, and beetles that spent last night dazzled by the ship's lights and now sit confused around the deck. When the sun comes up, the mynahs will strut like English starlings (their cousins) swallowing insects as they go.

Bows into the stream, we lie with our port side to the wharf. Three ancient hydraulic cranes wait to start the day. They have loaded ships here since Victoria's last days on Earth. Behind them is the town, a sprawling place of narrow lanes, warehouses, mosques, whitewashed government buildings, and the Catholic Cathedral of Our Lady of the Holy Rosary. The name Chittagong derives from *Chatigrama*: the village of lamp makers. The local mud must be just the thing for simple pots.

Across the river, apart from a sprinkle of thatched roofs, a level jungle sweeps to the eastern horizon. We gaze in silence as the stars fade. We don't confess to our thrills of rapture at the glory as the sky is shot with emerald when the tip of a new sun breaks the rim. A golden haze creeps over the forest. Morning comes with the pale blue of a robin's egg. The flow, no longer black, grows charcoal as silhouettes of lateen sails drift downstream. Once again, I bring to mind the words of Arnold, my sister's husband, onetime a ship's engineer with Elder Dempster: 'Never be a cynic, Harry. Take it all in. You'll see wonders.'

Dawn uncloaks the forms of men at the tillers of the sailing craft, the thin trails of smoke from their womenfolk's cooking. It is time for work. We assemble in the radio room, both in washed-out khaki shorts and shirts.

'Right, Harry, me old son, soldering irons today for both of us. We're here for a week, so we'll clear out those niggling faults. You work on the main receiver. Open it up. Trace the circuit. Any soldered joint that looks frosty, matt, or dull, cook it with the iron just long enough to see the solder flow and shine. No longer, mind. Don't over-cook, and don't forget the joints on the valve bases if you can get at them. I'll be in the radar hut, doing the same.'

'Fair enough. I did the joints on *Mahanada* with old Tommy Williams. That was after he had me painting anti-tracking jollop between every terminal in the radar. Took me a week.'

'Welsh Tommy from Anglesey. He's on the *Makrana* now. And about time, after fourteen years nursing *Mahanada* from new. That must be a record. Anyway, let's crack on. See you at breakfast.'

Redifon R50M receiver.
Image by Alfredo De Cristofaro.

I've got the innards of the R50M on the workbench. It's a formidable eight-band main receiver. My first job is to wipe the components free of felted dust with a damp cloth. Then pick out shrivelled corpses, sloughed skins, and specks of excrement voided by cockroaches that move into the gear for warmth in Atlantic winters. I track the superheterodyne's circuit path through the radio-frequency amplifier, from the mixer into the intermediate-frequency stage, the detector, and out via the audio amplifier, checking soldered joints on the way. There's a definite dry joint on the final stage, and four suspects earlier in the circuit. While the soldering iron cooks each joint, I add a touch of fluxed solder to help the bond, then wipe away surplus solder and flux with a scrap of chamois leather. Redifon, a London company, built the R50M in 1955. It's done five years service, but is now suffering. High humidity, wild temperature swings, corrosive salt air, and vibrations from the engines going full astern when navigating treacherous tropical rivers, have aged the wiring. The nimble fingers of young factory girls soldered the original joints, but a few show signs of hurried male touches at sea, the joints blobby and not wiped smooth. There's a spatter of solder across the 'breadboard'. I flick it off with the blade of a screwdriver, thinking: *whoever did that was in a rush.*

I admire the EC35, an elegant valve if ever there was. It's a triode-hexode frequency changer and is the heart of any decent superheterodyne receiver. Three-and-a-half inches tall to its top cap, the shapely glass envelope wears a painted screening coat of rich Mullard red. It has sloped feminine shoulders that swell to a comely hip before a narrowing sweep to an ankle-length hem... My forehead drips a bead of sweat onto the chassis. I've been at sea for too long.

Mullard EC35.
Triode-hexode frequency
changer.

8th November 1959: After a week in Chittagong, we slip downriver to the sea and steam east towards the mangrove swamps of the Sundarbans. It's difficult to judge where the Bay of Bengal ends and the tidal river system begins. Everywhere are creeks, and low islands smothered in jungle. On the 10th of November, the ship enters the deep river Pussur, one of the multitudes of outlets of the vast Ganges delta. *Mahronda* picks her way upstream, encouraged by the tide until, after sixty-eight miles of wet forest, home of the Bengal tiger, the trees give way to paddy fields where oxen drag ploughs. This is the port of Chalna. No wharf, jetty, shed or crane — just a broad hazardous river, paddy fields, palms, and vast skies. All *Mahronda's* anchors are laid out for and aft, and here we stay for a week. We are alone, except for canoes that dart out from a tiny village on the bank three-hundred yards distant. The brown men in turbans and loin cloths strain their necks and call. They beseech us to buy little green plantain bananas, scented papayas, and scrawny live poultry. We'll now have plantain and papaya for breakfast every day at anchor. Our agent turns up in a launch, so at least we have mail. Two days pass before a line of sluggish barges, piled with bales of jute, drift downriver. They come from Khulna, a town fifteen miles upstream.

Winches and derricks are soon at work hauling up the bales of jute, stacking them on top of the jute we loaded at Chittagong. Every bale a Pandora's box. We embark fresh regiments of cockroaches plus the occasional mouse, rat, or snake. How many tropical creatures will emerge in the jute spinning mills of Dundee? I dare say the old jute hands will laugh and the new girls shriek.

There's little to do except continue maintenance in the cool of morning and write letters in the evening. Just before we sail, I start a long letter to Beryl. Here are extracts:

Thursday 19.11.59: I've been ashore with Alex, Jim, and a couple of others. We hired a boat to take us to the river bank.

A tiny wooden canoe came out. The water was only an inch from the top of the sides. Two half-naked Bengalis paddled us, three at a time, across a three-hundred yard stretch of fast river. We had to bale, as the water was splashing in. I didn't think it very grand fun myself, that river is said to be full of crocodiles and the currents are treacherous.

We wandered along the river bank among the rice fields and came across some tiny villages. The headman and schoolteacher had us inside their huts and gave us fresh coconut. They were really friendly. We had a sit inside their bamboo-thatched huts and gave the kids a few barley-sugars, and the fellows, cigarettes. We felt like genuine Dr Livingstones among the primitives. They weren't primitive though, maybe they had bamboo houses and ate from clay jars but everywhere was scrupulously clean and the kids were all healthy and laughing.

One village we passed was further off the beaten track and the toddlers there ran screaming and howling into the houses when they saw us. Probably the first white men they had seen. But we soon made friends and they had us playing shuttlecock at one time.

The girls were kept out of our reach though, the women are always made to keep in the background. But we did catch glimpses of some very pretty young things. They were actually married with children clinging to them, the unmarried ones must have been locked away underground somewhere.

We returned safely to the ship and had a bit of a party to celebrate our leave-taking of Chalna for home. After Chalna we will be bound for Trincomalee, where we take on fresh water and stores.

Friday 20.11.59: Sneaking in a few lines whilst on watch.

The Maskeliya seems to be heading for Trincomalee too, from the Seychelles Islands though. We will probably be there with them, although only for six hours compared with her four or five days there. The Makrana is travelling home with us and she is calling at Port Sudan for cotton, so I hope that saves us a calling there. We are scarcely two-thirds full you know — heaps of empty space. But we have a load of jute and I'll bet Brocklebanks are getting a pretty penny for carrying that. Jute is a vegetable fibre from which sacking is made.

Dundee is the centre of the jute industry, hence our first port being Dundee.

Excuse me, Pet, I've got to do a little work now ...

At last a moment to spare. The station has been falling around our ears all day and we've done nothing but solder, search, and repair. This is the first minute we've had off today. Still, it's better that it happens now rather than on docking day.

The night is fine and the weather fair, and we are scorching along towards home. Only a few more lonely nights, darling. Twenty-five more and I will be stepping off the train into your arms ...

... Hope I don't have to coast, I don't want to miss this Xmas now. But of course I'm wishing for promotion to come along. I've still not shaved, there are only four beards remaining on the ship now. Wonder how many will go home. Most wives have objected, and you seem to be the only one who wants her husband to be whiskery on leave ...

Remember too, a nice rabbit and a chicken with suet pud for Xmas dinner ...

Depending on wind and weather, the East India Company's sailing ships voyaged for three to five months to reach home waters from this coast. With three stops for fuel oil, our steamer will take but one month. This is my fifth trip to the Indian sub-continent in two years, and I sometimes think I'm an 'old India hand'. But that is nonsense — I know so little of the interior. My experience is limited to coastlines, rivers, and the clamouring streets of seaports. If I give up the sea, that will be it.

I cannot tell how conditions and consequences will bring me back five times after a gap of thirty years. I'll stretch out on sunbaked rocks to watch women toss winnowing baskets in the stark valleys of the Karakorums. I'll gasp for scarce oxygen among snowfields on the Himalayan pass into the Shangri-La that is Zanskar. With Tibetan pilgrims, to chants of *Om Mani Padme Hum*, I'll circumambulate the spot where the Buddha reached enlightenment and meditate among them beneath the Bodhi Tree.

34

Homeward Bounders

A month at sea with three brief stops for fuel and water: Trincomalee, Ceylon; Djibouti, on the Horn of Africa; and finally the tiny Spanish enclave of Ceuta on the coast of Morocco, opposite Gibraltar. The Arabian Sea pitched us until we were weary of it, the Red Sea baked us, the Mediterranean chill made us don our heavy serge. Snuggled in bridge coats, we enjoyed the cold sparkle of the winter coast of Portugal. The Bay of Biscay flung us around. It was too wild for prostrations to Mecca on the open deck, and the cat did not venture outdoors. But nobody cared — we were nearly home.

The crew's eyes twinkled to see the officers infected by *The Channels,* that euphoria that comes with anticipation of homecoming and makes grown men act daft. Icy squalls blew us up the English Channel. Vermin migrated from the cargo into the accommodation in search of warmth. The North Sea was the usual biting green chop of winter. Men tidied workplaces, cleared out cupboards, hid small items of contraband, and packed suitcases. We clung to whatever was stable, toasted each other, played pranks, and sang until we came in sight of the jute mills and chimneys of Dundee.

We made fast on Thursday, the 17th December 1959, in good time for a precious Christmas at home. Three beards remain, and one is mine. Soon I will be on leave. In the gritty shopping streets of a West Hartlepool Saturday, I'll bump into people I know, old school friends, cycling club pals, and drinking comrades from the Volunteer's Arms. I can hear them now: 'Oh, hello, Harry. In from the sea again? When are you going back?' There'll be little interest in the glories I've seen, how the days flowed by on the trackless wastes, skies awash with stars, the scents of India before we saw the land. It will just be: 'Good to see you again. When are you going back?'

There's a letter for me:

> Dear Mr Nicholson,
> We are pleased to offer you promotion to chief radio officer. The position will be permanent on the understanding that you sign off deep sea articles and immediately sign coasting articles to take charge of SS Mahronda whilst she discharges at Dundee, and loads at Bremen, Antwerp, and Middlesbrough from where you may proceed on leave. We appreciate you will be disappointed to not be home for Christmas, but we have arranged that your wife, should she wish, is eligible to sign on Mahronda as a supernumerary crew member. She can remain aboard until you both sign off in Middlesbrough on or about 6th January 1960.
> Please telephone this office urgently to advise if these arrangements are acceptable.
> Yours sincerely
> Arthur Oram,
> Radio Superintendent.

I give a whistle, and my boss glances from his letter. 'You look a bit flushed, old son. Owt wrong?'

'I've finally got promotion. But it's on the understanding I coast the ship over Christmas. Arthur Oram says Beryl can join me for the trip round the coast. That'll be a fortnight she'll have aboard. Wintertime in the North Sea, though, and she has a job in an office.'

'From what you've told me of the lass, she'll jump at the chance. Congratulations on the promotion. Don't turn it down — you've earned it. It's been a treat to have you as a shipmate.' He gives me a steady gaze and a firm handshake. 'We'll not sail together again. I wonder what ship you'll get after this.'

'I'll be shoved in at the bottom, so it'll be an antique. Will you get a move up, John?'

'Nothing promised, so we'll have to see. Anyway, you'd best get ashore and phone the office. If you don't take the offer, they'll have to scrabble around for a volunteer. They'll have a job on to beg someone off their leave at this season.'

'I'd better phone Beryl's office right away. Brocks will have to wait.'

On the dockside, Scotsmen stand around waiting for our hatches to open. I weave between jute barrows to calls of: 'Here comes Father Christmas.' Whiskers are rare in Britain, except on the chins of philosophers on their last legs; if this is the reception I get, I'll not be keeping the beard for long.

Ethel, Beryl's hiking friend, answers the phone at Pounder's Plumbers and Electricians and puts me through to Miss Papple's desk. She huffs when I ask for Beryl, but I say it's urgent.

Beryl is both thrilled and taken aback by my torrent of explanation. She goes quiet when I ask her to give up her job. But I hear, 'Whatever happens, I think you should accept the promotion. I'll explain it all to your mam. She's been making plans and is bound to be upset. I'll talk to Mr Portiss and see if he'll give me time off. Give me the number of that phone box and I'll ring you back at eight o'clock tonight. Meanwhile, please do ring the company and accept their terms. Don't worry about me.'

At eight, in the shabby red telephone box by the dock gate, the phone rings. 'It's me. I bumped into my dad in Church Street. I asked him what I should do. Quick as a flash he said, "Your place is with your husband". I've done it! I leave my job tomorrow and catch the Dundee train on Monday. That'll give me three days to sort things out. What should I pack?'

'Yippee! Bring warm clothes. That brown coat you made, with a thick jersey, gloves, and a cosy hat. Flat shoes for the decks and ladders. No stilletto heels — they ruin the lino. And the little black cocktail dress your dad bought you will be just the thing for Christmas Dinner alongside in Dundee — you look gorgeous in it. Bring whatever else a winsome young lady might need. We sail for Bremen on Boxing Day.'

'Will I need a passport? I don't have one.'

'Oh, I hadn't thought of that. Don't worry — we'll sort something out. You'll be a crew member — a supernumerary on the handsome wage of one shilling per month.'

We have a splendid steward. He signed on in Calcutta. When I tell Noor Alam, son of Yeason Ali, that my wife will join me for two weeks, he squares his shoulders. 'Noor give cabin special clean for memsahib. Wash deck, polish wood, Brasso porthole. Make everything tigh hai.'

My bunk can be extended by eighteen inches and the 'Dutch wife' security bolster laid flat to fill the space. There's an increased risk of tumbling out, but we could hang on to each other when the seas are wild.

Appendix

The author's Seaman's Discharge Book. p1.

APPENDIX 263

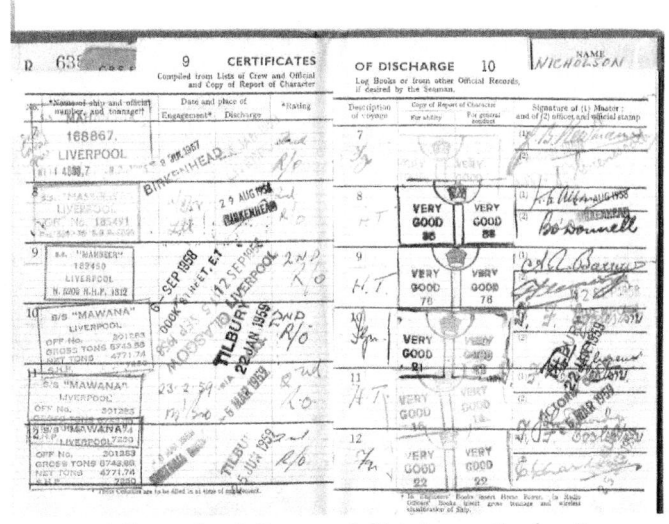

The author's Seaman's Discharge Book. p2

The author's Seaman's Discharge Book. p3.

About the Author

About the author:
Harry Nicholson now lives near Whitby in North Yorkshire. He grew up in Hartlepool from where his family have fished since the 16th century. He had a first career as a radio officer in the merchant navy. A second career followed in television studios. Since retirement, he has taken up art, story-telling, poetry and meditation.

To see more of his writing and art, please visit his blog: https://1513fusion.wordpress.com/

Also by

- This is book three of memoirs of my seagoing days. The years fly by, and I am surprised to be writing at the age of 84. With fair seas, I hope to write more. If you enjoyed these voyages of the golden years of the Merchant Navy, please leave a review. Thank you for reading.

- By the same author. In paperback and eBook on Amazon:
  Tom Fleck – historical novel of Cleveland and Flodden. Set in 1513.
  The Black Caravel – sequel to Tom Fleck. Set in 1536.
  The Best of Days – a memoir of the sea, book 1.
  You'll See Wonders — a memoir of the sea, book 2.
  Wandering About — poems 1994-2014.
  Green Linnet — anthology of short pieces.
  The Beveren Rabbit – a study of the breed.
  One Jump Ahead – the memoir of Lt Mann, SS *Vyner Brooke* escapes Singapore.

Printed in Great Britain
by Amazon